T0305577

CASE STUDIES IN FAMILY BUSINESS

ELGAR CASES IN ENTREPRENEURSHIP

Elgar Cases in Entrepreneurship offer an instrumental resource to fulfil the needs of instructors in entrepreneurship. Spanning numerous discrete fields, Elgar Cases cover state-of-the-art developments in real-world entrepreneurial endeavours, providing expert analysis with an international focus. Casebooks are edited by leading instructors, who bring together experienced and knowledgeable case writers to illustrate and analyse contemporary entrepreneurial scenarios. Each case offers a strong foundation for constructive discussion and includes learning objectives and summary questions to guide classroom discussion. Teaching notes for each case provide opportunities for instructors to further develop understanding and promote class engagement. An invaluable boon to course leaders and students alike, Elgar Cases in Entrepreneurship combine practicality, student engagement and international expertise to bring entrepreneurship alive!

For a full list of Edward Elgar published titles, including the titles in this series, visit our website at www.e-elgar.com.

CASE STUDIES IN FAMILY BUSINESS

OVERCOMING DESTRUCTIVE CONFLICT, DEVIANCE, AND DYSFUNCTION IN THE FAMILY FIRM

EDITED BY

ROLAND E. KIDWELL

Carl DeSantis Distinguished Professor of Management and Entrepreneurship, Department of Management Programs, College of Business, Florida Atlantic University, USA

ELGAR CASES IN ENTREPRENEURSHIP

Cheltenham, UK • Northampton, MA, USA

© Roland E. Kidwell 2024

All rights reserved. No part of this publication may be reproduced, stored in a retrieval system or transmitted in any form or by any means, electronic, mechanical or photocopying, recording, or otherwise without the prior permission of the publisher.

Published by
Edward Elgar Publishing Limited
The Lypiatts
15 Lansdown Road
Cheltenham
Glos GL50 2JA
UK

Edward Elgar Publishing, Inc.
William Pratt House
9 Dewey Court
Northampton
Massachusetts 01060
USA

A catalogue record for this book
is available from the British Library

Library of Congress Control Number: 2024936434

This book is available electronically in the **Elgar**online
Business subject collection
https://dx.doi.org/10.4337/9781035307357

ISBN 978 1 0353 0734 0 (cased)
ISBN 978 1 0353 0735 7 (eBook)

Printed and bound in Great Britain by
TJ Books Limited, Padstow, Cornwall

CONTENTS

FIGURES

TABLES

ABOUT THE EDITOR

Roland E. Kidwell, PhD, Louisiana State University USA, is Carl DeSantis Distinguished Professor of Management and Entrepreneurship in the College of Business at Florida Atlantic University (FAU). From 2015 to 2023, he served as department chair of management programs at FAU. He also served as director of the Adams Center for Entrepreneurship where he started the Family Firm Initiative, which provides advising services to family firms in South Florida and holds periodic panel discussions on issues of importance to sustaining family businesses. He is a fellow of the Family Firm Institute and the US Association of Small Business and Entrepreneurship. His research focuses on issues such as leadership succession, dysfunctional behavior, executive compensation, and corporate governance in family firms. He has published extensively in highly regarded academic journals over the years. In 2023, he received a Fulbright Scholar award to conduct family business research, including this book, at Hasselt University in Belgium.

CONTRIBUTORS

Folashade O. Akinyemi, PhD, is a Researcher, Senior Lecturer, and the Assistant Coordinator of the Business Development and Capacity Building Unit at the Institute for Entrepreneurship and Development Studies, Obafemi Awolowo University, in Nigeria. She lectures both at the undergraduate and postgraduate levels in entrepreneurship, business management, and financial accounting. She received her PhD in Business Administration from Wits Business School, University of the Witwatersrand, Johannesburg, South Africa. Her research interests are in entrepreneurship, business development and sustainability, family business and succession, resource management and environmental sustainability. She has more than 30 publications in both local and international peer-reviewed journals, book chapters, and edited books.

Pablo Álamo, PhD, is an international Distinguished Professor at the CETYS Graduate School of Business (Baja California, Mexico), Professor of Strategy, Ethical Leadership and Family Business Management in master's programs in business administration. He is a member of the IC-A, a Spanish reference center in corporate governance and president of the NLG, a think tank related to citizen freedom and good corporate governance practices. Professor Álamo combines his research and teaching work, specialized in case methodology, with strategic consulting for business families focused on Latin America. His research has led to publications in indexed journals, two case studies in Harvard Publishing, and business books such as *Long Live the Family Business!* (2019) and *Antioxidants for the Family Business* (2023).

Cristina Alvarado-Alvarez, PhD, is a Postdoctoral Researcher in Organizational Psychology at the Universitat Autònoma de Barcelona and member of the core team of KU Leuven Centre for Business Families. Her research agenda is focused on gender, leadership, and conflict management in family firms with a special interest in the business family system. She is a lecturer of mediation and conflict management in master's degree programs, a chartered psychologist, and a family counselor specialized in family businesses.

Unai Arzubiaga is an Associate Professor of Accounting, Management, and Family Business at the University of the Basque Country (UPV/EHU). He serves as associate editor in *Business Ethics, the Environment and Responsibility* journal and on the review board of *Family Business Review* and the editorial board of *Journal of Family Business Strategy*. Arzubiaga has also served as guest editor in the *Journal of Knowledge Management* and in the *Journal of Family Business Strategy*. He also belongs to the UPV/EHU Family Business Center. His interdisciplinary research is at the intersection of entrepreneurship, innovation, internationalization, and corporate governance, especially in the field of family businesses. His research has contributed to several high impact journals such as *Journal of Business Venturing*, *Journal of Family Business Strategy*, *European Management Journal*, and *International Business Reviews*. He has taught courses on family business at both undergraduate and postgraduate levels.

Myriam Cano-Rubio, PhD, is a Professor of International Management at the University of Jaén in Spain. She was a visiting scholar at the University of Calabria and postdoctoral visiting professor at the University La Sapienza in Rome. Her research interests are in family business, internationalization strategy, familiness, smart technologies, corporate governance, and circular economy. Before joining the academia, she worked as an export manager, R&D technician, and accountant.

John James Cater III is a Professor in the Department of Management and Marketing and the Director of the Center for Family and Small Enterprises at the University of Texas at Tyler. He is a fellow of the Family Firm Institute. Jim managed his family's retail furniture business in South Florida before earning his PhD in Management at Louisiana State University. Jim has published articles in the *Family Business Review, Journal of Business Ethics, Management Decision*, and other journals.

Martin C. Euwema is full Professor in Organizational Psychology at the University of Leuven, Belgium. He is chair of the KU Leuven Center for Business Families and past president of the International Association for Conflict Management. He was Weilung Professor at Tsjinghua University, Beijing, and visiting professor at the universities of Amsterdam, Copenhagen, and Seville. As academic advisor and practice he works with Deloitte on business and family dynamics. His research, teaching, and practice focuses on constructive conflict and mediation as instruments for growth of individuals, groups (business families and top teams), and organizations.

Sandra Fiedler is a Research Associate at Chemnitz University of Technology in Germany. She studied economics at the Fern Universität in Hagen and is an external doctoral candidate at the University of Witten/Herdecke. She worked for several years in the management of her family business. Her research interests are succession in family business, next generation, entrepreneurial family, family systems theory, and emotions.

Steve Gaklis is a Bertarelli Institute for Family Entrepreneurship Research Fellow and PhD researcher in entrepreneurship and family business. His research interests lie at the intersection of family business and entrepreneurship. The goal of his research is to investigate organizational sponsorship in the context of trans-generational entrepreneurship practices and understand how dynastic family firms use mechanisms associated with sponsorship activities to support new ventures. His research has supported new constructs in entrepreneurial habitus and applied theory in asymmetric paternalism. He received his PhD from the University of Strathclyde, UK and his MBA with specialization in statistics and finance from Babson College, USA.

Dagmar Y. Hattenberg is Senior Researcher at the Dutch Centre of Expertise in Family Business, at Windesheim University of Applied Sciences. Dagmar holds a Master of Science degree in Industrial and Organizational Psychology (Erasmus University of Rotterdam) and a PhD in Business Administration (University of Groningen) on the topic of understanding and developing the entrepreneurial mindset as an individual-level phenomenon. In her current research, she focuses on organizational and entrepreneurial processes in family firms and social wealth.

Annegret Hauer works as a Research Associate at the Institute for SME Research at the University of Mannheim (Germany). She completed a commercial apprenticeship at Dorint

AG and studied business administration at the University of Mannheim. Her research is focused on the importance of family businesses in Germany. She regularly publishes a list of the 500 largest family businesses in Germany and conducts research on succession and governance mechanisms in family companies.

María Jesús Hernández-Ortiz is a Professor in Business Administration at the University of Jaén (Spain), with four decades of experience in teaching and research. She held the Chair of Family Business at the University of Jaén between 2001 and 2017 and has continued as a member of the research team. Her research interests are in family business, social enterprises, entrepreneurship, and corporate governance.

Ellison Howard recently graduated with a PhD in Business Administration from Florida Atlantic University (Boca Raton, Florida). Her research focuses on family business, particularly deviance, theft, and fraud within family firms. She is also interested in studying the roles and unique theoretical implications for women and racial/ethnic minorities in entrepreneurship and family business. Ellison holds a BA in Journalism and Mass Communication from the University of North Carolina, and an MBA from Florida Atlantic University. Before graduate school, she owned a firm that provided marketing services mainly to family businesses.

Sally Kah, PhD, is a Senior Lecturer in Business Management at Leicester Castle Business School De Montfort University (DMU). Her research interests lie in social impact assessment, entrepreneurial bricolage, sustainability strategies, and opportunity recognition in the context of social enterprises. She has published academic papers in ABS-ranked journals and has presented her research at national and international conferences. Sally is a Fellow of the Higher Education Academy and a Member of the EMES International Network. Before joining DMU, Sally was a lecturer in business at Birmingham City University, where she led the Postgraduate Research Practice module.

Nadine Kammerlander is a Professor of Family Business and Associate Dean at WHU – Otto Beisheim School of Management in Vallendar, Germany, where she also co-leads the Institute of Family Business and Mittelstand. She received her PhD in Management from the Otto Friedrich University in Bamberg, Germany. Her research interests focus on innovation, governance, and leadership in family firms, and her articles have been published, amongst others, in the *Academy of Management Journal* and *Academy of Management Review*.

Christine Keller is a master's student at WHU – Otto Beisheim School of Management and a student assistant at the Institute of Family Business and Mittelstand.

Christopher Khoury is a PhD student and research assistant at WHU – Otto Beisheim School of Management at the Institute of Family Business and Mittelstand. His research interest focuses on external succession and financial investors in family firms.

Karumba Kinyua is a consultant with over 19 years of practical experience focusing on monitoring and evaluation, financial and risk management, business development, and strategic management. He has a Master of Science degree in Corporate Real Estate Finance and Strategy and a Bachelor of Commerce degree in Business Administration. He has extensive experience with international and regional institutions in sub-Saharan Africa, Europe, and North

America. He has worked for government agencies, financial institutions, agribusiness firms, faith-based institutions, and investment companies. Mr Karumba has authored a book titled *Wealth Beyond Generations: Strategies for Intergenerational Wealth Transfer.*

Astrid Kramer is a Senior Lecturer in the Department of Strategy and Entrepreneurship of Tilburg University. She teaches courses on strategy and entrepreneurship, conducts research on various facets of family businesses, such as governance, HRM, and the family in family businesses and is Associate Dean program portfolio and innovation of Tilburg School of Economics and Management.

Eric R. Kushins, PhD, is Assistant Professor of Management at the Campbell School of Business at Berry College in Mount Berry, Georgia. His research focuses on organizational culture, family businesses, interpersonal relationships, and organizational routines. He has published articles on topics ranging from race discrimination in the hiring process to R&D development in Chinese family firms. In addition to teaching undergraduate and MBA courses in Human Resource Management, the Art of Negotiation, Operations Management, and Social Entrepreneurship, he has trained hundreds of individuals in Lean Six Sigma over the past nine years.

Javier Macías is an active consultant, researcher, and speaker on next generations leadership, ownership, and corporate governance. He advises owning families in Europe, South America, and MENA countries. He co-founded the Family Business Advising Club in Spain, and the Iberoamerican Virtual Study Group in the Family Firm Institute. He teaches Family Business Governance in EAE Business School, Spain. He has been guest speaker at Universidad La Sabana, Colombia, and in other professional institutions including Chambers of Commerce, Family Business Associations, the Family Firm Institute, and Family Business Network. He is an BBA, MBA-ESADE, Psychologist, and Family Therapist.

Gaia Marchisio, PhD, is a family-enterprise researcher, consultant, educator, speaker, and writer with 25+ years of impact across global family enterprises, academic institutions, corporations, public-sector organizations, and others. She is currently a Senior Lecturer in Discipline and Faculty Director of the Global Family Enterprise Program at Columbia Business School. As program creator and researcher, Gaia has worked with the IFC (World Bank), the Family Business Network in Asia (as Chief Learning Officer), McKinsey, and others. As speaker, she has presented on wide-ranging topics at YPO, Egon Zehnder, Grant Thornton, and many others. Gaia founded the Family Enterprise Clinic in 2014 and continues to lead it, working with family enterprises on succession, governance, and other issues, collaborating with inter-disciplinary advisors.

Amaia Maseda, PhD, is a full Professor of Management and Accounting and principal researcher of the Governance, Entrepreneurship and Sustainability in Family Firms group, a Basque Government Consolidated Research Group of Excellence at the University of the Basque Country, UPV/EHU (Spain). She is also a founding member of the Family Business Centre at the UPV/EHU. Her research interests focus on SMEs and family businesses, with a specific focus on corporate governance, diversity, and entrepreneurship. Her research has been published in the *Journal of Business Venturing, International Journal of Management*

Reviews, Humans Relations, Journal of Small Business Management, International Business Review, Journal of Family Business Strategy, International Small Business Journal, and *Review of Management Science,* among other journals. She is Editor-in-Chief of the *European Journal of Family Business.*

William Murithi, PhD, is a Lecturer at Strathmore Business School, and a visiting scholar at the Center for Entrepreneurship Innovation, De Montfort University. He also taught as an adjunct at Ashesi University. He is a postdoctoral researcher at the Sisters' Blended Value Project. Previously, he was the Project Co-Lead for the Entrepreneurship Ecosystem Project. His research interests include entrepreneurship, strategy, family business, regional development, business model innovation, digital transformation, and sociocultural and institutional contexts within developing economies. He has presented his research at international conferences and published in ABS-ranked journals. He is a fellow of the Higher Education Academy (now Advance HE) and a Certified Management and Business Educator. He is also a management and enterprise strategy, project management, and curriculum development consultant. He serves in different capacities as an advisor and trustee in organizations in the UK, Ireland, Ghana, and Kenya.

Francisca Panadés-Zamora, PhD student, is a Professor of Human Resources at the University of Jaén in Spain. She was a visiting scholar at the University of Naples Federico II, Italy. Her research interests focus on family business, employee commitment, socioemotional wealth, and sustainability. Before joining academia, she worked as a human resources technician.

Robert Randolph, PhD, is Associate Professor of Family Business Management and research director of the Family Enterprise Center at Kennesaw State University, USA. He primarily studies the strategic management of family firms and other hybrid organizations using interdisciplinary approaches. Robert teaches strategic management topics across undergraduate, graduate, doctoral, and executive audiences. His research has been published in academic journals and covers a range of topics including strategic management, entrepreneurship, family business, information systems, hospitality management, and social enterprise.

Małgorzata Smulowitz is a Research Fellow at the Debiopharm Chair for Family Philanthropy at IMD. She has published articles in peer-reviewed academic journals such as *Human Relations* and practitioner-oriented work on numerous topics including cohesive giving, the use of blockchain in philanthropy, and impact. She co-authored the award-winning book *Family Philanthropy Navigator.*

Miranda Stienstra is a Senior Lecturer at the Department of Strategy and Entrepreneurship of Tilburg University in the Netherlands. She teaches several courses about strategic management and has done research on alliances and acquisitions. She is academic director of the Bachelor of Business Administration at Tilburg University and is therefore researching optimal teaching methods.

Jan Klaus Tänzler completed a banking apprenticeship at Deutsche Bank AG and then studied business administration at RWTH Aachen, the National University of Singapore, and UC Berkeley. He wrote his PhD thesis at the University of Mannheim on the topic of

Corporate Governance and Corporate Social Responsibility in German SMEs. Research stays of several months took him to the Western University of Australia in Perth and to Bank Indonesia. Following his dissertation, he was involved in the founding of various start-ups.

Manuel Carlos Vallejo-Martos, PhD, is a Professor in the Management Department, co-founder of the Chair of Family Business of the University of Jaén (Spain), and former visiting scholar at the University of New Haven (USA). He earned his PhD in the culture of family firms in 2003. His research has been published in different international journals such as *Journal of Business Ethics*, *Family Business Review*, and *Journal of Business Economics and Management*. Nowadays he combines his teaching and researching activities about family business management and entrepreneurship with some international research projects and with generational handover consultancy to family firms.

Ties van Daal is a master's student in Societal Transitions and Philosophy at Erasmus University Rotterdam and student assistant at Tilburg School of Economics and Management at Tilburg University. Based on his background in business economics and philosophy, he is interested in the philosophical aspects of organizations and innovation, such as technology, finance, and governance.

Judith van Helvert, PhD, is a Professor at the Dutch Centre of Expertise in Family Business, at Windesheim University of Applied Sciences. She holds a Master of Science degree in International Business Studies (Maastricht University) and a PhD in Business Administration (Jonkoping International Business School, Jonkoping University). Her current research activities focus on the impact of family values and dynamics on entrepreneurial activities in family businesses. Judith is co-chief editor of *Holland Management Review*, a journal for practitioners that offers articles on developments and trends in all current management themes.

Erik Veldhuizen, PhD, is an Associate Professor at the Dutch Centre of Expertise in Family Business, at Windesheim University of Applied Sciences. He holds a Master of Science degree in Business Economics at Erasmus University Rotterdam. In 2008, he received his PhD from the Faculty of Industrial Design Engineering at Delft University of Technology. His research mainly focuses on the social aspects related to family business succession, self-financing with multiple owners, and conflict management in family firms.

Peter Vogel is Professor of Family Business and Entrepreneurship, holder of the Debiopharm Chair for Family Philanthropy and Director of IMD Global Family Business Center. Vogel is also Director of the IMD Global Family Business Award. He was named by Poets&Quants as one of the world's best business school professors under 40 in 2022.

ACKNOWLEDGEMENTS

A book such as this one is only as good as its contributors. The editor wishes to thank the 34 researchers/educators/students who submitted cases and learning notes for this book as well as those contributors who provided reviews of other case submissions to help strengthen the quality of the cases and learning notes as well as the teaching notes connected to the book. Those who not only wrote cases but provided constructive comments and suggestions for improvement to their colleagues are Myriam Cano-Rubio, Jim Cater, Dagmar Hattenberg, Annegret Hauer, Astrid Kramer, Chris Khoury, Eric Kushins, William Murithi, Robert Randolph, Miranda Stienstra, and Jan Tänzler. And thanks to all the family firm leaders, family members, and family business advisors and therapists who gave confidential interviews to the writers of these cases. Also thanks very much to the editorial team at Edward Elgar Publishing, the US Fulbright Scholar Program and staff, and the administration, faculty, and students who hosted me at Hasselt University in Belgium this fall, in particular Anneleen Michiels and Wim Voordeckers.

Roland E. Kidwell

SUPPLEMENTARY MATERIAL

Supplementary materials for this book can be found online at:
https://dx.doi.org/10.4337/9781035307357

Introduction: dealing with the dark side of family firms, case by case

Roland E. Kidwell

Research interest in conflict, deviance, and dysfunction in family firms has expanded rapidly in recent years. Academic studies have investigated a variety of negative behaviors including theft, incompetence, bias against nonfamily members and women, aggression, fraud, and other forms of financial misconduct, corporate social irresponsibility, environmental degradation, tax avoidance, and evasion – the list goes on. While much of the inquiry compares the economic and social performance of family firms to nonfamily firms, more recent studies and reviews consider dysfunctional behavior across family firms, specifically why some members of family businesses are more likely to experience conflict or to engage in negative acts than others (Kidwell et al., 2024; Bettinelli et al., 2022).

The uniqueness that many family firms share – great difficulty in separating work roles from family roles, the tendency to reward based on needs versus merit, parenting style issues that carry over into the workplace when the children become adults, and altruistic behavior toward children that builds an entitlement mentality – can result in unfavorable outcomes for both the family and the firm. Combined with relationship conflict among family members, intense sibling rivalries, harmful nepotism, and the family's reckless pursuit of noneconomic goals, the unique factors can seriously damage the family firm as well as its stakeholders. These stakeholders include individual family members, nonfamily employees, customers, suppliers, governments, local communities, and other interests in the firm's external environment.

As family firms – large and small – make up a significant percentage of the world's economy, understanding how these firms and their family owners function is extremely important. Previous case books have largely focused on how family firms engage in the strategic decision-making process, encourage innovation and transgenerational entrepreneurship, and deal with the often-sticky problem of succession. Many of these issues involve the dynamics of a controlling family that seeks to mark the firm with its prevailing values, seeking positive outcomes and preservation of the family business into succeeding generations. In contrast, this book provides instructors and students with real-world examples that bring to life situations in which the family dynamic leads to more negative acts and results that hurt (sometimes unintentionally) the people, the business, the family, and the environment.

DESTRUCTIVE DYSFUNCTION: CASES OF FICTION AND FACT

The dark side of family business damages the happy prospect of families working together for the greater good of their loved ones, their businesses, and the societies in which they live. Unfortunately, negativity and evil are prevalent themes in media coverage of family business, whether it focuses on fraud committed against clients, stockholders, or governmental entities; aggression, harassment, and bullying within the family against each other or outsiders; theft from the firm by family or nonfamily members; or mistreatment of nonfamily employees and customers. There are many examples in real life (the Adelphia Communications financial scandal, the Parmalat fraud, the Samsung and Siemens bribery chronicles) as well as in fiction (recently popular TV shows such as *Succession, The Family Business*, and *The Fall of the House of Usher*). Family businesses that do society good, providing important products and services to the customers and employing thousands of workers, have not received as much popular recognition, at least in recent years. The Bailey Brothers Building and Loan of *It's a Wonderful Life* movie fame is a fictional company from a nostalgic movie made almost 80 years ago, but it is important to remember how that family firm transformed Bedford Falls for the better and how real family firms change their communities in a positive way.

While many family businesses and business families avoid the nasty conflicts depicted in the media and perhaps in this case book as well, it is important to recognize that many of the true stories presented by the authors here are representative of struggles and conflicts that occur in many family firms large and small, whether they concern parent–child relations, sibling rivalries, or disputes across more than two generations. Often these conflicts are connected to succession processes in a family firm or the workings of governance mechanisms or as the precursors of negative acts that damage the family and the business. The implications of these conflicts, largely based on personalities and relationships, are many. They include personal hurt and damage, subsequent dysfunctional behavior in the business, the stifling of innovation and transgenerational entrepreneurship, and potentially the destruction of the family firm. Yet, a positive side can be found as several of the cases included here reveal the means to address family feuds, succession issues, and governance problems.

As readers of this book probably know, cases are important because they provide a rich, detailed experience of an often-distant phenomenon. Yin (2014) posits that the goal of case studies is to help understand complex events and experiences such as those that occur in organizations. Case studies provide rich data that help build and test theory through the development of propositions and hypotheses. As an educational tool, case studies provide students and instructors with the opportunity to examine – in a real-world context – concepts and theoretical relationships that potentially impact organizational strategies, operations, and survival.

This case book provides in-depth examination and analysis of the phenomena of conflict and dysfunction in the context of real-life family firms. The cases are divided into four parts: Family Fights: Parents, Children and Siblings; Succession Struggles (and Successes): The Next Generations; Corporate Governance – or Lack Thereof; and Bad Behavior in the Family Business. With a couple of exceptions, all 19 cases involved the authors conducting personal interviews with family members or using personal experiences with the families involved to craft interesting and readable accounts. Each case is based on real families and family firms, but in all cases the names of people who were interviewed have been anonymized to protect their privacy. The case writers have used their network and community connections, persuasiveness, and relationship building to persuade these family firm members to pull open the curtain on what is not necessarily the most flattering view or outcome of their life's work. The authors deserve a great deal of respect and admiration for their successful efforts in finding and bringing these family business situations to a wider audience.

In each case, the authors provide a brief case overview, learning outcomes as all of these cases are designed for instructional use, discussion questions for students, an epilogue (spoiler alert) that tells the reader what happened after the narrative in the case ended, and a few suggested readings on related topics. Thus, each case can be used by instructors, students, consultants, and family business practitioners to shed light on current issues they face or will face in the future with their own family firms or others. Comprehensive teaching notes have been written by the authors for each case and are available via the publisher to those who are interested in adapting the cases for classroom use.

To set the stage for the rest of the book, a summary of each of the four parts provides evidence of the depth and breadth offered in this collection.

FAMILY FIGHTS: PARENTS, CHILDREN AND SIBLINGS

These six cases involve parent–child relationships and relationship conflict that may negatively impact the firm years later. A special focus on disputes among siblings is provided in several cases. This is particularly relevant in family firms as the relationships that sons and daughters have with each other tend to last a great deal longer than the relationships between parents and their children (Gilligan et al., 2020) and not always to a good end (Blake et al., 2022).

The first case, contributed by Gaia Marchisio, Eric R. Kushins, and Robert Randolph, tells the story of the struggles between Peter Peyton and his son Johnny, whose entry into his father's business turned it into a family firm. The case examines the issues that can occur when the lines between family and business relationships are blurred, and when a well-meaning homemaker/wife/mother, Maggie, gets involved in the father–son dispute by seeking guidance from business consultants.

The second, third, and fourth cases focus on disputes among siblings. Dagmar Y. Hattenberg, Erik Veldhuizen, and Judith van Helvert provide extensive coverage of the long-standing fights between Dutch brothers Herman and Henk, who are embarking on their 18th court case over a feud that originated over cash flow arguments but seems to have escalated when Henk's new girlfriend entered the scene. A different kind of dispute involves the three siblings of Luis and Carmen, whose business success in Spain allowed them to shower their children with positions, property, and protection and to tell their children that everything in the family firm would belong to them. Unai Arzubiaga, Amaia Maseda, and Javier Macías describe what happens between the three siblings when Julio refuses to join Felipe's and María's mutiny to go after the inheritance from their parents a little early, that is, before they die. The case illustrates the devasting effects of altruistic behavior by parents that instills an entitlement mentality among often ungrateful children. Finally, William Murithi and Sally Kah take the reader to East Africa where grocery chain Tuskys, having grown from a storefront to the dominant industry player in Kenya, faces potential ruin due in large degree to family infighting among allied siblings on a variety of fronts. The real Tuskys name is used in the case, but the names of the family members are disguised.

Chapters 5 and 6 provide a contrast between despair and hope. First, Sandra Fiedler recounts the sad story of intergenerational conflict between the first, second, and third generations of a German firm who cannot agree on anything, which eventually leads to the sale of the three-generation company. In contrast, Folashade O. Akinyemi presents Dee Doks, a third-generation Nigerian store owner who successfully operates what his culture traditionally considers to be a female business. The case reveals how the indefatigable Dee Doks successfully manages potential conflict and dysfunction with his sometimes unmotivated and less than honest employees, his seven children, and his three wives.

SUCCESSION STRUGGLES (AND SUCCESSES): THE NEXT GENERATIONS

The huge issue of passing the family on to the next generation and, even more crucial, who that successor will be is the topic of this group of cases. Potential conflicts that occur in the succession process can provide negative outcomes for the family and the firm (e.g., Cater et al., 2016; Cosson and Gilding, 2021). These cases focus on firm growth and operations and how the next generation is brought (or not brought) into the business, and how mismanagement of the process results in negative behaviors including insubordination, sabotage, theft, fraud, and family member impediment. Included also are positive succession cases that reflect some of the challenges that women in family firms have had to overcome to gain access to leadership of the firm as documented by family firm research (Campopiano et al., 2017).

In Chapter 7, Christopher Khoury, Christine Keller, and Nadine Kammerlander tell the story of CEO and father Joachim Schmidt who struggles with his desire to preserve his multigeneration family firm versus the family turmoil that would result if he asked his only daughter to take over the firm and divert her from her own career desires. The case evolves into a consideration of potential outside buyers of the business even as Mr Schmidt considers the possibility that by some means he may be able to keep the firm connected with the family. Chapter 8, written by Pablo Álamo and Unai Arzubiaga, presents a less optimistic picture for the matriarch of a 45-year-old ice cream business. The damage that distrust among parents and their children can cause is a key issue in the story of this Mexican family firm.

The last two cases involving succession reveal challenges in the process created by cultural differences involving the treatment of women and family quarrels among siblings and extended family members. But in both cases, the challenges are overcome. In Kenya, William Murithi and Karumba Kinyua outline the struggles of three sisters (the daughters of the founder) to take control of a supply business from an ill father who prefers to have a male successor, whether it be his disinterested son, a devious cousin, or an overbearing uncle. In the Netherlands, Astrid Kramer and Miranda Stienstra tell the story of CEO Gerald de Berg who is so determined to avoid a replay of his heartbreaking feud with his father and his brother that he sets up and administers a succession process for his daughters that he hopes will avoid the conflict that led to his estrangement from members of his family when he took over the firm years earlier.

CORPORATE GOVERNANCE – OR LACK THEREOF

These cases reveal conflict, misconduct, fraud, and other dysfunctions that impact not only the firm but external stakeholders as well, and have been frequent topics in family business research (e.g., Ding and Wu, 2014; Krishnan and Peytcheva, 2019). In Chapter 11, Małgorzata Smulowitz and Peter Vogel introduce John Johnson, a fourth-generation member of a European family firm selling luxury brands to high-end customers. John believes the earlier generations of the firm showed a strong commitment to helping others, but when he tries to establish a philanthropic mechanism so the firm can aid the less fortunate, he runs into a conflict of values with fellow family members. John is also blocked in establishing corporate governance mechanisms at the family business. Eventually, he can take control of the business and take it in the direction that is consistent with his values. Chapter 12, contributed by Jan Klaus Tänzler and Annegret Hauer, provides a story about price fixing charges and subsequent fines that threaten the survival of the Meyer family firm in Germany. The case documents the role that family factions and the lack of a family firm constitution or charter play in creating havoc when the current generation must deal with the sins of the past.

The next case, contributed by Miranda Stienstra, Astrid Kramer, and Ties van Daal, documents the wide-ranging problems that can accompany a CEO's passionate hobby to sponsor sports teams with his own name as well as the name of one of the Netherlands' largest family firms. Allegations of money laundering regarding the sponsors lead the CEO to face a criminal case and to inspire governance changes within the family business as the firm does not get the publicity it was seeking by sponsoring bicycle and auto racing teams. Finally, María Jesús Hernández-Ortiz, Manuel Carlos Vallejo-Martos, Myriam Cano-Rubio, and Francisca Panadés-Zamora close out this part by showing the dark side of professionalization. A Spanish family firm that has expanded and diversified in recent years hires an external manager to help move their various business divisions forward, and the owners are caught napping on their governance responsibilities, allowing a charlatan to loot the company at will and to threaten them when they consider involving the police.

BAD BEHAVIOR IN THE FAMILY BUSINESS

The final five cases show the outcomes that interpersonal conflict can have as an antecedent of dysfunctional behavior in family firms. Steve Gaklis provides insights into how destructive family disputes about how the business should be run eventually lead to firm-level conflict that threatens the company's future. John James (Jim) Cater III discusses succession issues that flow from long-standing conflicts between two brothers into a larger family tragedy when one of the brothers is mysteriously gunned down at the front door of his home. The family business matriarch is faced with the decision of whether to try to lure her surviving son back into the business to keep the family dream alive or close the business as it is in a declining industry sector.

The last three cases deal with specific dysfunctional issues that family firms may face at the intersection of the family and the firm. First, Cristina Alvarado-Alvarez and Martin C. Euwema present the story of a rogue second-generation family member whose apparent sense of entitlement and potential psychological problems are keeping his parents up at night with worries that the ownership shares in the firm they have given him may be wasted due to his behavior and that there might be something seriously wrong with him that warrants treatment. Then, Pablo Álamo and Unai Arzubiaga introduce a Paraguayan family firm CEO who attempts to remove his brother from the company's board of directors and ban him from the office because he is taking money from the business to fund his gambling addiction. The CEO's parents strongly resist firing their son out of love for him. But they don't realize they may drive away their responsible son who is effectively running the business despite his errant brother and is now considering leaving as CEO because the family resists his request to take action. Finally, Ellison Howard tells the story of how blind trust in a cousin of the doctor who runs a family medical practice jeopardizes the future of the practice. It seems the cousin who was hired because he was a family member has betrayed the doctor by fraudulently billing the government for reimbursements that end up lining the pockets of the fraudster cousin but leave the doctor responsible for the fraud. The doctor must evaluate his relationship with the cousin, who has been a close friend since childhood. He sorts out the implications of cooperating with the fraud investigation as he faces potential criminal charges as well.

CONCLUSION

A common thread – the connection of shaky family dynamics at early stages to bad family business outcomes later – runs through each of these cases to some degree and reflects the growing need for family business researchers to explore theoretical perspectives from the family science arena that further reveal the inner workings of the business family (Combs et al., 2020). Whereas interpersonal conflict often serves as a root cause of various negative outcomes in the family business, it can also stand in the way of solutions. Relationship conflict develops through parent–child interactions, disputes between siblings, or other triggers often operating below the surface of family firm member exchanges. Revealing, discussing, and resolving conflicts either within the family or involving the assistance of counselors and family therapists is a worthwhile endeavor that can head off a world of negative behaviors that threaten the future of the firm and the family. The cases in this book provide real-world examples that surface issues facing many family firms today. Avoiding remedies and hoping these conflicts and dysfunctional behaviors will go away only means prolonging them to a point where they will bring even more negative outcomes when they resurface or are allowed to continue unabated.

REFERENCES

Bettinelli, C., Mismetti, M., De Massis, A. and Del Bosco, B. (2022). A review of conflict and cohesion in social relationships in family firms. *Entrepreneurship Theory and Practice*, *46*(3), 539–77.

Blake, L., Bland, B. and Rouncefield-Swales, A. (2022). Estrangement between siblings in adulthood: A qualitative exploration. *Journal of Family Issues*. https://doi.org/10.1177/0192513X211064876.

Campopiano, G., De Massis, A., Rinaldi, F.R. and Sciascia, S. (2017). Women's involvement in family firms: Progress and challenges for future research. *Journal of Family Business Strategy*, *8*(4), 200–212.

Cater III, J.J., Kidwell, R.E. and Camp, K. (2016). Successor team dynamics in family firms. *Family Business Review*, *29*(3), 301–26.

Combs, J.G., Shanine, K.K., Burrows, S., Allen, J.S. and Pounds, T.W. (2020). What do we know about business families? Setting the stage for leveraging family science theories. *Family Business Review*, *33*(1), 38–63.

Cosson, B. and Gilding, M. (2021). "Over my dead body": Wives' influence in family business succession. *Family Business Review*, *34*(4), 385–403.

Ding, S. and Wu, Z. (2014). Family ownership and corporate misconduct in U.S. small firms. *Journal of Business Ethics*, *123*(2), 183–95.

Gilligan, M., Stocker, C.M. and Jewsbury Conger, K. (2020). Sibling relationships in adulthood: Research findings and new frontiers. *Journal of Family Theory & Review*, *12*(3), 305–20.

Kidwell, R.E., Eddleston, K.A., Kidwell, L.A., Cater III, J.J. and Howard, E. (2024). Families and their firms behaving badly: A review of dysfunctional behavior in family businesses. *Family Business Review*, *37*(1), 89–129. https://doi.org/10.1177/08944865241226739

Krishnan, G. and Peytcheva, M. (2019). The risk of fraud in family firms: Assessments of external auditors. *Journal of Business Ethics*, *157*(1), 261–78.

Yin, Robert K. (2014). *Case Study Research: Design and Methods*. Sage Publications.

PART I
FAMILY FIGHTS: PARENTS, CHILDREN AND SIBLINGS

1
Navigating relational rifts and communication clashes in the Peyton family firm[1]

Gaia Marchisio, Eric R. Kushins and Robert Randolph

CASE SUMMARY

In the early 1990s, Peter Peyton founded APS Inc., a B2B service company. Before start-ing his own company, Peter was the third-generation member of his family's business. Peter's wife is Maggie, and the couple have four children. Peter's dream was to work with his children in his business, which would provide them with a springboard for their own entrepreneurial careers. Peter is a devout Christian who grew up in an abusive household and his family is wrought with conflict and tragedy. Ostensibly to support the business, Peter exhibits dysfunctional workaholic behaviors and has an ultraconservative approach to spending money. Peter ran the business and Maggie was a stay-at-home mother. Peter was physically and emotionally absent from home life during this period but saw himself as the family patriarch with ultimate decision-making authority and expected his family to maintain this perspective despite his absence from home. After graduating from college and spending several years working for a consulting firm, Johnny, the eldest son, accepted Peter's invitation to join the firm, which doubled in size in two years. Johnny believed his success warranted him dominant control of the firm. The working relationship descended into daily fights and coalition sabotage for decision-making authority, hindering the firm's success. Maggie secretly seeks the help of family business consultants to address the rift between father and son, which is now hurting other members of the family.

LEARNING OUTCOMES

After analyzing this case, students will be able to:

- Describe how family-centered motivations and goals can inspire and guide entrepre-neurial behaviors of founders and the difficulties of translating those intentions and plans to the next generation.

- Explain how family structures and culture – in particular family members' religious values – can overlap with business decision-making and how that overlap raises a threat of family conflict resulting from actions taken in the family firm.
- Describe how conflict rooted in family roles can motivate seemingly destructive founder behaviors and shape how the next generation views and engages with the family business.
- Explain if and how nonbusiness family considerations influence salary and ownership decisions.
- Demonstrate an understanding of the "adultification" process (Ferguson, 2022) in which children transform into peer-like or partner-like roles in their parent's mind during the succession and professionalization processes within the family firm.

Maggie gripped the steering wheel as her car cruised through the picturesque countryside. The roads were flanked by tall trees, their branches reaching out like protective arms over the road, creating a tunnel of dappled sunlight and shadow. She glanced at the lush greenery, but her mind was miles away. Her hopes for the imminent meeting were as high as her fears. She felt as though everything in her life was at stake. Her family's legacy, her marriage, and her children's future all seemed to be at risk. In her mind she kept repeating the list of things she wanted to discuss with Louise and Marie. How would these two family business consultants she'd never met be able to understand their struggles? What she needed extended far beyond business advice; how could someone else really care about her family as much as she did? While her mind was driving as fast as her car, she went back to her mental notes to make sure not to miss anything.

She wanted to make sure that Louise and Marie appreciated what American Peyton Services (APS) Inc. meant to them. APS was founded by her husband Peter over three decades ago and since then it has been a cornerstone of their family life and identity. She wondered how to properly communicate the tireless devotion, countless sacrifices, and unwavering dedication Peter had poured into the business all those years. He was cut from the cloth of her entrepreneurial family, and she experienced how building something from the ground up required commitment that often spilled over into family life, and not always for the best.

Maggie also wanted Louise and Marie to understand her role in the family. Not holding a formal position in the family business, she had taken on the responsibility of raising their four children. (See Appendix 1A for Maggie's email to the consultants describing her children.) As the head of their household, she was sure to instill strong religious values and empathy, even as Peter's work to build the business came with its own struggles. Their marriage had truly been a partnership, even if their roles were different, and from the outside looking in, not always complementary.

As she drove, her thoughts danced between the well-being of her family and the impending meeting. How could she best describe the most delicate parts of the most recent complications regarding Johnny, their eldest son? He showed an impressive aptitude for the family business and made significant contributions that rapidly boosted the company's growth. How could she possibly explain that these accomplishments were simultaneously points of great pride for

Peter that reassured his hopes for the future but were also a source of incredible tension and excruciating emotional pain? Johnny was attempting to assume control of the company, going so far as threatening his own exit if his demands were not met.

Most of all, Maggie hoped she would learn how to better communicate the situation with Johnny, who, in his eagerness to be recognized and rewarded for his hard work, had inadvertently ignited contentious arguments with his father. How could she maintain both perspectives properly, while reporting them fairly to the consultants? Conversations about compensation, ownership shares, and even the day-to-day operations of APS Inc. were complicated enough to attend without the emotionally strained relationship between father and son. However, the fact that something needed to be done had never been clearer to Maggie. The conflict between Peter and Johnny was now impossible to ignore. It had escalated into hostile debates that were not confined to the family but had begun to bog down the business, adding even more strain to what she once thought were unbreakable familial bonds. Replaying this family drama with two strangers felt like betraying her beloved family. Trying to clear her mind, her eyes fixed on the road ahead. She knew Peter and Johnny were the core of her family, and it was her job to hold them together through both the highs and the lows. Unable to mend these fractures herself, Maggie reassured herself that taking the difficult step of seeking outside help was the right thing to do.

SETTING THE STAGE: MAGGIE'S PIVOTAL CONSULTATION

When she arrived at the meeting, Maggie had been driving in the car for a few hours. She was exhausted, yet hoping to finally gain some clarity on the concerns that had been mounting for a few years. She desperately needed her family back together and was no longer willing to sit on the sideline and watch as the conflict between her husband and her son was pulling the family apart. The breaking point was learning that her daughter-in-law, Johnny's wife, was not willing to attend the upcoming annual family vacation, a tradition that had always served as an oasis from business conflicts. It was a clear sign the current situation was no longer tenable.

She arrived at the conference room where Louise and Marie, two seasoned family enterprise consultants, were waiting for her. Despite being their first meeting, Maggie greeted them warmly with big hugs as if they had already known each other for a long time. She proudly and generously presented an adorned picnic basket containing a homemade pie, cookies, juice, plates, glasses, tissues, and forks. Then, very quickly, as though second nature, she plated and served both Louise and Marie while entertaining them with detailed stories involving family recipes and the pride she felt having passed these on to her children.

After breaking the ice, Louise and Marie asked Maggie a very broad question to kick off the conversation. It was important for Louise and Marie to see where she, Maggie, chose to begin. This is how Maggie started:

> To understand our story, we need to start with Peter's grandfather. He was the first entrepreneur in the family. He started a small metal parts manufacturing company in his

twenties. Peter's father grew it significantly, introducing automation and pivoting to focus specifically on the steel industry. He passed it to his two sons, Mark, my brother-in-law, and Peter. Mark is the oldest, which is the reason he got 60 percent of the shares from their father. Peter got the remaining 40 percent. There was never a discussion around either this decision or timing of the share transitions. Peter accepted his father's decision despite reservations and never considered alternative reactions. Peter worshipped his father as the patriarch until his last day, and in many ways still does. The fact that this reverence was never reciprocated in his own children is likely part of our problems today.

In addition to his father, Mark also played a major role in Peter's life. He had always been very bossy and cocky, even as a child. Don't get me wrong, I love my brother-in-law, but what I know from their childhood, Mark was a true antagonist in Peter's life. As children, when their playing got rough, Peter was punished when he fought back against Mark who would, for example, lock him in a small dark closet. Unfortunately, these abusive behaviors were either undetected or accepted, and nobody else in the family would stop Mark or help Peter.

As a result, Peter grew up learning not to address family issues directly. Still today, Peter avoids making any decisions and prefers postponing difficult conversations, emotionally shutting down when confronted. This has always been very difficult for me, especially when it comes to decisions around how to raise our children. My approach historically has been to "ask for forgiveness rather than for permission". There were times when Peter's delaying and postponing drove me crazy. So, I soon learned that it was less painful for me to go ahead and make calls without asking him and then deal with his upset mood.

Marie at this point interjected: "Maggie, that must not have been easy for you. How did Peter feel about this strategy?"

Maggie initially responded only with an intense glance, a tense smile, and what was the only minute of silence during the entire interview. Finally, after taking a long breath, she said: "I don't think he ever liked it, but he certainly got used to that." After some more thought, she added: "And if he doesn't like it, he doesn't mention it to me much. He has always spent so much time working in his father's business he barely knew what happened at home. I don't know what I would have done if it wasn't for Johnny."

Maggie changed gears and went back to talking about Peter's family.

In his early forties, Mark went through a difficult divorce. The aftermath of that challenging time was his total absence from the business, despite retaining all the decision-making authority. As a result, Peter effectively ran the operations during this time, which was very hard on us too, as we saw him even less. Unfortunately, as Peter was enduring personal sacrifices to support his brother making the business successful, Mark made a deal to sell the company to an international competitor, and only informed Peter when all the details were formalized. It was a total surprise. Peter was devastated and felt that selling the business was a betrayal to their beloved father.

Louise asked: "And how did you feel about the sale of the company?" Maggie tried to be positive in her description, but her eyes gave her true sentiment away.

> After the sale, it took Peter a while to get back on his feet. It was so difficult to see him being so lost. I did my best to support him every step of the way, but I also had to deal with three very young kids at home. Luckily things changed for us. Through his network, Peter found a business opportunity and bought a small business. It was one of his father's previous vendors. It was a service business: Scrap Metal Haulers. Peter saw great potential in this business. Not only for its expansion, but also for himself as well as our family. No longer being under Mark's shadow, he felt that being in charge would allow him to build the family business he always wanted. We started APS to create opportunities for our children to learn how to be entrepreneurs, deal with money, and be involved in the business.

Leveraging on her last comment, Marie asked Maggie to change the topic for a moment. "Maggie I couldn't help but notice you said you and Peter started APS together. Can you tell us a little bit more about you two as a couple?"

Once more Maggie's facial expression indicated it was not an easy topic for her to discuss. Yet, she had started feeling comfortable around Louise and Marie and quickly started sharing.

> We met through our church and have been married for 36 years. To be honest, I believe that our shared faith and church life has kept us together through the years and is at the core of how we raised the children. We intentionally "divided and conquered" our responsibilities according to what you may call "traditional gender roles". Peter took care of the business and I oversee the household.
>
> Peter is a workaholic. Since very early in our marriage, he has been physically and emotionally absent. Don't get me wrong, he is wonderful: he wants to inspire and support his community. He also wants to be considered a respected mentor, like he sees his own father. He is incredibly humble and modest, and very conscious about spending money. But he also struggles with being assertive and therefore tends to postpone conversations and decisions consistently. I am the opposite; while Peter shuts down when pressed, I talk about everything, sometimes too much.
>
> Peter identifies as the patriarch, with ultimate decision-making authority over everything at home and in the business. He expects everyone in the family to respect this role. I understand his desires, but to be honest, his lack of assertiveness, coupled with high levels of frugality, makes this impossible and has led to friction over the years. So, I must work behind the scenes to support him.

"Thanks for sharing this, Maggie." Louise responded. "I wonder how this way of avoiding difficult conversations played out in your parental role. How did you and Peter manage this despite the conflicts?" Thinking about her four kids, Maggie's eyes lit up. She took a moment to answer.

> That is a difficult question, but to be clear, being parents has always been our priority. To be perfectly honest, Peter's absence has always been a concern for me. I had to fill his void. I have been very present and involved in raising my children and developing their ability to be compassionate, and able to talk about difficult things. I certainly didn't want Peter to be their role model for that. I really wanted my kids to get along and have solid relationships. I was terrified that what happened between Mark and Peter could ever happen to my kids one day. Luckily, all our children are very supportive of one another and appreciative of their different talents without being jealous.
>
> Our youngest came up with a great idea. He created a family group chat where we share daily pictures, fun facts, requests for prayer, meaningful scripture passages, and achievements. I also use the chat to organize weekly gatherings with the family in the area, and we have group video calls with the siblings living away. My biggest win is to know that even outside the group chat the kids talk regularly. They share ideas, vacation plans, surprises for me or Peter. Everyone is deeply connected and invested in each other's life. That is a true blessing.
>
> Peter wanted to be like his father. He wanted to be a teacher for his children, so much so that sometimes he forgets to be a dad. He used each opportunity to teach them something: a skill, a value, a way of thinking, a passage from the Bible. This is all great, but he is less attuned to where they are in life. Always with the noble intention to equip them with wisdom and moral compass, he tends to turn any conversation into "preaching a sermon" rather than sharing his emotions with his children. I know this because the kids complain to me about it.

While scheduled for two hours, their meeting ended close to the three-hour mark. While Maggie had hoped to get specific solutions to convince Peter to finally sell his majority shares of APS to their son, she barely had the time to get to that part of the story. The new concept she learned, triangulation,[2] was intriguing. While she understood the need for and importance of her husband and son to talk more directly, she couldn't imagine Peter doing it alone.

Louise and Marie listened to her concerns and explained to her how some of her behaviors were potentially making the situation worse. While Maggie was taken aback by the idea that her impact might not have been effective, if not counterproductive, she started to understand the "importance of her doing less". She was clearer on their next steps. At the door, she thanked Louise and Marie, saying she "felt very hopeful that she wasn't alone in trying to fix this".

The last comment Louise made was to remind her of the importance of shifting language a little ... as words are powerful. Therefore, she said with a caring smile: "Maggie, one last thing before you leave. Remember, you don't need to fix them, actually you can't." Maggie nodded and smiled to indicate she got it, and that shift in mindset was probably the hardest for her to make. With a date secured for their second meeting she marched back to the car and drove back home.

A CALL WITH MARIE: THE PRESENTING ISSUE (2019)

Although sharing plenty of context in the first meeting, Maggie felt she failed to address the core of her concerns. Before the next meeting, Maggie decided to call Marie to share more information. This time she jumped into the conversation very directly.

Marie, as we speak, things are getting worse and worse. It has been five years since Peter and Johnny have been in business together, and they have reached a critical point. Tension is palpable. For the past eight months, Peter has complained to me almost daily about how difficult, arrogant, and demanding Johnny has become. And Johnny, my poor Johnny thinks that (again) his father doesn't want him to be successful. Isn't that horrible?

Johnny calls me weekly to chat about the boys and the plans for the weekend. I know my son; I can tell he is experiencing growing frustration and so I ask him questions, hoping to help. Our calls turn into a long venting session where Johnny criticizes his father's actions. He points out all the delays Peter creates in the operations and how the two see the issues of compensation and roles in the business differently. Johnny can't understand how his father refuses him the CEO title and a higher salary and bonus. In his eyes, this is unbelievable, given his contribution to the business, charisma, leadership style, and growing reputation in the industry. He deserves more.

The call went on for over an hour. Marie reassured Maggie. After the call, she collected all the additional information and prepared a memo to share with Louise for their team meeting, where to discuss next steps. To help better understand the whole situation, Louise and Marie organized a timeline of events.

HOW WE GOT HERE

2004: Peter acquires a small company, relocates its headquarters to his hometown, and rebrands it as APS, symbolizing his ownership. Both Peter and Maggie are committed to expanding the business with the vision of it becoming a platform for their children to gain business experience, collaborate, and utilize their resources. Peter forgoes a salary for a decade, reinvests profits to fuel growth, and aims to leave a substantial legacy within the company. He excels in operations and provides strategic guidance for stable organic growth over the next eight years. Additionally, he strategically builds a real estate portfolio that expands from a local to a regional scale.

2012: Peter relies on joint venture partners to expand to northern regions of the country. Johnny graduates from college and starts working for a prestigious consulting company. Peter thinks Johnny is not ready yet to join APS and hopes that a job in a big city will help Johnny learn a few more critical lessons about working hard, living on a budget, and making choices.

2015: Johnny's consulting career is going well. He gets his first promotion, a big salary raise, a company credit card, and a team to supervise. His boss gives him great reviews and more autonomy. Despite his young age, he has captured an extraordinary talent for sales and relationship-building with new clients. The company culture where he works promotes a very hands-off management style that helps inform Johnny's own management style.

2016: Peter's partnerships end, and he realizes he needs someone to handle the rapidly growing northern market. During a fall hunting trip, without previously discussing it with anyone, Peter approaches Johnny. As they sit in nature, Peter asks Johnny if he is interested in joining APS and building *their* company. He stressed how their complementary skills would be powerful.

Johnny, though surprised, considers the offer, even though he would take a significant salary cut compared to his current position. Peter emphasizes the benefit of a lower cost of living, of working for *their* company, and opportunities to match salary with a sales bonus. Johnny heard his dad referring to APS as "*theirs*" and assumed that was a clear invitation to joint ownership. The offer seemed attractive to him. Johnny was about to get married and his fiancée, Megan, would prefer to stay closer to home.

After the hunt, Peter and Johnny return to announce Johnny's impending role at APS. Maggie has mixed feelings. She didn't like that Peter approached Johnny without telling her, but at the same time, she was so happy to have Johnny back in the area. The family celebrating together is one of the more joyous memories Maggie shares.

The week after this decision, Peter calls a meeting with Johnny and shows him the updated operating agreement for APS Inc. Johnny reads: Membership in the company is being expanded as of 1 January 2017, including John Peyton, who joins Peter Peyton, the original member. Johnny is excited about partnering with his father. While he reads all the 20 pages of the agreement, he is most excited about the distribution of class A (90 percent to Peter, 10 percent to Johnny) and B shares (70 percent to Peter, 30 percent to Johnny). However, Johnny doesn't seem to pay attention to the details of the operating agreement, which mention that at least 85 percent ownership is required to make any significant decision in the company, effectively minimizing the power of Johnny's new ownership role. They finalize the deal, and Johnny purchases 10 percent of the shares with a low-interest loan from his parents.

2017: Johnny officially joins the APS team and travels north to keep building the business in this area. His sales and leadership skills quickly pay off. Revenue in his area doubles in only a few months. Johnny continues to focus on growth by extending services to new geographical markets and exploring new industries to serve. He is extremely successful in growing the business.

Peter is thrilled at Jonny's success and believes this performance is the outcome of their team efforts and synergistic skills. In Peter's mind, Johnny's expansion of the business is facilitated by Peter's focus on core operations and solid financials. Peter values the reputational capital he built over the years and knows the new growth would not have been possible if the company had not been in such a solid financial position.

Johnny begins making comments about how *finally* things are *now* working at APS. Johnny struggles with appreciating his Dad's contribution and regularly disparages Peter's role in the business in both their private conversations as well as when speaking with third parties such as clients, employees, acquaintances, or family.

Less than a year after joining the company, Johnny requests a salary increase and the right to purchase more shares. Peter agrees to consider the raise but privately finds Johnny's attitude arrogant and ungrateful. He doesn't share these concerns at home to avoid painting a negative image of his son.

Meanwhile, Maggie has consciously taken Johnny's side in the emerging conflict. Johnny describes the significant changes in the leadership team and how incredible he is at empowering and rewarding them. When asked what Peter thought about those changes, he responds by validating her experience with Peter as not being very action-oriented, justifying the lack of communication around some of those decisions, "As you say, Mom, better ask for forgiveness with Dad". These conversations hint at a deeper conflict. Johnny occasionally makes comments like: "I don't know, Mom, it feels like Dad doesn't want me to be successful."

As Johnny approaches the end of his first year in the business, Peter finally voices concerns to Maggie about Johnny's arrogance, extravagant lifestyle, and the need for humility and respect.

2018: A raise and a promising change in ownership occur. In the first quarter, without further conversation, Johnny receives a 20 percent salary increase. Peter feels this was too generous but hopes it will satisfy him, but Johnny is unhappy about it and believes it is too little. However, Johnny is still growing the business, there are new projects on the horizon, and he is on the road a lot. Toward the end of the year, Peter allows Johnny to purchase another 15 percent of class A shares, which in addition to the increased compensation structure, he hopes will satisfy Johnny's ambitions. The amended operating agreement includes the following changes: (1) The majority required for making decisions is now 75 percent; and (2) An optional buyout clause allows Peter to repurchase Johnny's shares if Johnny exits the business. Johnny doesn't express major concerns with these new terms but feels as though 25 percent of class A shares is only a small improvement of the situation.

Finalizing the new terms was not easy. Peter felt he was overly generous with his ungrateful son, while Johnny struggles to understand why it is difficult for his father to recognize his leadership and contribution. At the last minute, Peter adds a condition to the deal that they won't talk about redistributing shares for at least five years.

At the end of the year, Johnny asks for a meeting with his father to discuss bonuses and salary increases for *his* leadership team. Peter refuses the meeting, reminding Johnny it is not a topic up for conversation because he oversees it. Johnny shares his frustration and Peter pushes back, reminding Johnny that he is, and intends to remain, CEO of the company, and, as such, the conversation is over. Tensions and voices are higher than usual. A few comments shared by both are hurtful as the conflict threatens to spill over into their family life.

That year, during Christmas Eve dinner, the atmosphere is uncharacteristically tense. The friction between father and son is noticeable. While Peter remains silent, Johnny, at the prodding of his siblings, begins venting his frustrations to the family and sharing multiple details Peter considers inappropriate for the family dinner table. In essence, his concerns regard the many things not working in the business, his attempts to fix them, and how Dad is in his way and refuses to talk about it. The siblings' reactions are mixed.

Maggie observes the family's discontent solemnly. Over the holidays, she advocates for Johnny, causing more tension between her and Peter. Their marital relationship is strained, and old dynamics resurface.

2019: The conflict expands and reaches boiling point. During the first quarter, Johnny receives a higher paycheck with no prior conversations and no explanation. For Peter this is an attempt to go above and beyond to accommodate his son and avoid future conflict. He expects appreciation. Johnny acknowledges the effort, but clearly wants more authority and ownership and believes the additional compensation "doesn't reflect the total amount he believes he deserves".

By the end of the second quarter, Peter and Johnny have a significant argument around expenses. Peter finds out that Johnny has issued company credit cards for four leadership team members. The team is told to use them for lunch, even when they don't travel. Peter confronts Johnny and asks him to develop a clear and enforceable policy to define appropriate use of company cards and funds. Johnny refuses. In his view, this would communicate a lack of trust in the team. He concludes with an upset tone: "Why must everything be a fight about money with you? Why can't you be more generous like your father and let me run this place? People are happier here now." Peter shuts down. Johnny gets even more frustrated and leaves the office. That night both Megan and Maggie hear very different stories from their husbands.

Things get even worse when, returning from a problematic (yet successful) client trip, for which he had to miss his son's first recital, Johnny is surprised to learn that Peter has increased his own salary. This is infuriating for him. He looks for Peter in the office but doesn't find him. On the way back home, Johnny has enough time to ruminate on the current situation at APS.

> Since when does Dad take such a high salary? To think that my father believes he deserves to make as much as me is unbelievable. Why should Dad get paid to be in the office the whole day while I am out and about finding new clients? Why is my father the one making all the calls? After all, I'm now running the leadership team. This is also my company. Speaking of, where had they left the ownership conversations? How Dad can put a hold on for five years to have the conversation about more ownership, but this is no longer sustainable if Dad gets to make decisions like this. Honestly, at this point, what is the incentive for me to keep growing the company's value if Dad is the one benefiting from it?

As these thoughts flowed freely in his head, Johnny's resentment grew. Maggie calls at that moment to invite the whole family for dinner, and by his tone, Maggie knows something is wrong. The call lasts almost two hours. Maggie is worried but also upset with Peter. She finally decides it is time to intervene, even though she knows it could be a disaster.

When Peter gets home, she openly confronts him on this ownership topic. Peter is taken aback. How does she know that level of detail? Why is she having this conversation advocating for her disrespectful son over and over? Why isn't she supportive and helping him address Johnny's cockiness for once and for good?

From that day, mother and son, with an increased sense of urgency, started bringing up the need to sell additional shares to Johnny to prove Peter was seriously committed to their son's success. Johnny also demands a higher salary and more decision-making authority.

2020: When Covid-19 hits, Maggie and Peter had to isolate due to Maggie's health. They moved to their farm, and Johnny took over the business, hoping to prove to his father he could handle it without him. They communicated daily. Johnny hopes this is a successful test for Peter to enjoy retirement.

2020 became the most profitable year in the history of APS. Father and son are both very happy about the profit, far above the industry's average. Yet, they hold very different explanations for the performance of the business. Johnny interprets this success as clear evidence of the value of his role, and the first hint of the success of APS under his unconstrained leadership.

On the other hand, while Peter certainly recognizes his son's contribution, acknowledging his capabilities publicly and privately, he points out that this success would not be possible without APS being debt-free and financially stable. Additionally, returns from past investments made by Peter contributed to this fantastic year. Peter sees more of the partnership's efforts and complementary talents, while Johnny's view tends to be more skewed toward his own role.

Spending more time removed from daily operations, Maggie starts challenging her husband regarding what to do with the time together and what kind of retirement they can look forward to, given their overall financial situation. Peter is not ready for such a conversation, as he is not planning to retire, but instead, he enjoys the flexibility of working from home.

2021: Feeling slighted over Peter's lack of acknowledgement of his leadership abilities, Johnny is increasingly unhappy. He feels he is working very hard to create value in the business, but he cannot access such value enough due to the conditions set in the previous shares' sale agreement. Instead, he feels taken advantage of.

To get his father's attention, Johnny occasionally threatens to leave the business if he doesn't get another raise. Knowing that the five-year hiatus on share discussions is ending soon, he wants to redefine his base salary and bonus, and have the ability to buy more shares.

While reorganizing his office, he takes the chance to review the amendment to the shareholder agreement made in 2018 to better understand his situation. This time he reads it more carefully, and understands that his father, in his sole judgment and discretion, could potentially fire him and force him to sell all the shares back. That realization hits him profoundly, and he immediately calls Maggie. Without even saying hi, he begins the conversation by saying "How could my father do this to me?" During the same call, and the next day, he uses such words as "stunning", "world shattering", "devastating" and "unfathomable". Maggie is both devastated and furious.

Johnny's frustration is leaking into the leadership team. He also makes decisions in the business without informing Peter, unintentionally teaching the top management team that it is acceptable to bypass the owners when making decisions.

Peter also takes issue with how greedy his son has become. Father and son talk less and less, as every interaction is tense and strenuous. When Johnny offers his younger sister a position in the business without consulting their father, Peter is furious.

Maggie continues to support her son even at the expense of her marital relationship. Johnny changes his strategy, since threatening to leave has not gotten him what he wants. Instead, he begins withdrawing from the company. He stops complaining, but also stops actively working in the company, stops bringing in new clients, and stops fulfilling his responsibilities. Johnny claims he is no longer willing to work his tail off to make his father rich. Business growth stops, the leadership team is distressed, and one key member gets a job offer and contemplates leaving. In the family too, the situation is strained.

THE FUTURE OF APS INC.

In the past several months, tensions have worsened. For him to continue leading the company, Johnny demands his father sell him the majority of the company's voting shares, as he believes that the 25 percent he owns is no longer an appropriate representation of his crucial contribution and leadership. His father continues kicking the can down the road, initially indirectly, more recently very openly by dismissing these requests. Johnny's frustration turns to resentment after multiple attempts to sit and discuss the issue. Johnny's wife, Megan, sees how the situation is tormenting her husband. She is increasingly upset with her father-in-law and occasionally mentions to Maggie how miserable Johnny is.

APS is at an inflection point and a decision must be made. As it stands, Peter retains the majority of controlling shares and has no intention of selling anything more to Johnny. Johnny is now demanding at least 70 percent of the class A shares, or he is leaving with the leadership team. Maggie and her husband barely talk to each other as their conversations usually lead to a fight about Johnny. Peter feels abandoned by his wife. As a result, he becomes less engaged with all his children, as he tries to avoid questions about what is happening in the business, and he doesn't want to impact their relationship with their brother. Johnny is not as discreet and complains about how difficult it is to work with a father who doesn't recognize his contribution. The children don't know what to do, so they avoid spending time with the family, causing additional distress to Maggie, who doesn't understand how such a successful business can cause so much conflict.

Louise and Marie know this conflict is not just about ownership, but also know the sources of the conflict are multiple and complicated. Maggie solicits their help in resolving this conflict, but there is not a likely avenue available that will satisfy everyone. Maggie asks the consultants to develop a plan for the family and the future of APS.

DISCUSSION QUESTIONS

1. List all family members. What are your initial thoughts and feelings about each? Why do you believe those are your initial reactions?
2. Identify key elements of the Peyton family's history, culture, and family dynamics that help explain why this ostensibly successful family business suffers from such significant conflict.
3. Traditional family hierarchies often empower family patriarchs. When considering the personal conflict between Peter and Johnny, why do you think the Peyton family is unable to rely on family institutions and hierarchies to relieve this conflict?
4. Imagine you are a nonfamily professional member of the APS Inc. team, and you are trying to explain the current operating conditions of the business to a new hire. Briefly, in 2–5 sentences, how would you describe the situation between Johnny and

Peter and what advice would you give a new hire?

5a. Imagine you are a family friend of the Peytons and you have been approached independently by Maggie, Peter, and Johnny who are each seeking counsel from you. What advice would you give each of them regarding their situation and how they can move forward as a family?

5b. Imagine you are a business advisor (rather than a family friend). What advice would you give Maggie, Peter, and Johnny regarding their situation and how the business can be protected from negative spillovers from this conflict?

EPILOGUE

Within the realm of enterprising families, the Peyton family is no exception to the continuous process of evolution. Their ongoing transformation represents a pivotal aspect that demands careful consideration and understanding for effective management. Recognizing that no singular solution can comprehensively address every conflictual situation, the family acknowledges the necessity of a multifaceted approach that delves into the root causes of relational and structural concerns. Once they hit bottom, the Peytons aligned on the aspiration to enhance relational well-being, and it became a shared and mutual commitment, while also acknowledging the inherent risks involved. With all siblings now married, the family is actively engaged in integrating their spouses into the enterprise, navigating the delicate balance between familial and business dynamics. While Maggie and Peter conscientiously work on fortifying their relationship with the guidance of a marriage counselor, Johnny and his father find themselves in negotiations regarding a fair price for the transfer of control. Simultaneously, they purposefully cultivate the growth of the company in tandem. As the business expands, the Peyton family faces the imperative to seamlessly integrate the remaining family members into the evolving enterprise.

The very challenging years they experienced served as a profound lesson, revealing that their journey is an ongoing, perpetual, and ever-evolving process. Simultaneously, they came to recognize that their most valuable assets – human, relational, and spiritual capital – form the foundation of their shared experience, with the preservation of these elements emerging as their foremost objective.

NOTES

1. This case study is compiled from comprehensive interviews with and records of a team of advisors specializing in family dynamics including a family psychologist, a family enterprise consultant, and a compensation consultant. To safeguard the confidentiality of the families and organizations involved, the characters and their actions are composites based on recurring themes across multiple cases, fictionalizing background, location, and specific details, without compromising the authenticity of the situations explored and without identifying specific individuals or businesses.

2. Triangulation: the term "triangulation" is most closely associated with the work of Murray Bowen, known as family therapy. Based on Bowen's theory, under stress, a two-person

emotional system is unstable and may seek to include a third person. As the tension shifts around three individuals and now multiple relationships, a triangle can contain a greater amount of tension. Triangles contribute significantly to the development of clinical problems.

SUGGESTED READING

Ferguson, T.M. (2022). *Contributing Factors of Childhood Parentification: An Examination of Familial Characteristics.* (Publication No. 1410) (Master of Social Work thesis, California State University – San Bernardino). *Electronic Theses, Projects, and Dissertations.* https://scholarworks.lib.csusb.edu/etd/1410.

Garber, B.D. (2011). Parental alienation and the dynamics of the enmeshed parent–child dyad: Adultification, parentification, and infantilization. *Family Court Review, 49*(2), 322–35.

Gomez-Mejia, L.R., Cruz, C., Berrone, P. and De Castro, J. (2011). The bind that ties: Socioemotional wealth preservation in family firms. *The Academy of Management Annals, 5*(1), 653–707.

APPENDIX 1A: MAGGIE'S EMAIL TO LOUISE AND MARIE IN PREPARATION OF THEIR MEETING, CHILDREN'S PROFILES

From: Maggie Peyton
To: Louise and Marie
Subject: In preparation to our meeting – my kids

Dear Louise and Marie,
I look forward to finally meeting you next week. I can't tell you how exciting it is to have someone who can help us.

As per your suggestion, here is some information about my kids. I hope this will help create some context and maximize our time together. I did my best at picturing them in a balanced way. But they are awesome, and I am their mother. I know their interview is scheduled for the end of the month, so you will realize directly how wonderful they are.

Johnny – my oldest, is an empathetic and intelligent young man with great ambition, which are sometimes – according to Peter – "out of proportion, making him cocky". But I don't agree with Peter.

Johnny experienced the physical and emotional absence of his father. He quickly became very protective of me and always provided me with support, help, and a strong presence. Johnny has always been very critical of his father's lack of attention toward me. Only recently I learned that growing up, he was the one reminding Peter of my birthdays and anniversaries, he bought flowers for me on his behalf, and secretly booked dinner dates for us to ensure Dad didn't forget.

I am afraid he learned by observing me how to deal with Peter's procrastination and adopted the same strategy of not including Peter in decisions to avoid the pain of not connecting and evading essential and difficult conversations. At times, he also felt compelled to take the father figure role to his siblings, trying to encourage and support them in their choices. Johnny was an adultified child[1] and his father's proxy in the household. Thinking about all this now, I am concerned that all this set the roots for some growing anger toward Peter and ongoing unconscious competition between the two men.

I was so happy when Johnny married Megan, a bright, shy, and beautiful young woman. She is the only child of a very respected couple in another small town a few miles away from ours. Megan happily decided to stay home and raise their children God sent them. Johnny loves spoiling her with expensive gifts, long overseas weekends, and fun trips with friends, counting on Maggie's domestic work. Peter and I love spending time with their two little boys, Harry and Pete.

Johnny went to college and majored in English literature, he chose my same alma mater. After college, he worked for a consulting firm for a few years. When Peter's second partner left APS Inc., he thought it was the right time to ask Johnny to join. It was Peter's dream coming true. Johnny always knew about our plan to launch the children into entrepreneurship. So, he welcomed the invitation to join the company as a salesperson.

The business doubled in size in two years and continued its significant growth, thanks to his intuition to add new business lines. Johnny is very fast to act; he is persuasive and innovative. He has no tolerance for details, as he considers them annoying and irrelevant in the big picture. He resists when Peter shows him some critical clauses in the contracts he brings home. While Peter loves spending hours reviewing those documents and finds pitfalls that may create future problems, Johnny sees that as a useless waste of time, and his dad always (and annoyingly) wanting to save a few cents.

Jessy – My Jessy is so smart, sensitive, entrepreneurial, and incredibly caring. While in college, studying business, Jessy started her first successful business during her start-up class. She was the only one in her class to successfully launch the business she planned for as a school assignment and sold it after three years. With the proceeds, she began her second one, providing design consultation for shoemakers.

She is very close and caring of all her family members; she is great with her dad. She loves following in his footsteps, as she respects him, although she knows his limits. She carefully avoids asking personal questions, as she is aware that Peter isn't comfortable with being vulnerable, while she turns to Johnny for more personal struggles or life choices.[2] Jessy is engaged to Luke, a kind and driven young man who is an attorney in the M&A big firm. They have decided to get married but are still deciding about the date. They met through a youth group in college, although Luke is older. They both returned to their faith stronger after challenging it through life. They both feel very strongly about their beliefs. Everyone in the family loves Luke. Since he proposed, Peter told me they needed to get a prenup ready for him to sign. I am worried about it, but we can talk more about it when we get together.

Sandra – Everyone in the family (without envy) defines her as "Daddy's little girl". She has a BBA – Peter's same degree – from his same school. Sandra also has an outstanding ability to read people and situations and can diffuse tension while staying engaged in conversations, even when they get difficult. Sandra adores her dad and thinks the world of him. The feeling is mutual. Since a young age, she has had a passion for buildings and land. She is very concrete and down-to-earth. While Jessy is the daring dreamer, Sandra is the dependable doer. Peter is leveraging on that in the business setting, guaranteeing the sisters share ideas and perspectives regularly. Sandra developed an interest in real estate. After college, she joined a commercial real estate firm. Every day after work, she calls her dad and reviews the day with him. Peter loves that. They talk about everything she learned and could fill the gaps. She recently met a guy, Patrick. He seems really nice.

Sully – **Sullivan**, aka everyone's baby, is the youngest. Spoiled more by his siblings than by us, he was raised being adored by everyone. Sully developed some learning struggles that caused him to be slower in processing numbers and symbols. Extremely bright, he didn't let his slower pace get in the way of thriving. Peter never genuinely connected with Sully. While Sully was the most like Peter in his ability to capture details, they constantly focused on different kinds of facts. They spent many conversations bumping heads on which one was the most important or accurate, missing significant opportunities to connect. He saw his big brother Johnny as a hero, the only one who understood his struggles with his dad and the only one who could hold his footing with Dad. Sully picked liberal arts in college. He spent every summer working with either Johnny or Jessy. He wanted to learn more about business from them. Everyone in the family loved being in business, so he knew there must be something exciting about it, if only he could understand what it was. Sully is about to finish college. I want to help him find his way in the job market.

I hope this helps. If you have any questions, we can talk about it when we meet.

In the meantime, I send you warm regards.

Yours, Maggie.

NOTES

1. Adultification of children means exposing them to adult knowledge and engaging in behaviors understood as adult-like (such as taking on caregiving or provider roles in the family).
2. Johnny confirmed this, and stressed how important his role for his siblings is, as another example where he needs to balance for his father's lacking.

2
Brotherly battles at Brew Corp: "family firms should be forbidden by law"[1]

Dagmar Y. Hattenberg, Erik Veldhuizen and Judith van Helvert

CASE SUMMARY

This case focuses on Brew Corp, a second-generation family business, founded in 1960 on the family's farm. The business employs about 25 employees in the Netherlands, and was until recently owned by two brothers, Herman and Henk, who took over the firm from their parents in 1992. Henk started working for Brew Corp in 1985, while Herman joined a few years later. After the firm had been transitioned from the parents to the brothers, they decided to take on a bank loan to invest in a new production/filling facility. At the time, the interest rates were low, and thus the brothers felt positive about taking on the loan. Fast-forwarding to 2018, Herman noticed a shortage in liquidity, a shortage he could not fully explain, aside from increased purchasing prices. The bank urged a special management request to increase control over the liquidity issues. This moment served as the starting point for the brothers' legal conflict. The situation with the bank was the direct cause for the first court case about who should lead and own the business. In a period of four years, 17 court cases have passed. Currently, one of the brothers is still active in the business while the other brother no longer has any legal ties to the company. The brothers cannot seem to end their ongoing legal and emotional dispute. The relationship between the brothers had worsened when Henk started a new romantic relationship. According to Herman "this has been the root cause for all problems ever since". The new girlfriend allegedly tried to drive a wedge between the family and Henk, through gossip and hostility. A family conflict was born at this point.

LEARNING OUTCOMES

Through analysis of this case, students can be expected to:

*   Explain the situation of Brew Corp by using the Three Circle Model of family business systems.

- Describe potential sources of conflict in family firms related to family membership, leadership, and ownership.
- Use the principles of conflict resolution applicable in a family firm in explaining the available and relevant theories.
- Explain how differences in opinions and perspectives can be used for more effective decision-making and conflict resolution through different mediation styles.
- Describe the various instruments (formal and informal) of corporate governance that have the potential to facilitate decision-making in family businesses.

It is 2018. An official request is sent to the courthouse by Herman Garritsen to investigate suspected malpractice within his own family business, dating back to January 2017 and onwards from that point.

A few weeks before the official request was sent to the courthouse, Herman wrote in an email to the bank: "We would like to set up a meeting with you [the account manager] after July 19th, to discuss certain changes within the company."

The company is Brew Corp, a second-generation family business, founded in 1960 on a family farm. Nowadays, the business brews and produces gin-based drinks and employs about 25 employees in the Netherlands. In 2018, the company was owned by two brothers, Herman and Henk, who took over the business from their parents.

Two weeks after Herman sent his email to the bank, Henk sent the following email to his brother Herman: "Last week I told you I would also send an e-mail to the bank, and its content is – to say the least – not positive with regard to you and your role in the company. However, sending my e-mail might result in the bank quitting our collaboration and loan altogether."

When the bank invited both brothers for a meeting, Henk had let the bank know that he would not be available. Henk insisted that Herman prepare a proposal to buy Henk out. However, Henk did not accept Herman's proposal. When they tried to discuss the proposal on 29 July, the brothers ended up in a physical fight, resulting in Herman filing a police report.

A few days later, Henk wrote another email to the bank, in which he summed up numerous complaints about Herman. According to Henk, Herman had no oversight of revenues and costs, the stock accounts were incorrect, Herman invested in a new Enterprise Resource Planning (ERP) system that did not work, he dismissed a possible investor, and there was no way to communicate with Herman. He wrote that the lack of communication between the brothers led to a destructive polarization between them. The bank invited the brothers again for a meeting and indicated their worries about the continuity of the business. The bank let the brothers know they needed to find a solution that would also be acceptable to the bank.

After the bank's response, Henk wrote again to the bank requesting to withhold all accounts and block any usage. He wrote:

I would like to inform you that I will not be present at our meeting. I want to request that you block all accounts regarding Brew Corp, as well as Herman's private accounts. I am asking you to freeze the accounts to safeguard our money. At this point, my brother has transferred €50.000, to his private accounts. This is theft and only the bank can stop this by freezing the accounts. In addition, I convey my suspicions and the possible bankruptcy.

The email sent by Henk to the account manager of the bank resulted in a blockage of all access and usage of the company's bank accounts for both Herman and Henk.

HAPPIER TIMES AT BREW CORP

A flashback to the preceding decade paints an entirely different picture: two brothers who see each other as best friends, they can rely on one another through thick and thin. Both brothers considered following in their parents' footsteps as owners of Brew Corp as a logical next phase for the family business when the opportunity would arise. Herman describes it this way: "The transition was easy; we visited our family notary, signed the papers and from that moment on, my brother and I owned the company." The generational transition within the firm seemingly ran smoothly. However, in only a few years, the tables turned, and the brothers moved from one fight into another, well captured in the public eye through public court cases and newspaper articles.

In 1992, the two brothers – one of them described their relationship as always being incredibly close – took over the family business from their retiring parents. The parents (father, now 85 and mother, now 83) started their family farm in the southern part of the Netherlands. After six years of running their business, they moved to a different part of the country with more fertile ground. The business was relatively small though nationally known, and the brothers took over with the intention of (1) growing the business, and (2) keeping the business within the family, focusing on continuity. In these early years when the brothers still operated as a united front, the company served about 10 000 customers nationally. The business activities involved everything from the cultivation of ingredients to brewing and the delivery of gin-based drinks to customers, both B2B and B2C. One notable change they made to the firm's business model was the reduction of the cultivation and an exclusive focus on purchasing, producing, and selling.

While Herman and Henk officially took over the business together in 1992, Henk, the eldest brother who was born in 1967, had been working for the company since 1985. Herman (born in 1970) joined the firm in 1989. In the 1990s, after the firm was transitioned to the brothers, they decided to take on a bank loan to invest in a new production and filling facility. At the time, the interest rates were low, and thus the brothers felt positive about taking on the debt. The investment in the new production facility turned out positively and created substantial growth. New investments in machinery followed, partly financed with retained earnings and additional bank loans.

Fast forwarding to 2017, the business faced a shortage in liquidity due to rising purchasing and one-off costs. Upon noticing this liquidity shortage, the bank urged that company management increase control over the business's liquidity position. Legally, this moment was the starting point for the brothers' conflict, one that later turned out to be irreconcilable. In September 2018, the bank took the next step and decided to temporarily block the firm's usage of its bank accounts because the situation had not improved since the first notification of possible malpractice. In a letter, the bank expressed that it was extremely worried about the future of the company because of the long and intense disagreements between the brothers and the way they communicated with the bank. The bank's level of trust in the two brothers had decreased considerably. Bank officials announced that if the brothers were incapable of finding a reasonable and satisfying solution to their disagreements, the bank would withhold their credit facility and reclaim their outstanding balance immediately.

FIRST CRACKS IN THE BROTHERLY RELATIONSHIP

After an easy transition into the firm, the brothers had a smooth-running relationship during their first years of collaboration, because they both excelled in different areas of the business. Herman considered their skills as complementary: Herman being more strategic and sales driven, whereas Henk was described as more technical and production oriented. Both aimed at making the company more profitable, thus serving the continuity goal of the family firm.

Yet, while at first sight the relationship seemed strong, the first cracks started to show by the end of the 1990s. Brother Herman spent most of his time traveling around Europe to find new customers, something that triggered the jealousy of Henk. After all, Herman was doing "all the fun stuff". Herman had, however, a different perspective on this, because some of the traveling involved corruption and danger, especially in Russia and Ukraine: "In one of the occasions I was held at gunpoint with a machine gun. That made me sweat a bit." Herman explained that he would never pay bribes to the government for favored treatment as a matter of principle.

At the same time, Herman noticed the importance of Henk's work. Henk's technical expertise was very useful in helping the company produce efficiently and according to quality standards. Henk also designed a factory production layout that made it possible to grow the company further. Thanks to this factory production layout, the business was able to produce 5–6 million liters of gin-based drinks a year. From the inquiry report as requested by the courthouse, it became clear that the brothers' relationship took a turn for the worse by the second half of 2017, though the court's investigator claimed that already well before this time the relationship was no longer at its best. By mid-2018, the difficult relationship between the brothers had made it impossible to run the business together.

DEEPER CUTS IN THE BROTHERLY RELATIONSHIP

The relationship between Herman and Henk had worsened when Henk started a new romantic relationship. Henk already had two children, a son of 25 and a daughter of 30. After Henk broke up with the mother of his children, Herman took care of his brother and offered him a place to stay while recovering from heartbreak. Herman didn't have a permanent relationship at that time, but later fell in love with his current girlfriend, Martha, who already had two children, two boys 28 and 21 years old. Henk also found happiness again in a new relationship, something that Herman described as the significant point of change (which was later supported by the investigator).

Henk's new girlfriend, Gina, who is still in the picture, negatively influenced Henk, through gossip and hostility – in Herman's opinion. The girlfriend allegedly tried to drive a wedge between Henk and his family. The investigator noted in his report that Henk's communication style could be described as belligerent and obtrusive: Henk would write unprofessional and inappropriate emails to his brother, continually taking on an aggressive tone. The investigator suspected that Gina strongly influenced how Henk radically changed his communication and conflict management style from avoidance to confrontation, an almost sabotaging type of approach. Moreover, the investigator concluded that while Herman requested a meeting with the bank, it was due to the erratic behavior of Henk that the situation had escalated, and the bank was forced to temporarily close all of the firm's accounts.

FROM FAMILY TO BUSINESS CONFLICT

The family conflict turned into a business conflict when Henk started investing private money, which he borrowed from his girlfriend Gina, in the family firm. According to Herman, this was done because Henk made a business mistake earlier that cost the company some money, and by investing private money Henk wanted to compensate for his mistake. Around the same time, Herman invested some of his own money in a second home in Southern Europe. However, Henk and Gina felt this was unfair as they had invested their own money in the business. As it turned out, Herman's girlfriend Martha had sold a house in Eastern Europe and reinvested this money in a Southern European home. In an earlier in-company email, Henk had acknowledged this but kept blaming his brother for not investing his own money in the company, like he did. On the other hand, Herman believed that Gina wanted to obtain a stake in the family business. He believed this was the real reason why she lent funds to Henk and supported him to use the money for reinvestment in the business. When Herman found out that Henk was secretly transferring money back from the business to his private bank account, trouble started.

The violent escalation of the conflict in their office made the brothers realize that their current relationship was not a workable situation, and both agreed that one of them had to leave the company. Nevertheless, they both wanted to stay in the family business, and hold on to their shares. The question arose: who should leave and who should stay? This impasse of who would lead and remain within the company led to one of the first court cases where the brothers stood on opposite sides to each other.

After the devastating communication efforts with the bank, Herman filed a request for an investigation of the daily operations of Brew Corp and a request to dismiss Henk from his position and authority for the duration of the court case. Henk responded with a similar request for an investigation of the business and of course with a request for denial of his dismissal. Also, he requested that Herman be removed from his duties as board member of Brew Corp.

The brothers acknowledged to the court, through their lawyers, that they had disagreements about the question "who is guilty?", but they denied that the relationship between them as directors and shareholders was so bad that the company was out of control and, according to them, there was no reason to doubt the future of the company.

In the first court case, the judge decided, however, that there was enough evidence that the relationship between the brothers was harmed, and the brothers were not able to put their disagreements aside for the sake of the company. Moreover, the brothers were not able to reach an agreement about the unbundling of their (financial) interests. The disagreements between the brothers had even led to hand-to-hand fighting. In addition, Henk started to send out intimidating and negative emails to employees, which captured his enraged state regarding the troubles with his brother.

Of course, this situation created a backlash for the company. Decision-making in the board and in the general meeting of shareholders became impossible; employees had a lack of confidence in the joint governance of the firm, and daily work was greatly affected. The court said that based on the credit from the bank that was at stake, the continuity of the firm was in jeopardy. This gave the judge enough reason to doubt the policy and procedures of the company, and for that reason the judge ordered an inquiry.

In addition, the two brothers were dismissed from their roles as directors, and a temporary external director was appointed. The temporary director could decide whether he/she wanted the help of the two brothers in performing tasks. Both brothers agreed that the company's accountant would be allowed to make company payments during the time they were dismissed until the temporary external director was appointed. Furthermore, the brothers agreed that in the period before the temporary director started, Henk would only have access to the production area and would no longer enter the offices. As both brothers were the only shareholders of the company (each of them owned 50 percent) and could still exercise their rights as shareholders, the judge decided that the shares would be handed over to an independent manager. Therefore, Henk and Herman temporarily lost all decision-making power in the company (as shareholders and directors).

BREAKING POINT

The intensity of the conflict increased when Henk verbally threatened the externally appointed director on multiple occasions. Only six weeks after the first court case, the temporary director sent a letter requesting her own resignation and asking that another externally appointed director be assigned. The main reason for this was that she felt threatened by Henk and did not want to continue in her job. Henk had no confidence in her functioning (according to the court without objective justification) and treated her in an unacceptable way. The frequency, content, and tone of voice in emails from Henk to the temporary director were completely inappropriate and even made her feel unsafe. Moreover, Henk made her job to save the company almost impossible by sending messages to the bank about inaccuracies in stock valuation and complaining about her functioning as a temporary director.

The courthouse noted that the temporary director had done a great job, both professionally and with a great deal of commitment to Brew Corp and all of its stakeholders, by improving operational management and by preparing the sale of the company, which was in her opinion necessary to prevent insolvency. Indeed, the bank had declared in the meantime that it would end its credit line and was conditionally prepared to postpone their claim on the company of 2.6 million euros until April 2020. One of the conditions was that Brew Corp should present a plan to repay their loan. And there were only five weeks to prepare and present this plan.

Within the very short period of her appointment, the temporary director managed to show that a profitable continuation of the company was possible, but that an asset transaction was necessary to solve the bad liquidity position of the company. All parties agreed with this proposal. As the cooperation between the two brothers seemed to be permanently disrupted, and the bank was not inclined to continue financing the company with the current shareholders, all parties were aware of the urgency of the situation and the necessity of appointing an independent third person to guide the sale process of the company.

SELLING THE COMPANY

The idea of selling the company brought the brothers slightly closer to each other, as they promised, by letter to the courthouse, that they would cooperate professionally during the time of the sales process. However, as a preventive mechanism, the courthouse decided that Henk would receive a penalty of 10 000 euros (with a maximum of 200 000 euros) if he entered the company's premises after access was denied by a new temporary director.

Four months after the second court case, the supposed cooperation between the brothers in the sales process brought them to court again. In the meantime, Henk had changed his lawyer, which, in the course of time, would become almost a regular practice for him.

In a further attempt to reduce the bank loan, the temporary director discussed the potential sale of a 2.5 hectare piece of land owned by the firm. This plan had already been discussed with Herman, and he thought it was a good idea and would relieve the pressure of the bank on the company. Brew Corp already outsourced all cultivation activities, so this plan was completely aligned with the business strategy. However, Henk and Gina did not like the idea and offered to buy the land. For the sake of the company the temporary director sold the land to a third party and sent a copy of the agreement to Henk and Gina. This message was not received very well, and Gina sent an email to the bank (signed with 'Advisor of Henk') saying that the sale of land conflicted with earlier promises of the temporary director to her, that the sale price of the land was too low, and that the sale was disadvantaging the bank. The temporary director was not happy with this type of communication to the bank, as Brew Corp was dependent on the bank and did not yet have full liquidity to pay back the loan.

EXCLUSION FROM THE SALES PROCESS

In the meantime, the temporary director had decided that Henk was not allowed to access any of the company's premises (including the production facility) for a period of two months. As a reason for this, he mentioned the heavily disturbed relationship between Henk and Herman, and between Henk and most employees. In addition, Henk did not reply to the questions of the temporary director fast enough and was according to Herman "not indispensable for the operation of Brew Corp". The measure brought some relative relief to the company and the employees unanimously asked for an extension of it, which was indeed what happened.

Moreover, Henk and Gina were excluded from the sale process of Brew Corp by the temporary director. They were not allowed to buy the company as they were not dealing in the interests of Brew Corp. An example of their behavior was a message sent by Henk to a potential buyer: "If I let the bank go, the bank will pull back the loan, which will let Brew Corp go bankrupt. After that it will be much cheaper to buy the estate."

Henk and Gina sent many emails to the bank, the accountant, and the courthouse to make the temporary director look bad. Henk even created several WhatsApp accounts with fake names and pictures of the temporary director and the logo of his law firm to communicate with the bank and other parties. Before the judge, Henk admitted this, and he was ordered to stop these activities for the sake of the company and with the risk of receiving a penalty after further violations.

Of course, Henk did not accept his exclusion from the sale process easily. He asked the court to create a "level playing field" so that he would be treated like any other buying candidate. Furthermore, he wanted to receive all the necessary information for a potential takeover. The court concluded that it was indeed an extreme decision to exclude Henk from the sale process, especially because Brew Corp was a family business with a history of more than 60 years, founded by the parents of Henk and Herman followed by many years of cooperation between the brothers. However, according to the judge it was clear as the temporary director concluded that Henk was not dealing in the company's interest and therefore excluded him from the sale process. Furthermore, it was completely justified that the temporary director was careful about providing information about the company to Henk, as it might further harm the sale of Brew Corp.

Besides the exclusion of Henk from the sale process, the temporary director also decided to stop the payment of a monthly management fee to Henk. Unsurprisingly, Henk did not agree, and asked the court to revoke this decision. The judge decided that the decision to stop payments of his management fee was not unreasonable, because Henk did not work for Brew Corp any more, and this was due to an attributable shortcoming, namely his behavior, which made his functioning within the company impossible and even led to a denial of access to the company's premises.

When the sale process entered a crucial final phase, the tensions between the different parties increased. Within a period of one month Henk received 16 forfeited penalties involving a total amount of 400 000 euros. After the previous court case, Henk (1) was not allowed to frustrate or complicate the sales process; (2) had to tolerate that he was excluded from the sales process; (3) was not allowed to provide information about the upcoming sale of Brew Corp to third parties; and (4) was not allowed to speak or behave in such a way that was defamatory or threatening to the temporary director.

CLOSING THE DEAL

On 1 July 2020, the temporary director informed Henk that the closing of the sale was approaching and that there were several candidates. In addition, he offered Henk the opportunity to provide further information about what he deemed relevant for the sale of Brew

Corp, but what could not be derived from the administration, the management team, or the accountant. The next day Henk replied:

> How could I add information that is lacking, if I do not know what information is in the memorandum? When do you plan to retrieve the goods that are still here on my private property? Except for a few hundred grain cubes there is also a pallet of asbestos sheets and chemicals. In case of no answer, I will let them transport to Brew Corp and will calculate the costs of it.

In the legal procedure, the statement by Henk about dumping asbestos and chemicals at the gin factory was considered a threat, which would receive a penalty of 250 000 euros if it was executed. For each and every message that was sent by Henk and Gina against the orders of the court, the temporary director had already given them a penalty (as the temporary director was assigned by the court, he was allowed to do this). Then, the temporary director asked Henk to pay the total sum of money (400 000 euros) within two days, and when Henk did not react to this after seven days, the director seized his house, bank accounts, and his shares in Brew Corp.

One month later Brew Corp was sold to Herman and a company producing biological grain, an important ingredient of the gin-based drinks of Brew Corp. Herman became the majority shareholder. After this sale, the continuity of the firm was no longer at stake, as the bank loan could be paid off. However, Brew Corp still had financial claims and debts to the personal holdings of its previous shareholders, Herman and Henk, and an inquiry of the court was therefore still necessary to determine the final equity position of the firm.

PROOF OF MISMANAGEMENT

The inquiry resulted in a detailed report, indicating how, according to the investigator, the conflict between Herman and Henk had started. The inquiry investigator firmly concluded that during the time both brothers were involved in the business, they were incapable of running a professional operation in the firm. In 2021, the court discussed and ruled upon the matter in detail: while Henk accused his younger brother of being a fraudulent thief and while he accused the accountant of embezzlement and forgery when it came to the supply account, the court ruled otherwise. In December 2021, the court concluded that Henk was fully accountable for dubious behavior, sending out false accusations about current company members (i.e., his brother and the accountant). In particular, the court ruled on mismanagement and regarded Henk as fully responsible and accountable for such mismanagement practices. As an example, the court referred to several emails sent by Henk, for instance one where he withdrew his trust in the accountant, not taking the matter seriously. He was unable during the court sessions to support his claims and acts with arguments and facts. As the court case became public, several news outlets published the findings and rulings of the court.

Henk wrote a response regarding the inquiry report, a response that the investigator considered inconsistent with earlier statements provided by Henk regarding the malpractice of Herman within the firm. Nowadays, by order of the court, the business is owned and run by only one of the brothers and an external partner owns part of the shares. The family relationships are completely damaged, according to Herman: "If someone wants to ruin your company on purpose, and deals with his family in this way, then you never want to see him again."

At the same time, Henk had to sell all his shares to his brother, while a debt of more than 100 000 euros remained. Until Spring 2021, the shares were externally managed, and after the sale was completed Herman and his current business partner maintained all shares of the company. Notably, the court stated that Henk had been warned regarding his behavior on numerous occasions, during many of the trials that have taken place. Nevertheless, according to the rulings by the court, Henk continued with his destructive behavior, which severely escalated.

THE CONFLICT CONTINUES

The conflict remains ongoing and has touched upon multiple levels of conflict management: on the one hand, personal relationships have been damaged, involving the siblings, the significant others, the children, and the parents (the original owners). The parents feel very sad about the continuing fights between the brothers. In the past their sons were loving brothers and now their relationship is ruined. Gina and Henk do not want to see the parents and the rest of the family any more. Henk's children do not want to see their father and his girlfriend again, because they blame Gina and their father for the ongoing fights.

On the other hand, task-related/business relationships have been severely damaged, as there have been 17 lawsuits between the siblings over four years, costing both the family and the business millions of euros. Currently, Herman wishes to focus on growing the firm and selling it. While in earlier years the brothers discussed the continuity of the firm by keeping it in the family, this is no longer an option for Herman. He does not have children himself and he does not foresee handing over the firm to other relatives. At this point, after this experience, Herman even believes that "family firms should be forbidden by law".

During the conflict both brothers focused on their own interests and, in their opinion, the interests of the company. Their main goal was to grow the company that they inherited from their parents in what Herman called a very easy succession process:

> My brother and I went to the accountant without our parents, and we only had to sign the contracts. Even the accountant, their most trusted advisor, said it was an easy transfer of ownership, we did not have to pay a lot for the company. After the succession, dad would occasionally be hired as an advisor to provide for his pension.

Furthermore, Herman describes how he and his brother were raised in a warm and loving environment, based on family harmony. Moreover, according to Herman, both brothers were conflict avoidant: while there may always be minor disputes between brothers, both would rather move away from a potential conflict than communicate about it. When Herman now describes how his brother views the family firm transition, he strongly believes his brother's current perspective on the succession process is different from what it used to be: "My brother now looks back at our succession as a very annoying process. He even called it a bad contract that our parents saddled us with."

Of course, the conflict between the two brothers is frustrating and deeply troubling for their parents as well. Now, there is no communication between Henk and his parents although they are living only a short distance from one another. Henk even proclaimed that he does not wish to be mentioned on a mourning card in the event of the death of one of his parents, indicating how severely the relationship has been damaged at this point.

RULING JUDGMENTS

Upon current ruling, Henk has been convicted of several charges, including maltreatment, physical abuse, intimidation regarding nonfamily members of the firm and employees of the bank, and malpractice. The court ruled that the ongoing dispute has brought danger and instability to the firm and concluded that Henk is solely responsible for this escalation. According to the court, Henk deliberately painted a negative image of the company to influence the way the bank would respond to any requests, among others by impersonating a director and misleading his brother by using a fake account and requesting actions. Another request by Henk to regain insight into the administration has also been ruled over by the court. This last court case may allow Herman to finally file a damage claim towards his brother Henk, though it is still not known whether Herman will move forward with such a claim. What is known is that both brothers are preparing the next court case: number 18.

DISCUSSION QUESTIONS

1. What are the roles and interests of the various family actors involved?
2. What is/are the cause(s) behind the direct cause (the decision of the bank to withdraw the credit facility) for the conflict between Herman and Henk? And additionally, what is the tipping point (point of no return) of the escalation?
3. Do you think the family relationships of the brothers (and their parents as well as romantic partners) can be repaired and, if so, how?
4. The conflict between the brothers escalated in a short period of time. Which (alternative) conflict resolution mechanisms could have been used at which moments in time to manage the tensions that developed so quickly?
5. Conflict resolution theory, particularly within family firms, would suggest moving forward with mediation, especially in the early phases of the conflict. What type of mediation would have aided the brothers and in which stage would that have been helpful?
6. What family business governance practices could have helped to prevent this escalation?
7. If other companies were to come into a rather similar conflict where one family member uses disputable moral or ethical behavior, what advice could be provided to these companies to avoid a legal escalation (i.e., 17 court cases)?

NOTE

1. The company name and the names of the individuals were anonymized for this teaching case. The case is based on primary and secondary data. Primary data were collected via interviews with one of the brothers (Herman). Secondary data consist of press releases, newspaper articles, media coverage, and publicly available court reports.

SUGGESTED READING

Gilligan, M., Stocker, C.M. and Jewsbury Conger, K. (2020). Sibling relationships in adulthood: Research findings and new frontiers. *Journal of Family Theory & Review*, *12*(3), 305–20.

Glasl, F. (1982). The process of conflict escalation and roles of third parties. In G.B.J. Bomers and R. Peterson (eds), *Conflict Management and Industrial Relations* (pp. 119–40). Kluwer-Nijhoff.

Tagiuri, R. and Davis, J. (1996). Bivalent attributes of the family firm. *Family Business Review*, *9*(2), 199–208.

3
Feuding siblings: sowing the seeds of conflict in the family business[1]

Unai Arzubiaga, Amaia Maseda and Javier Macías

CASE SUMMARY

The case tells the story of Luis and Carmen and their children Felipe, María, and Julio. From humble origins, Luis and Carmen emigrated in the mid-1950s from a village in Spain, in the province of Badajoz, to Bilbao, a booming industrial city. They explored different trades and businesses until they reached the real estate sector, in which they worked as brokers (buying and selling) and ran a construction company as well as acquiring urban land and real estate in addition to buying a farm dedicated to agriculture as well as apartments to rent to vacationers. Luis and Carmen's vision was to work hard and save money to escape poverty and offer their children all the opportunities they had not had in life. With this aim in mind, they devoted their lives to helping their children in their attempts to make their own living, providing jobs in the family business for Felipe and María and for each child an apartment, a car, and several business premises and/or tourist apartments for them to rent out. They tried to distribute their wealth evenly among their children. Nevertheless, Felipe's and María's management of their respective family business units was not as prosperous as they thought. They have asked Julio to join them to ask their father, all together, for a donation of part of his estate to them during his lifetime. Julio does not understand this proposal; he believes the right thing to do is to help their parents and be grateful for all the things they have done for their offspring. Felipe and María see Julio's rejection as a betrayal, and the communication becomes aggressive among the siblings as in a contest with two sides of allies and opponents.

LEARNING OUTCOMES

After analyzing this case, students will be able to:

- Explain why sibling rivalry may not be the cause of family business failure but the consequence of a lack of leadership in both business and family, together with bilateral parent–child alliances.

- Communicate the significant differences between family business (with intention of continuity) and a business run by a family (self-employment without intention of continuity).
- Describe how the founder's vision shapes the organizational structure of the business and its future and, consequently, its expiration date.
- Explain how dysfunctional family dynamics and poor communication undermine the next generation's courage and motivation.
- Explain why pursuing personal and professional aims outside the family firm could be seen as a betrayal in some families, but in certain environments, a better way to grow and mature as an adult.

One morning in February 2015 Julio received a call from his sister María. Julio loved February mornings in his apartment in Fuengirola, on Spain's Costa del Sol. The morning sun streaming through the window produced a kaleidoscope of colors in his living room. However, the call from his sister would cloud that peaceful and luminous winter morning. The directive tone in his sister's voice already denoted that something was wrong. María told him:

> I have been talking to our brother Felipe, and we want to ask Dad to distribute his money and make living donations of part of his estate to us. It is incomprehensible that we are in need while he has one of the richest estates in Badajoz. However, we, the three siblings, must be united. If the three of us, all together, ask him for the money, he cannot refuse.

Julio was not surprised by this attempted rebellion. It was a subject that had already started to come up on other occasions among the three siblings: Felipe (the oldest brother), María (the middle sister), and Julio (the youngest sibling). For years, even decades, the two older siblings had maintained a distant relationship with Julio, the youngest. Both siblings, Felipe and María, had found a way to make a living from the family business, while Julio had chosen to make a living outside the family business. He had worked first as an employee in several companies and more recently had tried to become self-employed as a business consultant.

In fact, when Julio received this request from his sister, he had not yet established his professional career in the consulting field. He had recently worked as an employee for a financial institution. Julio's savings were small, and the consulting job market was subject to ups and downs. It was difficult for Julio to foresee the possibility of starting a family of his own in this situation. His sister's proposal was tempting. Receiving extra money would give him the security he needed to start a family and consolidate his new company. Moreover, by accepting his sister's proposal, he would become closer to his siblings again, sharing a common project. However, despite all these reasons for Julio to join the uprising, in the end, he decided to reject the proposal:

> I'm sorry, but do not count on me for this shipboard mutiny. First, our father's fortune is not as big as you think. I have been filing tax returns with Dad for years, and I am aware of the numbers. He has a modest heritage similar to what a successful manager working for a few years in a multinational company could have. Regarding our father's revenues… there

were better times. After the golden age of the 1990s and the beginning of the millennium, things changed. I do not know what has happened, but Dad does not have as much income anymore, while he keeps up the volume of expenses. He barely has any money left to save at the end of the year. I think that, instead of asking him for more money, we should work on our own and be grateful to him. Definitely do not count on me to become a part of this shipboard mutiny.

DISTRIBUTION IMBALANCES AND REBALANCES

Right after this conversation with his sister, Julio recalled how his parents, Luis and Carmen, had given each child an apartment and a car so they could start an independent life with a home of their own. Their parents used to say, "The married one wants a house." Moreover, Luis and Carmen had assigned the ownership of two business premises in Badajoz to the eldest son, Felipe, for him to rent. In addition to this allowance, Luis and María had granted him the management of the family lands. This management was given to him after helping him in two different businesses that ultimately failed: a burger business and a horse training business on one of the family farms.

María received similar treatment after her first marriage. Apart from the apartment and the car she received after the wedding, Luis and Carmen set up a picture framing store for the just married couple to run by themselves. María also received two apartments in Benidorm for her to rent out. After her divorce, she closed the store, but to balance her savings with her second husband, she received an additional dowry from her parents, consisting of two business premises in Badajoz and the right to collect the rent of an additional two business premises.

Meanwhile, Julio, the youngest, was observing these family events from a distance. He had decided to study business administration and management in the United Kingdom and, later, received an MBA at a prestigious business school in Spain. Julio, after his studies, developed his professional life outside the family business. Julio did not seem to be in such a hurry to get married as his siblings. Thus, Luis and Carmen decided to give him an apartment, a car, two business premises, and two tourist apartments when he reached the age of 30. Luis and Carmen believed that the distribution of property and businesses among their three children was balanced and provided them with sufficient means to be able to live and prosper.

Julio knew that he would become the "traitor" of the family after his refusal to join the siblings' uprising against their father. In fact, his brother and sister already thought of him as a traitor since he had chosen to make his own way outside the family business. Julio's intention was to honor his parents' efforts to make life easier for them. His aim was to live an autonomous and responsible life by making the most of his personal talents. Julio was aware of his siblings' rejection of his decision not to work in the family business. Felipe and María would make it clear that it was thanks to them that the family business continued.

On the other hand, when Julio helped his father to do the tax returns every year, he saw that the income from the family lands remained in the coffers of his big brother and that the income from the tourist apartments in Benidorm remained in the accounts of the middle sister. However, most of the expenses of these two business units were still the responsibility of the parents, Luis and Carmen. They paid most of these business units' bills. One of the times when Julio and his father were together to close the year and check the financial situation of the family businesses, Julio asked: "Why is there this inequality among the siblings? It does not seem to be an equitable distribution to me."

To which his father replied, "I try to help the one who needs it the most."

Julio respected his parents' decision. After all, the businesses and the family wealth were the result of many years of his father and mother's effort, and they belonged to them. Thus, Julio understood that he had no say in this.

Despite this fact, Julio had sought psychological help on this issue. He complained about feeling less loved than his siblings, since he was the one who had received the least from the family, in terms of both economics and attention. On one occasion, in a conversation with his sister, Julio brought up the issue and talked about the inequality. However, his sister disagreed because Julio's studies in the United Kingdom and, later, his MBA had cost the family an enormous amount of money.

ENTERPRISING COUPLE

Luis and Carmen knew each other for a long time before they got married. They were both born and lived in Zahínos, a village of about 3000 inhabitants in the province of Badajoz (Spain). A village where, at that time, most families lived in precarious conditions on the edge of poverty.

Luis and Carmen wished to leave the town to have a better life. Carmen was the eldest of four siblings and a hard worker from a very young age. According to her father's way of thinking, having a woman as a first born was a curse to the family. He needed the first born to be a man to help him in the fields, work for the landlords, and bring money home. Consequently, Carmen tried her best all her life to prove she was as capable as any man.

Luis felt attracted by the strong character Carmen had developed. Luis wanted better, for him and for his beloved girl. They both knew that remaining in the village would cause them to be poor forever and to live under their parents' tyranny. It was clear to the couple that they had to migrate in search of a better future, for them and for their future children. Luis found a way to leave the village with a secure job at his destination, thanks to his work as a deliveryman. Luis delivered eggs weekly to the home of a landowner whose engineer son worked in Bilbao. Therefore, he asked the landowner's family if they could recommend him for a job in Bilbao, a place with a thriving steel industry. Luis had no more education than the basics, which had enabled him to learn to read and write, add, subtract, multiply, and divide. However, he had earned a good reputation as a hardworking and honest young man both in the town and among all the bosses he had thus far worked under. Therefore, the family did not hesitate to write a letter of recommendation for him.

Thus, Luis left Zahínos at the age of 19 with the dream of starting a new life. The letter of recommendation allowed him to start working in Altos Hornos de Vizcaya, in its facilities in Sestao (Bilbao) as soon as he arrived. Altos Hornos was the largest Spanish company during most of the twentieth century. It was a steel and metallurgy company that sold high-quality

Basque iron both nationally and internationally. Luis entered as an operator to sweep factory floors, although soon after he was promoted twice. Luis studied elements and chemical reactions to apply for this position.

Luis' work in Altos Hornos was interrupted when he was drafted into compulsory military service. Once he finished his service, he married Carmen, with whom he returned to Bilbao to start a life together. They were a hardworking couple with ambition and a desire to do business together. While Luis worked at Altos Hornos, Carmen contributed to the family income by trying self-employed businesses, such as sewing raincoats, cooking and washing clothes for the guests they lodged in an apartment they offered as an inn, and running a fish shop.

Luis, on the other hand, worked as a construction laborer after his workday at Altos Hornos. This situation continued until one day a friend encouraged him to sell portrait-holders to neighboring houses. After a few months, Luis and Carmen organized their own picture framing workshop in their home. Luis went out to sell pictures, while Carmen framed the pictures at home. Everything was going well until the introduction of electronic door entry systems, which complicated the cold call sales that Luis knew. This new entry system made it difficult for him to socialize and talk with potential customers, which was his primary sales strategy.

For this reason, Luis returned to the construction business. He started a company with two business partners to construct a building for workers' housing. The working-class population of Baracaldo (Bilbao) was increasing, as was the need for housing. However, upon completion of the first building, the company was dissolved. Luis and Carmen joined forces with Alberto, who had been the accountant of the construction firm, to start a new company. In this new firm, Luis assumed the roles of builder, developer, and salesman, while Alberto, together with Carmen, oversaw accounting, salaries, and purchases from suppliers.

BUSINESS IDEAS

The new firm's business model was based on the organization of homeowners' cooperatives. Individuals interested in a home would advance money for the construction of the building, receiving a new home as their own property upon completion. One of the most difficult tasks was to find enough buyers to advance the money. The risk was high for both parties, buyer, and construction firm. However, this was a way for the buyer to save up to 80 percent of the property's value. Luis and Carmen's ability to build trust made the task of finding a minimum group of buyers to start the cooperative to construct the building relatively quick.

Finally, Luis resigned from Altos Hornos de Vizcaya, since his entrepreneurial activity was demanding full-time attention, and his earnings were much higher than the payment received from the corporation. Luis and Carmen were engaged not only in the new construction of cooperative housing but also in the purchase and sale of homes. They acquired apartments that needed a small renovation, renovated them, and put the property back up for sale. This business had a shorter turnover cycle than the construction of buildings, and the returns were sometimes close to 200 percent by that time. Luis and Carmen obtained bank loans to finance the renovation of houses. In addition, Luis and Carmen had learned to negotiate and process mortgages with the banks, an experience they also put to good use advising and processing mortgage loans for third parties.

At the end of the 1960s, Luis and Carmen had their own successful business. They were buying and selling real estate almost every week and had built five residential buildings in Baracaldo. During this period, their two first children were born, Felipe and María. Most of the housework and childcare was Carmen's responsibility, who continued to work in the businesses. A fighting spirit, instilled from her earliest childhood, was very strong in Carmen. In their entrepreneurial ventures, Luis and Carmen had equal decision-making power and participation.

In the mid-1970s, when Felipe was entering his preadolescence and María was still very young, the couple decided to return to Badajoz to be closer to their extended family. By that time, Luis and Carmen had business in both places – Baracaldo and Badajoz.

In the early 1980s, the entrepreneurial couple had already settled down in Badajoz running their own construction company. Then, they tried to create a new business: raising cattle. It was a complete failure, but Luis still had a desire to own property in the countryside. Owning land was important for him. Luis finally bought several plots (160 hectares – about 400 acres – in total) and subsequently bought machinery and tractors and hired a family of farmers to work for him in the fields.

WEALTH MANAGEMENT

At the end of the 1980s, Luis and Carmen decided to abandon construction activity. They had business premises to rent in Badajoz, located in central streets of the city, and apartments to rent in Benidorm, a major tourist center in Spain since the 1970s.

Felipe and María were eager to emulate their parents' entrepreneurial activity. That's why they were constantly searching for new business opportunities and proposing new projects to continue the business. However, all the projects Felipe and María proposed were rejected and never taken seriously by their parents.

Gradually, as the enterprising couple grew older, real estate activity also slowed down. With their children already grown up, with all their dreams of well-being achieved, and with a good amount of savings, Luis and Carmen decided to stop doing business and enjoy life just by managing their wealth. However, this prosperous situation could only be maintained for two decades.

Two main facts threatened the business. First, Badajoz was losing a young population with an entrepreneurial spirit. On the other hand, Benidorm had been the focus of construction companies during the real estate bubble in Spain (late 1990s until 2008). Thus, Badajoz was losing demand for business premises, while Benidorm had a vast supply of newly constructed buildings that were attracting renters, leaving the family business apartments empty. Given this situation, family income decreased substantially.

LEGAL ARCHITECTURE OF THE BUSINESS

When Luis and Carmen decided to leave the construction business and focus on wealth management, they dismantled all their limited liability companies and partnerships. Thus, the new legal structure was as self-employed freelancers. They paid taxes based on a 50/50 distribution between the couple.

Luis' vision was that he would continue to run the business until he was no longer competent. Luis' position about continuity was confusing. He used to say, "All these are yours." Moreover, sometimes Luis and Carmen communicated that they would be proud if their children were eager to continue the business.

However, the legal architecture of the business made it difficult. Each member of the family was a freelance employee, owning personal property, and having separate income. Moreover, each sibling thought they had the right to lead the family business. Felipe, the eldest sibling, thought it his birthright to run the business because he was the eldest. María, the middle sister, thought she had the right because she talked with her parents frequently and had helped them to solve certain situations with the tenants in the past. Julio, the youngest, thought he had the right because he had the training and handled the family finances and related paperwork.

Felipe had signed a rental agreement with his father that enabled him to work on the family lands in exchange for a symbolic amount of money. However, Felipe did not behave as a tenant, and Luis did not behave as the landowner either. Given the symbolic meaning this land had for the family, the father and child were constantly discussing the weather, how to farm, or which cereal was the best to plant in the next season. Luis liked visiting the family land and seeing how the plant seeds were growing in the fields. Carmen liked to visit the family land too and spend time with Felipe while taking care of the farm animals he kept in his village house. Carmen was also in charge of helping Felipe invest in developing his agricultural business, such as a new barn and sometimes new machinery.

Despite all his parents' efforts to make Felipe happier, he claimed to be a self-made man who had never received any help from his parents. He claimed that his father had deceived him in the past. However, when somebody tried to clear up this misunderstanding, it ended up as an emotional and verbally violent situation. Moreover, every member of the family was aware of Felipe's mood swings. Certain situations could trigger him into a violent argument. Some triggers were known, but others were not. His parents got used to these unexpected and changing moods and were experts in handling Felipe's behavior. However, these emotional breakdowns became stronger as the entrepreneurial couple got older and even more so after Felipe's divorce.

After a divorce from her second husband, María, the middle daughter, had signed rental agreements with her father in exchange for a symbolic price to acquire the right to manage seven apartments located in Benidorm owned by her father, Luis. She also signed a ten-year note for a €100 000 loan from him for her to have cash to renovate the apartments. Luis and Carmen were getting old, and they didn't feel like going to Benidorm any more. Therefore, María moved in to her parents' apartment in Benidorm. Luis and Carmen were very happy that María was now in charge of all the family properties in Benidorm. María had refurbished the seven rental apartments and now was advertising them as seasonal rentals using websites on the internet. Once María settled down in Benidorm, Luis and Carmen quit their usual winter holidays there. Nevertheless, María and Carmen talked over the phone frequently, and María was updated on everything new in the family business. Luis and Carmen were still in good shape to manage the rental properties in Badajoz, as well as their investments in funds and stocks.

Julio did not have a defined role in the family business, but he helped his father in managing his business rentals in Badajoz, income tax payments, and anything else that could be useful. Julio was now involved full time in his consultancy work in Madrid. However, this job allowed him a high degree of flexibility. On each visit to Badajoz, he took several days to be with his parents and help them with whatever they needed. The frequency of these visits increased as his parents aged.

ALLIANCES AND FAMILY DYNAMICS

Felipe and María's plan to claim their father's inheritance during his lifetime was supported by their mother, Carmen. However, it was a shifting alliance. Julio knew that despite their mother's initial support, an alliance between the three children against their father would have caused Carmen to disapprove of the plan. On many occasions, Carmen reminded her children that the most beautiful part of their life as a couple had been dreaming together about the future of the family and the business. Therefore, although the mother could support her children's whims, as a wife she was never going to turn against her husband and business partner.

Julio's position about the heritage distribution was different. Julio had to endure difficult situations at work, such as moody bosses and competitive peers. He experienced being an employee with limited rights and many obligations, while he had to constrain himself to a rigid schedule. Thus, when he experienced his first failures at work, he asked his father for either a position in the family business or a business unit for him to run. He had wanted to become a manager at the family business because he could not become one at his current company. Still vivid in his memory was the day when his father had not given him the option to stay in the family business:

> This is not a business for you. This business has been set up by an illiterate foolish village guy like me. You have studied, and you can do more interesting things in your life. I do not understand why you want to stay at home. I have already given you a career, for you to fly. Thus, now it is your time to fly!

It took Julio a while to understand Luis because his father's behavior confused him. Luis was telling him to fly. However, as soon as Julio started a new position, Luis phoned him asking for advice. Sometimes Luis asked Julio for his opinion on stock market investments. Other times, Luis was asking for help with problems he was having with his rent management. Julio understood this phone call as an indirect way to involve him with the family business. Julio also knew about the business since his father had given him responsibilities during his summer holidays when he was a student. However, these calls were not related to the intention to involve Julio again in the business. They were just a way to acknowledge him, to make him feel valuable and connected with the family business.

In addition, Luis knew his son Julio would be able to work both as an employee and as a casual advisor to help his parents in the family business. Luis was fascinated by the children of other family members who came home on weekends or vacations to help their parents in the fields, while during the working week they kept their regular jobs in factories or in other companies in the city. Luis came from a generation where life was work and where the extended family was there to help each other with all their needs.

THE EXERCISE OF POWER

Luis told his children incessantly, "All this is yours." He intended to raise his children's commitment to the family firm with these words. However, his offspring saw it the other way around: "If it is mine, then I can dispose of it as I please. Give it to me."

Julio had tried to open a dialogue with his siblings, trying to make them understand that this sort of syllogism was wrong. Moreover, Julio tried to make his siblings remember their father's saying: "I will continue to run the business until my head fails me." However, these conversations among the siblings never ended well. Felipe complained about his father's treatment and all the disqualifications he had received throughout his life. On the other hand, all of them were able to acknowledge in these sibling talks that their father was going to hold power until his final day. Finally, it looked as if Felipe's solution to this problem had been to fight Luis' hold on the company through resistance, encouraging his siblings to join him on his crusade.

FAMILY COEXISTENCE AND CONFLICTS

For years, the family had become accustomed to four of the family members "having fun together" – Luis and Carmen, Felipe, and María – doing their own business and private agreements, while Julio, the youngest, was excluded from the family conversations and dynamics. Now that Luis and Carmen were getting older, Julio became more present at family gatherings, as well as in handling the paperwork of the family business. While Julio was not involved in day-to-day management, he was helping his father do the income tax and regularly reviewed all the family business's accounts books. Consequently, Julio knew all aspects of the business in detail, even the private agreements his siblings had set up with their father and mother.

Moreover, Julio's closer physical presence meant that the "*colaciones*" (casual donations in life) that Felipe and María received from their father whenever they demanded them were less frequent and less generous. Maybe because their father knew that now Julio, the silent observer, was closer. Whether for this reason or another, Julio's physical presence bothered his siblings, who confronted him at every possible opportunity.

Julio could not understand how these misunderstandings were taking place in a family moved by unity, love, and affection. However, in recent years, the family atmosphere had become tense, as family dynamics changed due to alliances, coalitions, and verbal confrontations. Luis valued honesty and integrity. He had taught his children: "Your businesses must be honest. You must be able to sleep peacefully every night."

Julio wondered if these values (i.e., honesty) were truly shared by his siblings. He also wondered about how and why this situation had developed, how it could have been avoided or prevented, and what could be learned from it all.

DISCUSSION QUESTIONS

1. Do you think this family has made good decisions regarding the professional career design of the second generation? Why or why not?
2. How have mature dependency or immature dependency relationships been promoted in the second generation?
3. Analyze the following three variables considering the case facts: (a) conjugality; (b) parentality; (c) partners, and how they explain the family conflict.
4. Is the firm in this case a family business or a cyclical circumstantial family business? What is the difference?
5. What recommendations do you think could have prevented the family conflict from escalating in the case?

EPILOGUE

Julio took the initiative to open a family office in one of his father's business premises while maintaining his consulting business that he attended from afar. He asked his father for permission to conduct an audit of all the family's assets. He traveled regularly to Badajoz from Madrid (where he worked as a consultant) for two years to actively support his father in the management of the estate and to put Luis' affairs in order.

In 2020, Luis appointed Julio as administrator and delegated the management of the parents' estate to him. His siblings, Felipe and María, were upset about Julio being appointed as the administrator of their parents' estate and pressured him more directly to share all of the parents' patrimonial information. Luis made it clear to Julio that he was not to share the financial information with his siblings, a confidentiality that Julio preserved as if it were just another client.

The discomfort between the siblings was growing until Luis decided to "buy peace" by promising to make three lots of assets to donate to his three children. The apartments in Benidorm for María, the farmland for Felipe, and the business premises in Badajoz for Julio. The differences would be compensated in cash.

Julio communicated his disagreement with the distribution because the business premises had no real value; they could not be rented out or sold. He also expressed his disagreement because, according to his point of view, the family should be talking about how to take care of the aging parents and about the economic needs of the parents at this stage, not about how to divide the "loot."

In any case, it was the decision of the patriarch, whom Julio respected as the head of the family. Conflicts among the family members escalated until Carmen's death changed the scenario. Now, the inheritance paperwork and distribution are in the hands of Julio and the family lawyer. Felipe and María must wait until they receive their inheritance to relieve their suffering.

NOTE

1. This case, based on an actual family and family business, was compiled by conducting several interviews with a key family member. All names of individuals, the company, and other details have been changed to protect the identities of the family.

SUGGESTED READING

Eddleston, K.A. and Kidwell, R.E. (2012). Parent–child relationships: Planting the seeds of deviant behavior in the family firm. *Entrepreneurship Theory & Practice*, 36(2), 369–86.
Jaskiewicz, P., Uhlenbruck, K., Balkin, D.B. and Reay, T. (2013). Is nepotism good or bad? Types of nepotism and implications for knowledge management. *Family Business Review*, 26(2), 121–39.
Kaye, K. (1996). When the family business is a sickness. *Family Business Review*, 9(4), 347–68.

4

Tuskys Supermarkets: the good, the bad and the ugly in the Kago family business[1]

William Murithi and Sally Kah

CASE SUMMARY

The case discusses the rise and fall of the Kago family as founders and owners of Tuskys (formerly known as Tusker Mattresses), a business that started as a small retail store selling mattresses in Rongai, and later diversified to groceries and other consumer goods, on the outskirts of Nakuru town located in the Rift Valley in East Africa. The supermarket chain was started by Mzee Kago, and later joined by his five sons, who helped grow the business to a leading retail store in Kenya and beyond. The exit of Mzee Kago in the early 2000s, and his death in 2002, dealt a blow to the family. However, the business seemed to be taking a new path and in good hands, as Sitivo took control of the family business. For the next decade, Tuskys enjoyed a growth period that rivalled their competitor Nakumatt supermarket, which was the leading retail chain both in assets and market reach. However, trouble started in 2012 when one of the siblings, Yosefu, Director of Sales and Marketing, accused his brothers Sitivo, the Managing Director, and Gacheni, of financial mismanagement and fraud. Yosefu alleged that the two siblings had siphoned off over KES 1.64 billion (US$20.88 million) and transferred it to subsidiaries and privately owned businesses without the knowledge of the directors. These accusations did not go well with Sitivo, and when his brother failed to withdraw a case he had filed seeking the courts and Criminal Investigation Department (CID) to investigate the allegation, he punched him in the face. The battles for control among the siblings went full throttle after this incident. Any efforts to reconcile the siblings failed. Several attempts were made to rescue the leading retailer but the capital injection in the form of merchandise from the suppliers and efforts to bring in investors failed. At the press conference, Sitivo admitted that the Kago family has contributed to some of the woes that have faced the supermarket chain. But the question is, will the siblings be able to bury the hatchet to save the family business?

LEARNING OUTCOMES

After working through the case and assignment questions the students will be able to:

- Identify the leadership elements/style within family businesses that contribute to conflicts.
- Evaluate management and governance mechanisms within family businesses.
- Describe the entitlement that family owners and subsequent generations can have regarding their family business.
- Explain the need for professionalization in family business: a coordinated and planned recruitment of professional nonfamily managers and directors at different stages of the business.

On a sunny morning in 2021, a seemingly jovial Sitivo Kago emerged for a news conference followed by his siblings. The media representatives who had gathered were eager for the much-awaited results of the deliberations between the owners of Tuskys Supermarkets, a leading retail chain in Kenya, and suppliers and investors who had expressed interest in discussing how to save the firm from collapse.

The long-serving Tuskys general manager revealed that Tuskys' had received a financial boost of KES 1.2 billion (US$10.909 million)[2] in working capital from its suppliers in the form of merchandise (Wambu, 2021). For the first time, Sitivo publicly admitted that the trouble witnessed at the failing supermarket was the family's fault. He appeared to own up to the mistakes the Kago family had committed to stop a downward freefall in the operations of the family firm. He further revealed he had personally "broken down" expressing remorse in his role in the siblings' infighting, and conflicts that had led the family to almost lose grip on the family jewel. He stated: "I own everything that has happened in this organization ... I own that 100 percent; the success of this organization is for us all, but the failure is mine, we are going to make it good because we are committed as a family"[3] (Wambu, 2021).

It appeared that Tuskys was finally getting a lifeline. But the question was whether it was enough to save the once towering supermarket chain in the Kenyan and East African retail market. However, a lawsuit that pitted Sitivo, the third son and Managing Director, on one side, and three of his other brothers Yohana (firstborn), Samutei (secondborn), and Yusefu (fourthborn) on the other side, accusing him of mismanagement, was still in court (Ng'ang'a, 2022). Additionally, Yusefu had vowed to scuttle any efforts to close deals with potential investors interested in buying the outfit before the case was resolved. The situation was deteriorating, and the clouds surrounding Tuskys' governance and management were becoming thicker by the day. As the microphones were switched off, one could not help but wonder whether the efforts made so far were enough to save the retailer.

The onetime largest Kenyan supermarket with over 65 branches across Kenya and Uganda, and over US$500 million a year in revenues was in jeopardy (Nga'ng'a, 2022; Mburu and Wasuna, 2023; Mwaura, 2023). The proverbial elephant that had towered over the retail sector was losing its tusks after successfully operating its branches for the last 36 years. A retail business that started from humble beginnings on the outskirts of Nakuru town in Rongai, long ago, was knee-deep in debt. It currently owed bank loans and suppliers totalling KES 20 billion

(US$71.203 million[4]), with an estimated asset base of KES 6.5 billion and US$46.3 million[5] (Wambu, 2021). The increasing likelihood of the creditors seeking to liquidate the firm was looming. Thus, was the capital injection enough to save the business? Were the siblings capable of putting aside their unresolved conflicts to save the business their father, Mzee Kago, built from scratch and left for them? Was the family business finally going to close down and see thousands of employees' dreams buried with it?

TUSKYS: A RISE FROM HUMBLE BEGINNINGS

The story of Tuskys began in 1982 in Rongai, a settlement on the outskirts of Nakuru, which is the central business town in the Rift Valley in the East African country Kenya (The East African, 2012). For several years, Joram Kamau Kago (hereafter, referred to as Mzee Kago) had been a dedicated employee of Nakuru Mattresses, a retail business that first specialized in selling mattresses and clothing, which was owned by the Shah Brothers. During his many working years at Nakuru, Mzee Kago married his lover, Hanisa, and together they had eight children; five sons (Yohana, Sitivo, Samutei, Yosefu, and Gacheni) and three daughters (Maki, Moniri, and Ganjiku).[6] The family lived a humble life in Nakuru with Mzee raising his family with the earnings received from working at Nakuru Mattresses. He was a trusted pair of hands who had risen to the rank of a supervisor at the retail stores.

In his prime, Mzee Kago had given his all to the Shah Brothers. In his late forties, he began contemplating calling it quits and beginning a new venture. He knew it would be a big risk, especially considering the big family that depended on him, but this opportunity presented an adventurous journey in realizing his dreams. After years of contemplating, and battling his doubts, as well as many dissenting voices from his family members, he finally quit working for Nakuru Mattresses and embarked on his wildest dream: pursuing his desire to venture into retail.

A DREAM COME TRUE AFTER A SURPRISE TWIST

In 1982 Mzee Kago decided to sell one of his prized bulls he had acquired a few years earlier and use the money to start his own retail business. He had worked for Nakuru Mattresses for several years and was well acquainted with the retail business. In honour of his service and to reward his blood and sweat, the Shah Brothers decided to give him one of their retail stores located in Rongai (The East African, 2012). Mzee Kago was surprised because most employers would rather not see a former employee competing with them. But the gesture was well received by Mzee who already was geared to start a retail business with his savings and the income from the sale of the bull. He wasted no time, named it Rongai General Stores, and went ahead to venture wholeheartedly into running his retail store.

Over the years, while working for the Shah Brothers, Mzee Kago had developed a unique relationship with them. At the onset, he had arranged with the brothers to supply him with goods at a generous rate of credit, which he would sell at a very low price. The store specialized in selling mattresses and clothes, following in the footsteps of the Shah Brothers (The East African, 2012). This earned him a loyal clientele, shifting allegiance from his competitors. Through this arrangement, the Shah Brothers ensured that the store was well stocked and extended goods on credit to ensure that the business thrived. With the support of the Shah Brothers, Mzee Kago grew the business and expanded his reach into the central business district of Nakuru town.

Since the onset, Mzee Kago's dream had been to establish a family business, perhaps motivated by his former employers. However, his vision to run the retail store as a family business began to unravel when he introduced his children to the business. He had always dreamt that after a lifetime of working in the retail sector, he would one day have his store and have his family join him in working there.

The thirdborn son Sitivo joined his father's shop in the 1980s right after high school, as a shop assistant helping his father in the business. His presence in his father's business nurtured the entrepreneurial skills that would later be instrumental in transforming the business from just a general store in the outskirts of Nakuru to a giant supermarket chain that would at one time be the largest in East Africa (Mwaura, 2023). Alongside his father, Sitivo worked tirelessly in contributing to the gradual yet steady growth of the store in the early 1990s.

Given his experience in the retail industry, Mzee Kago was determined to ensure that he succeeded just as his previous employers had. He set up his first grocery store in 1982 in Nakuru. A year in, with the help of his wife and children, Mzee Kago opened his second store, Gitwe General Stores (Kiragu, 2016). After six years in business, they needed to expand further. In the 1990s, the family opened its first self-service store, Magic Stores at Nehu Pundit Road, a more suitable location for the business given the footfall and access it enjoyed (The East African, 2012; Kiragu, 2016) (see Wanjala, 2016, p. 4).[7] This was a game changer in the emerging retail business as it was from here that he began expanding the business even further.

For the next seven years, Mzee Kago and his family dedicated their time and resources to growing their business and reinvesting their profits. Despite the desire to spend on other family needs and expenses, Mzee Kago had ruthless discipline when it came to finances. He had the good fortune of having had the opportunity to taste his dream, and he was determined to see the stores follow the track of the Shah Brothers' Nakuru Mattresses, which transformed into Nakumatt supermarket, and by the mid-1990s, Nakumatt had grown to be a powerhouse in the retail business, second only to the government-owned Uchumi Supermarkets (The East African, 2012). Mzee Kago was determined to expand rapidly beyond his hometown of Nakuru. He wanted to attract the attention of most businesspeople and media houses, just as the Shah Brothers had with Nakumatt.

In the later 1990s, the Kago family made a bold move through its maiden expansion to the capital city, Nairobi, by opening its first branch, Magic Stores (later renamed Tuskys Magic supermarket) (The East African, 2012). This was not only a big milestone for the Kago family but a move that would later transform the retail business landscape in Kenya and beyond its borders. The Kagos had become the new Shah Brothers.

GENERATION 2.0

In 1998, Mzee's son, Sitivo, took a leading role in the family business and his work was instrumental in expanding the business from Nakuru to the city of Nairobi following their mentors' footsteps and now competitors, Nakumatt supermarkets. Sitivo seemed most likely to take over management of the business from their father, who was aging. Not only had he worked in the business the longest, but he was all in from the beginning (Ng'ang'a, 2022). Sitivo had a front-row seat when his father had successfully managed to kick-start a revolutionary journey that would transform their small store in Rongai, Nakuru, to leading the move to Nairobi and finally to a leading supermarket chain in Kenya with presence in all the major and minor cities and towns (Ng'ang'a, 2022).

In the early 2000s, Mzee Kago, who had gradually taken on less work in the business, had begun to have health complications. This meant that his involvement in the business scaled down immensely as he focused on recovering from his ailments. Unfortunately, in 2002, he suffered a major health setback that he would not recover from. All was not gloomy; he was laid to rest in his mid-80s having achieved success and boasting eight Tuskys stores. His was a legendary story of rags to riches (Mwaura, 2023), a tale of passion, hard work, a generous employer, and a formidable family that supported him. At the time of his demise, he left his family eight very profitable stores.

Unlike other family businesses that would run aground with the passing of the founder, the Kago family business was not severely affected by their father's demise. Many family businesses suffer a void in leadership due to a lack of potential heirs. This was not the case for the Kagos. The baton was passed to the thirdborn son who had served in the business for close to two decades alongside his father (Ng'ang'a, 2022). Sitivo was chosen as he had a deeper knowledge of the business and experience in steering the business in the absence of their father.

General Manager Sitivo, who had proven to have a knack for business as everything that he touched seemed to thrive, relentlessly pursued an expansion strategy for the business (Ng'ang'a, 2022). Under his leadership, the Nairobi branch proved a success and expanded both in terms of size and with new branches. Defined by his innovative and go-getter nature, Sitivo seemed to embody his father's spirit. The other siblings had no qualms with him heading and growing the company.

In 2003, a decision was taken by the Kago family to form Tusker Mattresses Limited (later rebranded as Tuskys). This brought all the stores under the Tusker Megastores brand, Jolly Stores, and Rongai General Stores together into one company: Tusker Mattresses Ltd (Kiragu, 2016; Ng'ang'a, 2022). This gave rise to the proverbial "Elephant Tusk" as Tusker Mattresses adopted the easily recognizable tusk as its symbol. They successfully managed to copy their competitor, Nakumatt supermarkets, which had earlier rebranded with an elephant head and two tusks as their logo identifier. In 2006, Tusker Mattresses now resembled the rebranding of Nakuru Mattresses, with just the tusk, and adopted the name Tuskys Supermarkets.

During this time in the early to mid-2000s, the leading retailer, Uchumi, was suffering major financial losses due to gross mismanagement by the senior leadership. Cases of conflict of interest with senior managers being the top suppliers to the chain brought the giant crashing down (Ombulutsa, 2016). A huge gap was created in the market when, in 2006, the trading

Table 4.1   The ownership distribution (%) among the seven Kago siblings after restructuring

Sibling name	Ownership (%)	Ownership company
Yohana* (first born, later Chairman of the Board of Directors, after taking over from Hanisa,* their mother)	10 per cent	Green Pharm Investments
Samutei* (second born)	17.5 per cent	Future Group Ventures Investments Limited
Sitivo* (third born and first Managing Director)	17.5 per cent	Mitiki Investments
Yosefu* (Director of Sales and Marketing)	17.5 per cent	Not known
Gacheni* (later CEO after the departure of Danili* (nonfamily CEO)	17.5 per cent	Aliann Investments Limited
Maki* (deceased, 2011)	10 per cent	Kendan Investments Limited
Moniri*	10 per cent	Njowawa Investments Limited
Ganjiku*	No shares	N/A

Note: *The names have been changed to protect their identity.
Source: Case authors.

of Uchumi shares was suspended by the Nairobi Stock Exchange (now Nairobi Securities Exchange) following the chain's insolvency (Ombulutsa, 2016). Nakumatt quickly took up the number one spot and was branded as the premium supermarket with the slogan "All under one roof". Tuskys was close behind, taking Uchumi's niche using the slogan "Pay less, get more, every day" (The East African, 2017).

The strategy for Tuskys' expansion was simple: locate a store on the ground floor of a building that is right next to a bus station. All the footfall coming in and going out of the bus stations was a guaranteed market as customers did not need to worry about carrying heavy bags while shopping as they headed home. This new strategy proved more than successful for the family. Each new store was profitable and big money started pouring in. What began as a general retail store on the outskirts of Nakuru town had now grown into a mega powerhouse supermarket chain in the Kenyan retail landscape. As the firstborn son and Tuskys board chairman, Yohana noted: "We have held onto this formula; expanding into the residential estates and peri-urban areas in line with our long-term vision of becoming a successful brand on every street corner" (Kiragu, 2016).

All the merged and new stores were managed under one holding company: Orakam Holdings Limited. This meant that Orakam Holdings owned the Tuskys chain of supermarkets. Additionally, the Kago family decided to restructure the ownership of the supermarket's chains through the holding company as shown in Table 4.1.

After the successful reorganization, Sitivo, together with his siblings, embarked on an aggressive growth of the supermarkets, becoming the fastest-rising retail chain that, at its peak, reached over 60 outlets across the country and in the neighbouring country, Uganda, and more than US$510 million[8] in revenue yearly (Business Daily, 2012; The East African, 2012; Ng'ang'a, 2022; Mwaura, 2023). This was the golden decade of Tuskys.

TROUBLE IN PARADISE

Upon the death of the founder, Mzee Kago, who served as the board chair, the family turned to his aging widow, Hanisa, to serve as the board chair. While the business was thriving and doing well, there were bouts of infighting and tension within the family (Mwaura, 2023). In a bid to calm the rising tension, the Kago siblings decided Hanisa would be best suited as the chairperson since she had played a key role in establishing the first store in Nakuru. The siblings had hoped that she would be the right person to steer the family through the turbulence. However, it turned out that her presence on the board did not yield the expected fruit and things started going downhill really fast. In her mid-seventies, Hanisa had worked behind the scenes for the business for over 30 years and would rather have stayed away from the limelight. Further, she lost a daughter, Maki, in 2011. She no longer had the energy to steer the family ship and handle the turbulence rocking it. Thus, she eventually stepped down, passing the baton to her firstborn son, Yohana.

Trouble began in 2012, when one of the directors and administrators of the late father's estate, Yosefu (fourthborn), accused two of their siblings, Sitivo (thirdborn and then Managing Director) and Gacheni (fifthborn) of financial mismanagement and fraud of close to KES 1.64 billion (US$20.88 million) (Business Daily, 2012), which was diverted to more than a half dozen other subsidiaries (The East African, 2012). These companies were registered by some of the family members and directors of Orakam, but it was not clear whether they were part of Orakam Holdings. Yosefu demanded that his brother Sitivo conduct a forensic audit of the retail chain's financial operation and the adoption of new governance structures (Wambu, 2021). Yosefu said in a letter dated 3 March 2012, "It is noteworthy that the proposed forensic audit is to rule out fraud and therefore prudence would suggest that aggrieved parties should seek to require the management of the company to provide information they may deem unclear" (Business Daily, 2012). "By resolving and setting out clear structures and guidelines, conflict will be avoided, and the business environment will be improved by causing involvement of all stakeholders and staff in their respective agreed roles" (Business Daily, 2012).

After a protracted silence, Sitivo responded with an acknowledgment of the complaint by Yosefu and proposed that the shareholding of Orakam remain in the hands of the seven siblings. The subsidiaries that were to be fully owned by Orakam Holdings were as follows: Tusker Mattresses Limited, Tusker Mattresses Limited UG, Enkarasha Department Stores (K) Ltd, Enkarasha Department Stores Uganda, and Dykaka Investment Ltd. The other subsidiaries were conveniently left out of this list (Business Daily, 2012).

During this stand-off, the then company secretary (Livingstone Associates), the legal advisor, and Finance Director Firamu tried to intervene to conduct a restructuring, as suggested by the Managing Director (The East African, 2012). However, Yosefu dismissed the proposals, by stating that their interventions were unwarranted and were deemed unsatisfactory as the dispute was between directors and shareholders. Yosefu further instructed his legal advisor, Murgor & Murgor Advocates, to file a formal complaint with the Criminal Investigation Department (CID) to investigate financial misconduct and fraud within the company (Business Daily, 2012; The East African, 2012). He alleged that some of the directors (his siblings at the helm of the management of Tuskys Supermarkets) had illegally invested the company's funds into subsidiary companies they owned. After several attempts to reconcile the feuding parties through a litigator and Tuskys auditors, the rivalry between Sitivo and Yosefu escalated when Sitivo allegedly punched his brother for refusing to withdraw the criminal charges filed against him. Further, Yosefu wanted nothing short of a criminal investigation.

What was unearthed in the process was a decade-long rot that rocked the family to its roots. There appeared to be a sweet deal between some nonfamily senior directors and the executive family members (Sitivo and Gacheni) where the nonfamily directors' ventures benefited from trading with the main family business in various capacities as either suppliers, development partners, or consultants (The East African, 2012). It was also discovered that the nonfamily senior directors used the supermarket chain as a guarantor for lines of credit for businesses that were not even part of the family. Money was also taken from Tuskys Supermarkets to fund various subsidiaries, some of which were under Orakam, and others that were not. Some monies could not be accounted for (Mwaura, 2023).

In good faith, Yohana and Samutei, as the older siblings, had allowed their younger siblings to take over the running of the family business. It was unlike many family businesses in Africa where the older sons automatically took over the helm of running the business without question. Having noted the close relationship between Sitivo and their late father, the two older siblings trusted that the company would be safe in his hands. However, early investigations uncovered a complicated web of corporate betrayal, espionage, sabotage, and misappropriation inside Tuskys' boardroom, allegedly orchestrated by the two brothers, Sitivo and Gacheni (The East African, 2012). The Kago siblings entered a series of Mexican stand-offs[9] regarding their future and that of the firm.

THE GRAND HEIST, THE THIRD GENERATION, AND THE STAND-OFFS

The period between 2012 and 2015 was a very messy time in the Tuskys boardroom. It was akin to the climactic iconic movie scene in the 1966 movie, *The Good, the Bad and the Ugly*. No one was a friend to anyone; everyone was an enemy, and the bounty would be collected by whoever shot first and swiftest. No one wanted to negotiate. The family fabric frayed as if it had outlived its wear.

The first stand-off was between Sitivo (thirdborn) and his brother Yosefu (fourthborn). At the helm of the supermarket, Sitivo and his younger brother Yosefu were pitted in a stand-off that ended in court over accusations of fraud, misappropriation of funds, abuse of office, and a personal assault. Sitivo had allegedly punched his younger brother in a heated altercation over criminal charges. This resulted in Yosefu instructing his legal representative to institute legal redress in court, first for the fraudulent transfer of Tuskys funds to the siblings' subsidiaries and secondly for the assault.

After a prolonged court case, Sitivo was forced to step down from the helm of Tuskys. Yohana, the eldest sibling, became chairman of the board taking over from their mother, Hanisa. Further, a nonfamily member, Danili, was installed as the CEO of retail supermarkets. Danili joined the family business from Speed Capital, an SME financing company, and had previously served as head of audit at Tuskys in 2012 (Ngechu, 2016). This was the first time the company was led by a nonfamily member after over 25 years of existence.

Finally, it appeared that the Kago family ship was starting to steady from a storm that had threatened to topple it. However, since the underlying issues were still unresolved, animosity was being witnessed among the warring parties, particularly the third and fourth siblings. Yosefu appeared to have some personal scores to settle with his sibling Sitivo. Yosefu also did not support the appointment of Danili as the CEO (Riaga, 2015).

In mid-2015 through 2016 the second stand-off started brewing between the nonfamily CEO, Danili, and the group calling itself "the third generation" (Ngechu, 2016). The third generation consisted of some of the late Mzee's grandchildren who had banded together in opposition to a nonfamily CEO. Less than a year after Danili was installed at the helm of the retail chain, "the third generation" stormed Tuskys' headquarters offices on 23 February 2016, fully armed with news cameras, to eject the CEO (Ngechu, 2016). The group accused him of defying a termination letter issued to him a month earlier that was supposedly signed by four directors. According to the termination letter, Danili had breached his employment contract by being a majority shareholder of Artemis Africa Ltd, which provides staff outsourcing services to Tuskys Supermarkets. He was further accused of not respecting the stakeholders and of causing a decline in the performance of the company compared to the previous year. This entire spectacle played out on prime-time news for all of Kenya to see.

In a statement, the Tuskys chairman, Yohana, distanced the board from the actions of the children that had led to the ousting of the CEO. Yohana, the firstborn and chairman, stated, "We would like to state that the children acted on their own volition and not on behalf of the Board of Tuskys" (Macharia, 2016). He condemned the children and promised to investigate the incident and issue full details.

A drama that was largely a family affair had spilled out of the boardroom onto the employees and the regular customers on the supermarket floor. The third generation, in their very public display of power, indicated that there was trouble in paradise. Unfortunately, they could not take their actions back. They had publicly humiliated a CEO and displayed their broken family to the public. Whispers began on how greed had taken over the family and the ungrateful grandchildren left a bad taste in the mouth of many a Kenyan. The family's reputation and that of the supermarket chain were muddied.

As things began to cool off for the family (at least publicly), the operations of Tuskys were not drastically affected. If anything, in September of 2017 when the Shahs were going through their fair share of troubles with Nakumatt, the Tuskys board came out publicly to state that they were exploring ways of working together to save Nakumatt. Things seemed to have calmed down for Tuskys, and it became the number one retailer in the country after Nakumatt was forced to close its doors in 2019.

As this was happening, another stand-off between the company and ex-employees/Kenya Union of Commercial, Food and Allied Workers (KUCFAW) started to brew. In 2021, the employees wrote to Tuskys through the KUCFAW, warning them against taking any drastic measures against the employees including, among other things, forced unpaid leave to save costs in the ongoing business operational realignments. Tuskys, through a letter from its human resources manager, announced it was going to lay off some of its workforce: "It has become apparent that the company's performance in the last two years has been on the decline. As such the company has embarked on a process of restructuring its operations to ensure viability" (Juma, 2020).

At its peak, Tuskys had grown to more than 65 branches across the country and neighbouring Uganda, with over 6000 employees (Juma, 2020; Mburu and Wasuma, 2023). Due to worsening performance and the effects of the Covid-19 crisis, Tuskys went ahead to axe over 1000 employees. It was clear the supermarkets were not going to survive without taking rigid cost-cutting measures (Mburu and Wasuma, 2023). Employees became immediate victims, particularly temporary staff based at the facilities department who had only been given a month's notice. Trouble continued when several employees took to the streets to protest salary delays. By the look of things, it appeared the employees were not going to receive their arrears due to the worsening financial situation.

During the period between 2012 and 2017 when the siblings were busy fighting and dragging each other to court, the grandchildren brought in the media to humiliate the CEO, and various power struggles continued, no one was keeping an eye on the operations of the business (Ngechu, 2016). There was usually no one person responsible for what was going on in the retail giant's operations, and even when there was, there was fierce opposition and forceful removal. There is no telling how much the business and the family lost in that period – no one was looking. Whether there was theft by employees, you couldn't tell. Whether there was further financial misappropriation, no one knew. By the time the family came around to see whether they might have been losing the family fortune, Equity Bank and others were already in court. The matter was now almost out of the family's hands.

THE STROKE THAT BROKE TUSKYS' BUSINESS

Several attempts were made to rescue the Tuskys ship from sinking. The directors, with advice from friends and consultants, had resolved to reconstitute the board of directors and appointed Banadi as the board chair. He became the first nonfamily member to lead the board and completed the nonfamily takeover with Chalamu, who had joined after the departure of Danili in 2020 as CFO (Otieno, 2022). Chalamu had served as the CFO for Tuskys and was seen as the best person to assist with the search for a new capital injection from strategic investors to pump in much-needed funds to rescue the chain (Otieno, 2022). He had also served as the CFO for Uchumi[10] Supermarkets, another troubled retail sector business.

The search for strategic investors appeared to be heading in the right direction as expected. At some point, over ten private equity firms had expressed interest in acquiring a stake at Tuskys. However, most strategic investors had presented a nonnegotiable condition that, for any deal to sail through, they must take over 100 percent ownership of the retailer's remaining stores in Kenya and Uganda. Such a deal would mean the Kago family gave up not only their shares but their father's investment over the years in Tuskys. This looked far-fetched and unrealistic, yet it would be a promising offer that would rescue the giant. Despite their continued fights for control of the firm and the bleak future they were facing due to increasing pilferage, deteriorating stakeholder relationships, and piling debt, the siblings were determined to keep the business within the family.

The news of an interested strategic investor from Mauritius who had put in a bid of KES 2 billion (US\$14.24 million) was a good indication that Tuskys would be saved (Mburu and Wasuma, 2023). The funds were aimed at stabilizing operations to make Tuskys more attractive to strategic investors. The CEO immediately began the process by disbursing over KES 500 million (US\$3.56 million) to improve their working capital including partial payment to staff, suppliers, and property owners (Mburu and Wasuma, 2023). Additionally, Tuskys had notified the Competition Authority of Kenya (CAK) of its intention to engage strategic investors to revive the dying "Elephant", and avoid the possibility of being choked to death by ballooning debt. The CAK engaged Tuskys and its suppliers to try and broker a series of agreements to seek a win–win situation as Tuskys shopped for a strategic investor (Juma, 2020).

Tuskys began talks with suppliers to extend a line of credit on merchandise worth KES 1.2 billion (US\$8.57 million) (Juma, 2020). However, for this deal to go through, the suppliers had requested that sales from the supermarkets be deposited in an escrow account. This was to ensure that payments owed to the suppliers would be sent to them directly and the balance given to Tuskys. In addition to the deal, Tuskys had agreed to pay a debt of KES 2.4 billion (US\$17.12 million) owed to suppliers in instalments for the next two years (Juma, 2020). Finally, the CAK required that Tuskys seek approval before paying bonuses to directors, opening more branches, or starting new businesses, which aimed to protect the cash to pay its suppliers. It was the first time the CAK had given orders that appeared to interfere with the supermarket's management. The measures taken by the CAK forced Tuskys to prioritize the interest of suppliers ahead of other parties such as shareholders and employees.

Despite all efforts to save Tuskys, it appears that the sibling feuds, particularly the stand-off between the two brothers, were the proverbial straw that broke the elephant's back. As talks with strategic investors continued, Yosefu vowed to fiercely oppose efforts to sell Tuskys to external investors, arguing that allegations of fraudulent payments of Tuskys funds to subsidiaries owned by his siblings should be investigated. Further, he accused his siblings of excluding him from talks with investors. The investors who had expressed interest in the retailer appeared to be backing off, because of the continued sibling fights for control. Tuskys had sent several signals that all was not good within the Kago family and of course the business itself.

After several attempts to secure a strategic investor to help the business with a much-needed capital injection, board chair Banadi resigned from Tuskys in 2022, citing his age (77) and the demanding challenges at the retailers (Otieno, 2022). Banadi had served for three years after taking over from the eldest sibling, Yohana. Shortly after Banadi's departure, Chalamu also resigned from the retailer, and his position was swiftly filled by Gacheni, the fifth son, who had been co-accused with Sitivo the thirdborn. The question was clear. Could Tuskys survive the continuing family feud now that a controversial family member was back in as CEO?

DISCUSSION QUESTIONS

1. Generally, the family business literature indicates that family-owned and family-run businesses tend to have a long-term view of the business, particularly when the founder is involved. When Sitivo (thirdborn son) took over from Mzee Kago, he was considered the best bet since he had worked alongside their father, and his leadership, innovativeness, and go-getter attitude propelled the business to a path of growth to become the leading supermarket chain in the East African region. Despite Sitivo's success in growing the business, what could have led to the disgruntlement and conflict among the siblings?
2. What are some of the management and governance strategies that could be implemented by the Kago family to help with conflict resolution?
3. Do you think the Kago family was genuine in bringing the nonfamily CEO and chairman into the business or was it a ploy to convince investors? Explain? How could they have approached the recruitment of nonfamily executives into the business?

EPILOGUE

The battle for control of Tuskys continued through the decade with the warring parties unwavering between 2012 and 2022. In 2022, several investors expressed interest in taking over the family business. The investors wanted to buy out the Kago family and take control of the supermarket chain. However, due to the unending fights within the Kago family investors pulled out and left the retailer to battle on itself. Sitivo, the thirdborn son, and long-serving Managing Director, died in 2022 at the age of 64 (Ng'ang'a, 2022). After a protracted court fight through a case filed by the creditors (including suppliers and financiers), the court through Judge Mjanja[11] granted their wish to liquidate Tuskys to recover their debt (Kiplagat, 2023). The judge appointed a liquidator for Tuskys to help with the clearance of debts amounting to over US$130.76 million owed to suppliers and debt providers.

NOTES

1. This case was compiled from information collected using secondary sources, written articles, and media news items. The prolonged nature of the Tuskys business dispute and challenges has received much media coverage and attention. Due to the sensitivity of the business' situation, it was not possible to get consent from any of the family members to be interviewed. Though the information about the disputes, the conflicts, and sibling rivalry is public, an effort was made to anonymize the names.
2. US$1= KES 110.
3. See: https://www.standardmedia.co.ke/financial-standard/article/2001408506/family-curse -businesses-become-graveyards-when-founders-die.

4. US$1 = KES 140.442 (June 2023, totalling KES 10 billion).
5. See: https://www.businessdailyafrica.com/bd/corporate/companies/tuskys-rejects-push-reveal-secret-investor-3394344.
6. The names of key actors in the case have been changed to anonymize their identity.
7. See: https://www.slideshare.net/JoanneWanjala/tuskys-news-002?from_action=save.
8. US$I = KES 78.541 (https://www.ceicdata.com/en/indicator/kenya/exchange-rate-against-usd).
9. A Mexican stand-off is a confrontation where no strategy exists that allows any party to achieve victory. Any party initiating aggression might trigger its own demise. At the same time, the parties are unable to extract themselves from the situation without suffering a loss.
10. Uchumi Supermarkets was created as a government parastatal that operated in the retail sector. Uchumi closed down, albeit temporarily, and was placed in receivership during June 2006 after 30 years of business.
11. Not the real name of the judge.

SUGGESTED READING

Bennett, R.J., Thau, S. and Scouten, J. (2005). "I deserve more because my name is on the door." Entitlement, embeddedness, and employee deviance in the family business. In R.E. Kidwell and C.L. Martin (eds), *Managing Organizational Deviance* (pp. 287–300). Thousand Oaks, CA: Sage.
Dias, M. and Davila Jr, E. (2018). Overcoming succession conflicts in a limestone family business in Brazil. *International Journal of Business and Management Review*, 6(7), 58–73.
Eddleston, K.A. and Kellermanns, F.W. (2007). Destructive and productive family relationships: A stewardship theory perspective. *Journal of Business Venturing*, 22(4), 545–65.

REFERENCES

Business Daily (2012). Tuskys retail chain hit by fierce sibling rivalry. *Business Daily*. Accessed 28 March 2023 at https://www.businessdailyafrica.com/bd/corporate/companies/tusky-s-retail-chain-hit-by-fierce-sibling-rivalry--2004852.
Juma, V. (2020). State stops Tuskys directors pay, new branches in Sh1.2bn debt row. *Nairobi News*. Accessed 5 June 2023 at https://nairobinews.nation.africa/state-stops-tuskys-directors-pay-new-branches-in-sh1-2bn-debt-row/.
Kiplagat, S. (2023). How Judge Majanja put Tuskys to death. *Daily Nation*. Accessed 20 November 2023 at https://www.businessdailyafrica.com/bd/corporate/companies/how-judge-majanja-put-tuskys-to-death-4283546.
Kiragu, P. (2016). Tuskys inspiring story of growth second to none in the retail sector. *Tuskys News*. Accessed 12 September 2023 at https://www.slideshare.net/JoanneWanjala/tuskys-news-002?from_action=save.
Macharia, K. (2016). Tuskys CEO hounded out of office by grandchildren of the founder. *Capital Business*. Accessed 16 June 2023 at https://www.capitalfm.co.ke/business/2016/02/tuskys-ceo-hounded-out-of-office-by-grandchildren-of-founder/.
Mburu, P. and Wasuma, B. (2023). Only dust, memories linger on in Tuskys last outlet as retailer limps to its deathbed. *Nation Media*. Accessed 25 May 2023 at https://nation.africa/kenya/business/only-dust-memories-linger-on-in-tuskys-last-outlet-as-retailer-limps-to-its-deathbed-4152884.
Mwaura, W. (2023). The tragedy of Tuskys and the slippery retail business. *Citizen Digital*. Accessed 14 June 2023 at https://www.citizen.digital/news/the-tragedy-of-tuskys-and-the-slippery-retail-business-n315977.
Ng'ang'a, A. (2022). Tuskys' Mukuha played central role in growth of retail industry. *Standard Media Group*. Accessed 2 May 2023 at https://www.standardmedia.co.ke/business/opinion/article/2001439480/tuskys-mukuha-played-central-role-in-growth-of-retail-industry.

Ngechu, W. (2016). Drama as Tuskys CEO is kicked out of office. *Citizen Digital*. Accessed 13 June 2023 at https://www.citizen.digital/news/drama-as-tuskys-ceo-is-kicked-out-of-office-115695.

Ombulutsa, W. (2016). Kenyan regulator penalises former Uchumi executives. *Reuters*. Accessed 14 September 2023 at https://www.reuters.com/article/ozabs-uk-kenya-uchumi-regulator -idAFKBN13E080/.

Otieno, B. (2022). Two top officials leave troubled Tuskys in two weeks. *Business Daily*. Accessed 10 March 2023 at https://www.businessdailyafrica.com/bd/corporate/companies/two-top-officials-leave -troubled-tuskys-in-weeks-38876566.

Riaga, O. (2015). Tuskys Supermarket is planning to join NSE amid sibling rivalry. *Chetenet*. Accessed 28 November 2022 at https://chetenet.com/2015/11/22/tuskys-supermarket-is-planning-to-join-nse -amid-sibling-rivalry/.

The East African (2012). Trouble in the empire: An inside look at Tuskys Supermarkets family drama. *The East African*. Accessed 12 February 2023 at https://www.theeastafrican.co.ke/tea/news/east -africa/trouble-in-the-empire-an-inside-look-at-tuskys-supermarkets-family-drama-1308490.

The East African (2017). How Nakumatt found itself in a perfect storm. *The East African*. Accessed 14 October 2023 at https://www.theeastafrican.co.ke/tea/business/how-nakumatt-found-itself-in-a -perfect-storm--1370766.

Wambu, W. (2021). It is all our fault, now says Tuskys sibling on retailer downward spiral. *Standard Media Group*. Accessed 10 June 2023 at https://www.standardmedia.co.ke/financial-standard/article/ 2001382875/it-is-all-our-fault-now-says-tuskys-sibling-on-retailer-downward-spiral.

Wanjala, J. (2016). My father's legacy lives on… *Tuskys News*, p. 4. Accessed 12 September 2023 at https://www.slideshare.net/JoanneWanjala/tuskys-news-002?from_action=save.

5
Stahlmann GmbH: everything lost due to intergenerational conflict[1]

Sandra Fiedler

CASE SUMMARY

This case deals with the failure of a small German family business in the third generation. When the daughters joined the family business, an intergenerational conflict quickly arose: the three generations – consisting of grandmother, father, and daughters – fought for the family business, but the younger generation went in a different direction from the older generations. The daughters took over the management of Stahlmann GmbH in 2017, but the ownership shares were not changed, and the change in management – which was also not communicated to the employees or other stakeholders – did not resolve the conflict. On the contrary, the conflict escalated for years. In the spring of 2022, the sisters filed for insolvency, and in the summer, Stahlmann GmbH was sold to a holding company.

LEARNING OUTCOMES

Through analysis of this case, students can be expected to:

- Describe the consequences of conflicts from two sides: a younger generation and older generations.
- Communicate the importance and specifics of succession for the survival of family firms.
- Explain the core concept and main stages of conflict escalation.
- Describe concepts from family systems theory that relate to the case.
- Evaluate how the intergenerational conflict that prompted the sale of the family firm could have been resolved.
- Explain how family conflicts can thwart business performance and lead to business failure.

"That it had to end like this ... because this family can't agree!" Claudia Schuster muttered to herself as she left the company headquarters in June 2022. Claudia had worked as an accountant for Stahlmann GmbH for 37 years, and today was her last day of work. Stahlmann

GmbH had filed for insolvency in the spring of 2022 and found a buyer shortly thereafter. In July 2022, a holding company took over the family firm on the condition that the family leave the company completely. At that point, Claudia decided to retire early. The following family members stayed active in Stahlmann GmbH until summer 2022: grandmother Gerda, father Ralf, sisters Christa and Karin, and Christa's husband Andreas. In recent years, "the old" and "the young" had faced off against each other as if in a war of positions. The generational conflicts continued to grow until all sides could only lose. Hence, the family was eroded, and the family business failed. Claudia wondered, "Could anything have been done to save it? So many jobs lost, and lives affected."

FAMILY AND COMPANY HISTORY

First generation: Willy and Gerda

Willy Stahlmann, founder of Stahlmann GmbH, grew up in a children's home after losing both parents in World War I. He married Elisabeth, and, in 1940, his only son Ralf was born. Tragically, Elisabeth died a few days after giving birth, while Willy was fighting in World War II as a sergeant major. After the war, Willy married again; his new wife Gerda was only 12 years older than Ralf. Andreas, Ralf's son-in-law, reported:

> Willy was a militarist through and through, and even in the years after that, when Ralf was of school age, he didn't take much care of him. He practically pushed Ralf off on Willy's sister-in-law and uncle. Ralf grew up with his parents-in-law, and at the age of 10, he went to boarding school until he graduated from high school. He was occasionally allowed to come home during the vacations, and, at those times, he had a little room with his parents.

The 1960s were the time of "economic miracle" in West Germany. In 1963, Willy Stahlmann founded Stahlmann GmbH to manufacture metal products, especially steel and stainless steel products, including grids, baskets, wires, and tubes. Stahlmann was only able to establish and finance the startup because Gerda was a wealthy heiress. The company quickly flourished and moved to a larger production area in 1967, a property that Gerda had inherited. The company is still located there, in a medium-sized city (about 50 000 inhabitants) in northern Germany. The company developed well under the tight management of Willy Stahlmann, while Ralf was growing up.

Ralf Stahlmann had a rather difficult relationship with his father, Willy. Willy focused entirely on the company; neither Gerda nor Ralf experienced emotional closeness with him. Ralf's stepmother, Gerda, was the only one who showed him affection, and therefore she still means much to Ralf today. Andreas provided a description of Ralf's relationship with his stepmother:

> And when Ralf finished school, he did a commercial apprenticeship, and that's when his stepmother, Gerda, gave him his first car: a Volkswagen Beetle. He felt taken in by her, and she often backed him against his tough father, hence the dependence, the emotional bond

to this day. […] Because he was only her stepchild, he felt emotionally committed to her until the end of time and always gives her heaven on earth.

Claudia, the accountant, described Gerda as dominant and assertive: "If you're that fit at 94, hats off to the old lady. She had a better grasp of business contexts than Ralf. Gerda pulled the strings in the background."

Second generation: Ralf

After finishing school, Ralf followed a career path that conformed to his father's ideas. Ralf's daughter Christa recounted:

His father told him that he should first do a commercial apprenticeship and then become a paint engineer. For three years, he went to Krefeld, where there is a technical college for surface technology. And then he joined one of Gerda's relatives' paint stores. He was plant manager there for a few years. Willy was then in poor health and therefore Ralf also had to become managing director at Stahlmann GmbH. So, he didn't really know much about metal either. He continued his education at night school to become an industrial foreman. He always switched: in the morning he was in the paint store, and in the afternoon at Stahlmann GmbH.

Ralf's second daughter Karin said:

My father built up the company together with his stepmother, and he was grateful to be allowed to work there and that he was there. He also always had a kind of obligation to my grandmother and still has it today. It's a certain gratitude, a sense of obligation, that's actually quite extreme for him.

In 1980, Ralf took over the management of Stahlmann GmbH. Ralf breathed fresh air into the organization; soon, Stahlmann GmbH invested in bending machines and other equipment, significantly expanded its product range, and acquired key new accounts. Ralf brought a completely new product area into the company with street furniture (products such as park benches, trash cans, bike racks, etc.), which developed very promisingly. After annual sales had stagnated under Willy in the last years of his leadership, Ralf was able to increase them continuously, and the number of employees increased from 48 in 1979 to almost 60 in 1985. After Willy Stahlmann passed away in the mid-1990s, his shares in the company were transferred to Gerda.

Ralf married early and had two daughters with his wife Renate: Christa and Karin. Ralf had an emotionally distant but purposeful marriage; he was heavily involved in his job, and Renate understood that the family's prosperity depended on Stahlmann GmbH. Ralf was often at work, even at weekends, and the family rarely went on vacation, but Renate did not complain, instead supporting her husband and taking care of the two daughters. The daughters, Christa and Karin, also learned that a family business requires the full attention of the entire family. Karin said: "I don't have the best relationship with my mother. We've never had a conversation

that wasn't about the company. The company has always dominated the family." Christa con-
curred: "I grew up with the company always coming first. And the company was important,
and we lived for the company. You get that drummed into you from the cradle. And so I went
there, too. Yes, I've often regretted that." Given the company's importance to the Stahlmann
family, Christa and Karin were given little autonomy in their choice of careers, as Andreas
recalled:

> My wife [Christa] wanted to study something completely different from economics. But she
> was told that she would have to join the company later, so she had to study this and that. It
> was the same with my sister-in-law [Karin]: she studied business administration. But I did
> electrical engineering so we could complement each other. There are things that don't suit
> you, but you still have to do them.

The family internalized that ownership has obligations; after all, they had a great responsibility.

At company celebrations, Gerda sometimes reminded people that the establishment of
Stahlmann GmbH was due to her family's heritage. Gerda liked to emphasize that the success
of Stahlmann GmbH and the prosperity of the family had come in no small part because of
her familial relationships with other companies in the metalworking industry and her real
estate company. (Gerda inherited the land on which Stahlmann GmbH was located, so for tax
reasons, a real estate company was founded to manage Gerda's land and property; this real
estate company rented space and buildings to Stahlmann GmbH and another family firm, BSS
GmbH.) Karin reported:

> At that time, we still had two companies; BSS painted aluminum rims for the automotive
> industry, [it] was a pure paint store. I was involved there quite a lot, with vacation jobs and
> so on, and was actually quite deeply involved and tended to go in that direction. A large
> paint shop was also built there, and I was basically there for the first three years after my
> studies, doing accounting.

Third generation: Christa and Karin

Ralf and Gerda were still in management roles when Ralf's daughters, Christa and Karin,
joined the company in 2010 and 2015, respectively. After working outside the family business
for a few years and earning her stripes, Christa came back to the family business. Christa
recounted:

> And then my father proudly walked me through the company, I remember that, and
> showed me everything all over again, right up to the changing rooms and so on. And he
> asked me what I thought of it. I said, "Dad, your company is a pigsty." Literally. I'm always
> very clear about that.

Ralf was offended and didn't understand his daughter: didn't she see what he had built? There used to be no showers at all in the company, and the social building with sanitary facilities and break rooms had been completely rebuilt under his leadership. Claudia said,

> The girls didn't have a good start. Christa came from a large company and often barreled through. But in retrospect, they were still keeping their heads down at the time. There wasn't any real trouble until later, when the young ones only argued with the old ones and everything got worse and worse.

In Claudia's eyes, the sisters had too little respect for their father's life's work: "Mr. Stahlmann did a very good job. Without his perpetual canvassing, also outside Germany, and the major orders from Deutsche Bahn, this development would not have been possible."

Despite Christa and Karin being well educated, it seemed that "the old people" did not trust the sisters to be able to run the family business in the future. Karin said:

> But for my father, he's more of the generation that thinks that girls belong at home, while the son belongs in the company. But he stupidly had only two daughters. For him, it was unthinkable that a girl could study and go into manufacturing and be able to do something. Perhaps he didn't want to put his daughters through that. As a father, you want to protect your daughters; the poor girls – you can't put such a burden on them.

Christa's husband had been with the company since 2007 and specialized in street furniture; he described Ralf's leadership this way: "The right impulses were no longer set. At the time, I suggested using a different wire welding machine that was less labor-intensive than the other production processes. I fought for it for two years, discussed it, worked hard to convince people, prepared profitability calculations, et cetera." Andreas quickly convinced Christa and Karin, but while they and Andreas praised the advantages of the new machine, Ralf and Gerda were skeptical, because the investment sum was too high for them. Ralf finally ended the heated discussions decisively, as Karin recounted: "Then he [Ralf] decided in a single day that my brother-in-law had nothing more to say, and then we had a family quarrel." Andreas said: "That was very bitter and annoying. The result was that we had no communication for more than a year. That's the unpleasant thing in a family. The parents are often already grandparents, so the relationship with the grandchildren was hurt as well."

Gerda reassured Ralf that it was right to assert oneself and that one must remain firm. But this break led to the young generation growing even closer together. Andreas realized disappointment: "Ralf's prevailing opinion was that we didn't want to grow any more, that we would stay as we were – small and manageable. So that continued, and no further investments or modernizations were made." Christa affirmed: "We were thwarted. And then such frustration arises." When the younger generation – Christa, Andreas, and Karin – wanted to keep the company on a course of growth, the older generation – Ralf and Gerda – slowed them down and blocked strategic decisions. Figure 5.1 shows the network positions of the family members. The intergenerational conflict intensified over many years and led to problems in business decision-making. At a point of further escalation in 2016, Ralf overrode the jointly made decision

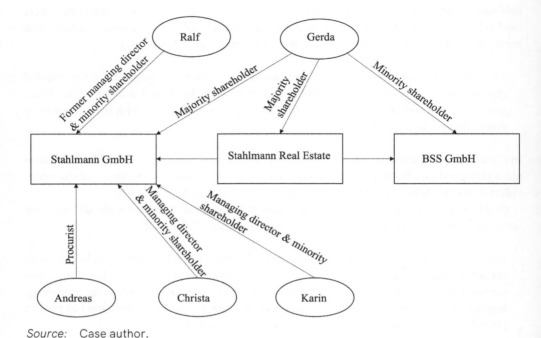

Source: Case author.

Figure 5.1   Stahlmann GmbH network and positions: early 2022

not to deliver any more goods to a major customer until their outstanding invoices had been settled. It was a fatal mistake – one that cost the company a great deal of money. Christa said,

> It was also that decisions made jointly in the committee were no longer valid the next day. That was one of the reasons why we got into this mess. And that was with one major customer. We lost €1.1 million. But that was because my father simply ignored the decision not to deliver anymore.

For her part, Gerda did not want to know about wrongheaded decisions, and when such decisions were made, she always claimed that she had not been sufficiently informed. Claudia reported:

> Yes, the thing in 2016 was a disaster and the beginning of the financial problems. I could understand that Mr. Stahlmann didn't want to upset the major foreign customer he had painstakingly recruited and developed. He was gullible, and that cost us a lot of money. Maybe the order was also just a bit too big for us.

The conflicts were now piling up. The more conflicts arose in the company, and the more clearly the "fronts" between young and old solidified, the greater the emotional distance between the generations. Privately, the sisters had less and less contact with their parents and grandmother. Even at family celebrations, arguments quickly flared up, so they preferred to stay out of each other's way. Andreas remembered: "These family celebrations, like birthdays, weren't fun. When a topic like that came up, you knew right away that it would escalate within five minutes. Things were thrown at you, and that was not okay."

Outside help was sought to pacify the generational conflict. Andreas said that tax advisors and other consultants with a business focus tried to resolve the conflicts early on:

> Everyone tried, even when we did this process optimization a few years ago, to articulate clearly in this direction. But it all went in one ear and out the other. Or was even brusquely rebuffed the second time around. There was no willingness on the part of the old people to take that step, to stay out.

Andreas made it clear that not letting go of the old guard – that is, Gerda and Ralf – was the main problem that could not be solved.

Claudia reported: "At the end of 2016, the young suddenly wanted new offices. There was quite a bit of thick air in the executive floor for months." On this topic, Karin said:

> That's when it got to the point where we said we'd either do the offices or all three of us would go. That was the first time we took to the barricades like that. And then in 2017, I took to the barricades the second time. At some point, I said, "Look, either something changes here now in the management or I'm leaving."

Ralf's health made it increasingly difficult for him, at age 77, to run the company. Everyone wanted the family business to continue, and that was only possible with the younger generation. A few days after Karin's ultimatum, Ralf and Gerda finally agreed and left the management, which Christa and Karin took over. Even so, all four family members still held shares in the company, meaning that the change in management was not accompanied by a complete change in ownership. Furthermore, Claudia said, "There was never a real company handover, never an official statement to the whole workforce that the leadership had been handed over, that the younger generation was now doing something."

INSOLVENCY AND SALE

Christa and Karin were appointed managing directors on paper, but practically nothing changed in the company: three generations were still fighting over the family business, but in different directions. Claudia described the years 2017–2022 as difficult, because there was no unity in the management of the company. She recalled disagreements over personnel matters: Karin terminated a production employee, and the next day Ralf rehired him. This was an exposure for Karin that all the employees witnessed. Gerda and Ralf still used their spacious offices on the executive floor, their executive parking spaces, and other privileges, despite the scarcity of space in the growing company. A newspaper article from 2018 wrote about Ralf Stahlmann thusly: "He is not really retired yet anyway. He runs Stahlmann GmbH: 'I'm still there every day,' says Ralf."

Table 5.1   Key financial figures, Stahlmann GmbH 2017–2020

Key financial figures	2017	2018	2019	2020
Balance sheet total	€4,074,050	€3,993,030	€3,974,647	€3,259,899
Turnover	€8,700,000	€8,600,000	€8,600,000	€7,100,000
Turnover CAGR (4 years)	8.4%	2.8%	0.9%	−14%
Equity	€3,365,842	€3,242,064	€3,385,043	€2,811,113
Equity ratio	83.2%	81.2%	85.2%	86.2%
Profit (Loss)	Not specified	−€123,778	€142,979	−€573,930
Return on sales	Not specified	−1.4%	1.7%	−8.1%
Return on equity	Not specified	−3.8%	4.2%	−20.4%

Source: Case author.

Karin and Claudia reported that due to the loss of €1.1 million in 2016, money was very tight in subsequent years. Table 5.1 provides key financial figures for 2017–2020. Karin recalled the years 2021 and early 2022:

> We saw no way to restructure the company ourselves or in family hands. Of course, money could have been raised, but we simply couldn't expect any success because of the family situation, which also led to the insolvency. There was a long discussion about winding down the company ourselves in insolvency, because we were never illiquid.

Christa and Karin finally filed for the insolvency of Stahlmann GmbH in March 2022, due to impending illiquidity. (Under German law, companies must file for insolvency in the event of illiquidity, impending illiquidity, or overindebtedness.) Stahlmann GmbH was very short of cash in 2022, but not bankrupt.

In the summer of 2022, Stahlmann GmbH was sold to a holding company, and, at the express wish of the new consortium of owners, the family had to completely abandon the company. His daughters report that Ralf Stahlmann has since fallen into depression. The family has almost completely disintegrated; while Christa, Karin, and Andreas now have a very close relationship with each other, they maintain almost no contact with Ralf and Gerda. The sisters hardly visit their parents any more, and Ralf increasingly withdraws and suffers from growing health problems.

Karin summarized the causes of the insolvency thusly:

> There was never a real handover of the company to me and my sister. My grandmother was 94 on her last day at the company in 2022, and my father was 82. They haven't been actively involved since the end of 2017, but they still had a say in all of the big decisions. And they either completely blocked a lot of things that are essential for a company or talked them

down until we simply no longer had the strength to go through with it. It's actually a huge intergenerational conflict. The generational transition failed completely. We had no chance to assert ourselves.

The younger generation, though partly aware of the problems, was unable to separate family issues from business issues; as a result, the family could not solve its conflicts.

Christa also saw no possibility of developing a sustainable solution for Stahlmann GmbH with the older generations:

> My grandmother is the type of person who you can never please. You never get the right price there [i.e., on selling the firm]. So, I had to argue about every single pencil I sold. She would have grilled and grilled us, and no one would have been able to stand that. I don't think that there was any ill will involved. They [Gerda and Ralf] always wanted the best for the firm. But times change, and you have to let go sometimes, even if it's difficult. I think my father would have been able to handle it better on his own; my grandmother is the one who's distrustful and who always believes that others can't do things better than her. She also gave him little room to say, "I'm going on vacation now, going to go away for a while and let the girls do it." Even at 75, he still had to argue that he could allow himself to go on vacation for three weeks. That came very much from her, and because she's so suspicious. My father was over 50 before he had a say.

Andreas painted a different picture and identified two main causes for failure: first, not letting go of Gerda and Ralf, and second, the unfavorable ownership relationships associated with the failure to let go. Although Christa and Karin took over the management of Stahlmann GmbH in 2017, the ownership shares largely remained with Ralf and Gerda. In fact, Gerda held most of the company shares until the family firm was sold.

Claudia, as a nonfamily member, had little insight into family relationships. She said Gerda always wanted to retire but often disagreed with Christa and Karin's management. Gerda viewed Stahlmann GmbH to be mainly her property and insisted she make the decisions about Stahlmann GmbH. Gerda probably had to agree to the sale in 2022 because there was no longer any possibility of keeping Stahlmann GmbH in family hands. Claudia summed it up: "Yes, we faced very big challenges. But where there's a will, there's a way. We could have done it if everyone had pulled together. To this day, I can't understand why the girls threw it all away."

DISCUSSION QUESTIONS

1. How would you describe the family relationships:
   a. between the sisters Christa and Karin and their father Ralf?
   b. across generations in general?
2. How has the intergenerational conflict escalated over time? Please identify several stages in which the conflict between the successor generation and the previous generations escalated and refer to text passages.
3. How could the intergenerational conflict have been resolved? Discuss and present

your findings.
4. With regard to the key economic figures of Stahlmann GmbH, what can we assume about the impact of the conflicts on business performance?

EPILOGUE

After the company was sold, the older generations, Gerda and Ralf, retired. Christa continues to manage Stahlmann real estate, which owns land and several buildings. Her husband Andreas has taken a career break. Karin has set up her own coaching and consulting business. When Stahlmann GmbH was integrated into the holding company, most of the employees were retained. This was an express wish of the Stahlmann family when the company was sold.

NOTE

1. This case is based on confidential interviews with family members, employees, and business partners as well as other data sources (internet research, brochures, and newspaper articles). The names of the people and the business have been anonymized, and other details have been changed to protect the identities of those involved.

SUGGESTED READING

De Massis, A., Chua, J.H. and Chrisman, J.J. (2008). Factors preventing intra-family succession, *Family Business Review*, 21(2), 183–99.
Eddleston, K.A. and Kellermanns, F.W. (2007). Destructive and productive family relationships: A stewardship theory perspective, *Journal of Business Venturing*, 22(4), 545–65.
Qiu, H. and Freel, M. (2020). Managing family-related conflicts in family businesses: A review and research agenda, *Family Business Review*, 33(1), 90–113.

6

Dee Doks' family business conflicts: culture or nurture?[1]

Folashade O. Akinyemi

CASE SUMMARY

Dee Doks is a third-generation supplier of provisions and household items in Ile-Ife, Nigeria. He has expanded a family business that he inherited in the 1980s from his mother and grandmother from the hawking of snacks and a few provisions on a tray to a large building with a warehouse and three branches in Ile-Ife, each operated by one of his wives. Even when the popular notion that polygamy was the breeding ground for unending conflicts as well as the major reason behind the fall of many family business empires in Nigeria, Dee Doks has been able to use his iconic skills and managerial wherewithal to reduce and resolve conflicts both at home and in business. He also carved a niche in a business primarily dominated by women. This case focuses on the fact that human behavior is principally formed and guided by certain norms and culture. And by extension, the degree or extent of deviations, misgivings, and dysfunctions are dependent on the family background, religious tenets, mindset, and experiences. Some very challenging circumstances, which seem unbearable and way beyond one's threshold to address, are often an extension of those that some individuals grew up with, survived, and even thrived under in their various professions and life endeavors.

LEARNING OUTCOMES

Through analyzing of this case, students will be able to:

- Explain the impact of culture and religion on family business from the angle of curbing and reducing conflicts in a polygamous setting.
- Observe and describe how a business leader's efforts to make deliberate preparations for succession go a long way to influence the behavior and expectations of family members and workers.
- Describe how the success and continuity of a family business are not solely dependent on the nature/type of work but mainly on the personality, passion, maturity, and managerial skills of the owner/manager.

- Explain how a cause for conflicts in one family business could be the major motivation for continuity in another if family members understand and are guided by the same religious and cultural values.

In a Nigerian community where women traditionally dominate the provisions, food, and beverage segments of the market, we find instead a man – Dee Doks – behind the counter. He is plump and stout in stature, looking cheerful as ever as he mans the cash till. He is sincere and trustworthy, very encouraging, and enthusiastic about his customers' welfare. He is quick to recognize faces and always inquires about a customer's satisfaction after new products are recommended or introduced. Dee Doks is also a distributor of some imported goods (drinks, cereals, milk, vegetable oil, etc.). He has become such a magnet that people call to find out when he'll be in the shop and would not mind awaiting his arrival just to buy goods from him. Yet, his work and home life are not without complications and conflict; all three of his wives work with him in the third-generation family business. Dee Doks' polygamous relationships have allowed him to expand the family firm to several locations.

NIGERIA'S INDUSTRIAL SETTING AND BUSINESS CHOICES

Back in the 1930s, Nigeria was still under British colonial rule and most of the economic activities were agriculture, arts, and crafts. The major exports were crops such as cocoa, groundnuts, and rubber. In Western and Southwestern Nigeria, the Yorubas were predominantly cocoa farmers and produced large quantities for export. In the 1960s, Nigeria experienced a steady growth in the oil sector, and in the 1970s, there was an ample oil boom that led to a buoyant economy and the exchange rate was £2 to 1 Nigerian naira. By the early 1980s and 1990s, poor leadership and corruption issues led to the neglect of other sectors of the economy (Ighoshemu and Ogidiagba, 2022; Awofeso and Odeyemi, 2014). Moreover, the proceeds of the oil boom were not properly managed and gave rise to many political and economic problems, leading to a serious decline in the agricultural sector.

Nevertheless, some noticeable economic activities continued, only a handful of the population were educated, and lots of job opportunities were available, so much so that university students had job options and were assured of a luxurious life after graduation. Company officials went to conduct interviews in all the few tertiary institutions available at that time. Large department stores such as Leventis, manufacturing industries such as the Ajaokuta steel rolling company, Nestlé, Cadbury, Bata, Michelin, John Holt, and Peugeot as well as oil companies such as Shell and Chevron were mostly foreign-owned and were the major employers.

The Nigerian business environment had a concentration of foreign expatriates in many organizations, traces of colonial legacies, and a little reflection of Indigenous traditions. That is, most of the organizations were inclined more towards the formal than the informal sociocultural system (Murithi et al., 2020). Hence, the activities within those organizations were mostly guided by orientations, values, and behavioral patterns drawn from Western civilization due to colonization. Indigenous family businesses were not common, and the popular businesses were either small trading stores or small shops operated by artisans. So, most parents encouraged their male children to get university degrees to have the options of choosing among the most attractive jobs in well-established organizations.

The women, because of cultural sentiments and economic conditions, were not often allowed to go further after secondary education. The very select few who had the privilege of attending higher institutions were those who obtained scholarships or came from very rich families. Most women had to learn either a trade such as tailoring, hairdressing, and cloth weaving, or the buying and selling of foodstuffs, food ingredients and provisions. Some of the women benefited from and found solace in the heroic deeds done by some matriarchs who trained other women and encouraged them to be entrepreneurial (Dagoudo et al., 2023). The reality for most women led to Dee Doks' grandmother and mother's involvement in the retail and wholesale trading business.

THE BUSINESS AND BUSINESS OWNER

Dee Doks' business is a wholesale and retail outlet for provisions, foodstuffs, and household goods. It is in Ile-Ife, a historic city in Southwestern Nigeria that is often referred to as the Cradle of Mankind. It boasts a rich heritage of Yoruba culture (Adebara et al., 2020) and has grown to a population of 750 000. A brief description of the city and its location in Nigeria can be found in Appendix 6A.

The third-generation business was started in the 1930s as a little trading outfit by Dee Doks' grandmother Agnes, before it was passed onto his mother Rachel, from whom he inherited it. In 1978, Dee Doks got a salaried job in Obafemi Awolowo University. While working as a nonacademic member of staff in the university, he helped his mother with the family business part-time, and kept observing and learning the trade from his mother until 1981, when he resigned his university job and became fully involved in the family business.

> My father was one of the elites who brought Islam to this town but he died in 1964 when I was in primary school and my mother refused to remarry. I was the second son but third child out of five. My elder brother was bent on going to school so I felt obliged to support my mother in every way that I could. My siblings used to tease and call me "Mama's Boy" and make fun of me when I resigned but later, they got used to seeing me in her shop and accepted my decision.

After his mother's death, he took over the business and continued to increase the scope of its operation. He then registered the business as Dokun Ade General Commodity Merchants and has been able to establish three other branches. He has been running the business for over 40 years and has a staff of almost 20 workers. He recalled:

> Back in those days, when girls were often married off early and not allowed to go to school, my grandmother started by hawking a few clothes on a tray. By the time she had my mother, she had a small shop, continued selling clothes, and added some provisions and foodstuffs.

After her demise, my mother took over the business and I used to go on business trips with her to bring in goods from major cities like Lagos and Ibadan. I was so fond of my mother that I resigned and supported her fully in the business…

Dee Doks manages the main location (situated very close to the major town market in Ile-Ife). It is open from Monday to Saturday 8 am to 7 pm daily but sometimes shut on Fridays when he goes to the mosque or when he is out of town on business trips. Activities in the main shop are usually at their peak after the locals finish work. So, during such periods, he ensures that more store employees are around to move the traffic through efficiently. Previously, he entrusted his workers with the running of the business, buying of goods, and handling the cash proceeds, but after a series of unpleasant experiences he changed his business policy and started monitoring everything himself. Now, whenever he is not around, he always locks the store, but when he is there, he oversees the cash till to make sure it stays under lock and key. He also collects and banks the sales proceeds himself. Meanwhile, he has handed over the other three branches of the business to his three wives, who oversee the businesses and report to him from time to time.

FAMILY BACKGROUND: RELIGION, POLYGAMY, AND MARRIAGE

Dee Doks comes from a lineage of Muslims and well-grounded Yoruba culture where polygamy is often encouraged. For him, this combination provides ample opportunities and freedom to attain maximum potential of both procreation and business empire. The concept, history, and practice of polygamy dates as far back as the pre-colonial era (Fenske, 2015; Nnabuife et al., 2019). It was particularly rampant in African feudal societies where subsistence farming was the major economic activity. More hands were needed to boost farm yields, they had to work for little money, and be easily accessible. Back then, and even now, hiring external or professional hands was not easily affordable. There was no mechanized farming, and plentiful harvests were needed. It was more convenient to marry more wives and have many children to fill the need. So, polygamy has been present in many Nigerian cultural settings before the advent of colonization and education. Even after the colonial period, the polygamists also argued that there are more women than men and, therefore, believe they are helping society by marrying more than one wife.

The Yoruba culture and communal lifestyle, to date, still permits and sometimes encourages polygamous marriage. In some sects, it is seen as a sign of wealth and is often rampant among the rich and royalties. Some Yorubas who embraced the Muslim religion instill this culture in their children right from childhood. Therefore, these two tenets (culture and religion) seem to have a strong grip in shaping people's lifestyle, the acceptable norms, and behavioral patterns. When asked about family issues and growing up, Dee Doks said:

I come from a Muslim family and polygamy is common among Muslims. So, when I married my first wife, I told her there was the possibility of marrying a second or third wife if need be but I assured her that I would take good care of her and her children. And she agreed...

When asked if polygamy runs in his family, Dee Doks replied "no" and added that his father only married his mother but died in 1964. His mother had five children with his father and did not remarry until 12 years after he died. Her second husband was a widower and much advanced in age. Culturally, it was unacceptable for a woman to remain single, and any woman whose husband died at an early age was often accused of killing her husband. So, Rachel was always being taunted until she finally agreed to remarry.

Dee Doks added that he deliberately resorted to polygamy for two reasons: first, because of his religious beliefs and, secondly, as a reward for honesty. So, when his business began to grow and expand, he felt he needed more hands, so he decided to take a second wife. Some years later, the third wife, who was one of his workers, came on board. He married her because she refused to connive with some of the workers who hid some sales proceeds, which was a huge sum of money. She exposed their plans to steal the funds and helped him to recover the very large amount of money, which would have severely hurt his business if the employees had got away with it.

CONFLICTS AND DYSFUNCTIONAL BEHAVIOR WITHIN THE BUSINESS

Conflicts, either at work, home, or play, have often been deemed inevitable where two or more individuals coexist, cohabit, or cooperate. Moreover, the business world does not exist in isolation so it cannot be void of some of the cultural, religious, and moral values operating in the external environment. The onus is therefore on the business owners and managers to ensure the conflicts become stepping stones with potential to move their businesses forward. Dee Doks recalled having observed several conflicts, dysfunctional behaviors, and outbursts in the workplace. He also noted that he had observed some conflicts peculiar to his own polygamous family businesses and made attempts to prevent such conflicts in the foreseeable future.

Employee theft

Initially, to ease the traffic at the main location, Dee Doks hired one manager, three sales reps, and five laborers to help customers carry their goods to their vehicles. So, the modus operandi was for each sales rep to collect the sales proceeds from the customers and hand them over to the manager, who oversaw the business and financial records, to vet and bank the proceeds. For instance, during most of their periodic briefings at the beginning of every month, Dee Doks starts by thanking everyone for their contributions towards the progress of the business, urges everyone to put in their best, and assures them of better pay packages as the business grows. He turns to the manager and says:

> Please, ensure the sales proceeds are promptly banked to avoid the risk of keeping huge sums of money in the till. Be smart about the timing and manner in which you bank the

proceeds to avoid being trailed or attacked by armed robbers. Also, cross-check the stock levels with the quantities sold so we know when to re-stock…

He reminds the three sales reps to ensure they remain polite, cheerful, and treat customers with respect. Then, he appeals to the laborers to handle the goods with utmost care and ensure the customers' goods are intact, adding that goods damaged by them will be deducted from their wages.

Trouble occurred when, on a weekly basis, Dee Doks found discrepancies either in the amount remitted, amount recorded, or amount banked. On several occasions, Dee Doks had to summon the manager and sales reps to settle quarrels. Often, when asked to go on business trips, there were shortfalls in the amount given to the manager to restock and the amount paid for the supplies, which sometimes brought about embarrassments, inability to meet customers' demands, and delay in receiving goods from the external suppliers.

Dee Doks recalled one scenario when he gave his manager about five million naira (more than US\$34 000 back then) to buy goods in Lagos with the company truck. He also gave the manager 30 000 naira (more than US\$200) for fuel and 20 000 naira (about US\$140) for contingencies. The trip, there and back, usually lasts for two days but the manager did not return at the expected time, claiming that the truck had flat tires and engine issues. The manager ended up spending beyond the budget and even took money from the amount designated for goods, hoping that the suppliers would give him (the manager) and the driver the needed goods and then allow them to pay the balance later. Unfortunately, one of the suppliers refused, informed Dee Doks his reason for declining the request, and added that this behavior was becoming the norm whenever Dee Doks' manager or workers came to buy goods from him. Dee Doks was surprised to find out that his manager and driver had been conniving behind his back to syphon funds from the business. He smiled as he recalled the incident and exclaimed:

> That was the last stroke that broke the camel's back! And that was the last time I ever gave them money or asked any of my workers to go and buy goods for me. On many occasions, I've had serious conflicts with my employees, including the drivers, because of missing goods and funds. These conflicts stopped when I started going with the driver myself. And then, when banking apps came, I started paying for goods online and sometimes in advance before going to bring the goods from Lagos…

Inventory control

Dee Doks is in charge and fully involved in running the main office. Some of the seven children from his three wives – two boys and five girls – used to participate in running the business during their holidays from school. Their father used to sit at the counter and collect the sales proceeds, the children, together with other workers, took orders from customers, helped with the items' selection, packaging, and delivering the goods. He also hired workers who helped carry goods into the warehouse and gave instructions on how the goods should be arranged and selected when demand arose.

For instance, goods are usually sold on a first in, first out basis, but conflicts have arisen on some occasions when the workers have been reluctant to bring out the goods in the warehouse and kept selling the new arrivals until some of the old stocks expired. So, on a weekly basis, Dee Doks would instruct the manager to check the expiration dates and conditions of the goods every Saturday before closing. First thing on Monday mornings, Dee Doks would confirm the reports and condition of the goods before they start selling. Also, the quantity of damaged goods and conflicts arising from workers bumping into each other reduced when he started deducting money from the salaries of those at fault. He also ensured that he spelled out the rules and regulations, terms, and conditions of service before hiring workers.

When customers are around, Dee Doks first attends to them directly, takes their orders, writes out the amounts, collects the money, and then delegates his workers to bring out the goods from the warehouse while he ticks them on his invoice paper. Whenever he needs to restock or buy more goods in Lagos or Ibadan, he always locks up the head office where he manages, and sometimes goes with one or two of his sons when he needs more hands and makes sure nothing is missing from the shipment.

Dysfunctional succession

Dee Doks confessed that one of his major fears was the possibility of his wives and children fighting over the business after his death. He had heard of such trends in some polygamous families after the founder's demise, with some family members using evil means to usurp authorities, chase away some of the founder's wives and children, take over the businesses and mismanage things till the businesses plummeted. There were even cases of the founder's offspring becoming impoverished after such incidents. When asked if he specifically knew of any such cases, Dee Doks bowed his head for a while, shook it as he smiled, and raised his two fingers (the index and the next) to give two instances that he could easily recall. He said:

It is a pity we don't keep records or document events the way the whites do. Otherwise, you would have read or heard about some of these stories, because some of you were not yet born or probably infants back then. But I will never forget the case of a very wealthy cocoa merchant in Ilesha, one of the neighboring towns where my late mother used to hawk her wares. He was very rich and had many wives but fell sick and died. Hmm… the contention over his cocoa plantation, business and properties was so much that his family members started using diabolic means to fight against each other. Some died in the process while some could no longer sustain the luxurious lives they had been living before his demise and left the town. Another similar case happened here in Ile-Ife, where one of the princes married three wives. He was into the car business and real estate. He kept two of his wives in this town and one in Port Harcourt but after his death, there was contention till the children all went their separate ways and the family business is now moribund.

To prevent such conflicts during succession, Dee Doks established three different branches and handed one to each of his three wives to manage. He periodically sends goods to them to sell and asks them to use the proceeds to cater for their children, while he maintains the head office and pays his children's school fees from the proceeds. He takes turns spending time with each of his wives. While being commended for his feats so far and asked about retirement or how the main office would continue to be run, he said:

> I have three wives, but we are not living together in the same house. And to avoid envy and bitterness brewing among them, I treat them equally and I don't give them the impression that anyone is more preferred than the other. I built houses for each of my wives and set up businesses for them using the family business name. I have also instructed my wives and children to work extremely hard and build their businesses to become independent. I made it clear to them that I would not hand it over to any of my wives but might sell it or hand it over to any of my children who can handle it well on behalf of everyone…

Dee Doks added that he has been observing some of his children who have been showing interest in the business and has also been supporting those who have interest in other kinds of businesses to establish them. So far, two out of his five grown children seem to be very interested while the other two are into other kinds of businesses, and one is a university lecturer. The last two are teenagers.

Conflict with the workers

Dee Doks recalled that some days are hitch free while some days are hectic, with conflicts arising due to lateness, and especially during peak periods when many customers are around, or when one of the workers starts on a wrong note and begins to be too absent-minded or edgy. Then there are arguments, yelling, and emotional outbursts.

One beautiful Friday morning, 25 November 2022, one of Dee Doks' regular customers, Rex, had called, informing him that he was coming to buy ten bags of rice, five kegs of vegetable oil, and six big tins of tomato puree. On arrival, Dee Doks delegated some workers to open the shop, arrange some goods on the shelves, and bring out the needed goods. Everything seemed to be going fine until three of the workers (Bill, Drake, and Sam) started arguing among themselves about who should carry the tenth bag of rice. Bill accused Sam of negligence of duty and always being slothful. Drake said it was his turn to arrange the goods on the shelves and take stock, then went off to do so, while Sam said he was too hungry to lift the last bag. The argument continued until the three workers agreed to all carry the tenth bag and then carry subsequent bags in turns when customers came. Thankfully, the conflict was resolved before Rex arrived and Dee Doks noted that when he introduced the "more-work, more-pay" concept among his workers, each worker was eager to work more and even set personal targets for themselves to earn certain amounts of income and bonuses.

By mid-December 2022, some workers felt they needed a raise, that things were tight, and kept making excuses for lateness. They requested loan advancements or half their salaries before the end of the month. Dee Doks gave them half their salaries and promised an additional 10 percent before Christmas. Then Sam and Drake hardly came in to work in the remaining days in the month of December when sales were high. Dee Doks got fed up issuing queries about their attendance and fired them. He asked four of his children who had just returned for the holidays to help at the main office till he was able to hire new workers.

Family arguments in the workplace

The older children in tertiary institutions such as universities and technical colleges report to the headquarters/main office during holidays and get paid to work overtime. Two are from the first wife while the other two are one each from the second and third wife. Since they were living separately and had to report to the main office by 7.45 am, two out of the four were always more punctual and most times would have worked for almost an hour before the others arrived. This often led to arguments whenever benefits/money were to be given, until Dee Doks introduced the deduction policy whereby a certain amount would be deducted for late-ness. They all agreed, then the frequent bickering, which sometimes escalated to exchange of words, ended. Daily registers were made and in no time the diligent ones were earning more.

Dee Doks smiled as he recalled those moments when the resumption dates for schools were fast approaching, and each child would present his/her lists for school requirements.

I love having my children around me and I used to enjoy those moments when we sit down together in the workplace after closing hours to have our tête-à-tête. We did not all live together under the same roof and did not use to have the regular family gathering except during the Muslim festivals. Also, as a matter of principle, we don't discuss our family matters when the other workers are around. I usually settle the workers first and ask them to go while my children and I sit back to go through the records and summarize the day's activities.

So when the holidays are coming to an end and I start looking at their school lists, they sometimes argue when I say I'm giving the girls or their elder brother extra pocket money. You'll start hearing the younger ones saying "Daddy, it's not fair, we worked more than them and we need more money than them" and sometimes they'll say "Daddy, they're never punctual and you said laziness must not be encouraged, so please don't give them any extra money. Instead, please, give us the extra pocket money because we worked hard for it."

Then the elder ones would try to shush the younger ones and counter their claims. It would then become a debate and each party would try to prove their points until they suggested the use of a register and deduction policy. So everyone knew what to expect at the end of the break period and worked extra hard to get some extra benefits. Hence, that issue has been finally resolved and there haven't been any more quarrels along that line...

THROUGH THICK AND THIN

The traffic at Dee Doks' main office is not as much as it used to be. Most of his regular custom-ers are caught in the web of "Japa Syndrome" (the popular slang used for the many Nigerians relocating abroad) (Okunade and Awosusi, 2023). All his children are grown and well settled in their various fields of endeavor. His eldest son is a university lecturer in Calabar, Nigeria while the second sells automobile spare parts in Lagos. His second daughter relocated to Canada while the other three are married and living with their respective husbands. Some of his children come to visit him from time to time while others make video calls so their children can say "hello" to Grandpa Dee Doks.

Early in 2023, Dee Doks was found at his main office, sitting behind the counter, looking cheerful as ever and chewing bitter kola from time to time as he attended to customers. Most of the payments were being made electronically, and Dee Doks ensured he received the bank alerts before releasing the goods to the customers. Dee Doks is now in his sixties, looking healthy and strong. He said he maintains a healthy lifestyle with a good social network among family and friends, and ensures he's well rested before coming to work each day. The author observed that the number of staff had reduced and most of the workers were not from Yoruba land. When asked, Dee Doks said:

> I fired all my Yoruba workers because of the countless problems they were causing. Their hassles were too much and their demands unbearable. In fact, I now hire people from other tribes, especially from Calabar because they are less troublesome and more hardworking than our fellow Yoruba people. And I am expecting some more workers soon…

Dee Doks added that, initially, there was pressure from some family friends and fellow kinsmen to reconsider his stance and hire their wards. Some had even come to remind him of his previous good deeds, kind nature, the need to avoid societal gossip and maintain a good reputation among his kinsmen, and the possibility of earning a chieftaincy title if he remained in their good grace. But he said he had to choose between bowing to cultural sentiments or working towards the sustainability of the business. After noting and considering the implication of each option, he resolved to stop hiring his fellow Yoruba kinsmen.

Dee Doks' family business has continued to thrive despite the storms and hurdles. They were not spared during the Coronavirus pandemic in 2020. Business activities were generally low as movement was restricted but the business was able to bounce back. In February 2021, when a fire engulfed many shops at the main town market, the shop of one of his wives was destroyed. But Dee Doks and his two other wives, friends, and family members rallied round to help her start afresh. The insurance policies in this part of Nigeria are often ineffective and are not often taken up at grassroots level, thus many small and medium businesses resort to informal contributions as well as family and friends in times of need.

Aside from the initial family firm, Dee Doks has been able to add another line of business, just like his mother, who started with clothes and added provisions. He is also involved in real estate business whereby he builds houses, hostels, and sublets. He says he is thankful for all the lessons learned, hurdles crossed, and challenges overcome, as well as the blessings that accrue therein. He is proud to have successfully overcome various conflicts and dysfunctional behaviors that have arisen within the family, the firm, and the community over more than 40 years of operating his family business.

DISCUSSION QUESTIONS

1. Identify the business strategies and practices that reduced conflicts in Dee Doks' family business.
2. Have adequate measures been taken to address all the possible levels and dimensions of conflict envisaged in Dee Doks' family business? If not, what other strategies can be suggested?
3. If Dee Doks were a woman, in the same cultural setting and with the same religious inclination, whose business grew and flourished as it did, would he have established the same family pattern or managed the business the way he did? Why?

EPILOGUE

Dee Doks still sits behind the counter and operates the main office. He controls the purchase and delivery of goods to the branches, and does the weekly routine checks of goods. The frequency and magnitude of conflicts have greatly reduced but spike every now and then, especially when new workers are hired. Nevertheless, Dee Doks still beams with joy and maintains his cheerful outlook.

NOTE

1. This case, part of a larger study on gender issues and polygamy in Nigerian family firms, was developed from several interviews with Dee Doks, public records, and personal observations. The names and some details have been changed to protect the identity of the business family and the family business.

SUGGESTED READING

Alrubaishi, D., McAdam, M. and Harrison, R. (2021). Culture, convention, and continuity: Islam and family firm ethical behavior. *Business Ethics, the Environment & Responsibility, 30*(2), 202–15.

Murithi, W., Vershinina, N. and Rodgers, P. (2020). Where less is more: Institutional voids and business families in Sub-Saharan Africa. *International Journal of Entrepreneurial Behavior & Research, 26*(1), 158–74.

Nnabuife, E.K., Nwogwugwu, N.O. and Okoli, I.E. (2019). Polygamy and family-owned business succession in Nigeria. *International Journal of Management Excellence, 13*(1), 1891–7.

REFERENCES

Adebara, O.B., Adebara, T.M., Badiora, A.I. and Ojo, D.B. (2020). Exploring spatial pattern of residential property value around cultural heritage sites in Ile-Ife, Nigeria. *International Journal of Real Estate Studies, 14*(1), 110–22.

Awofeso, O. and Odeyemi, T.I. (2014). The impact of political leadership and corruption on Nigeria's development since independence. *Journal of Sustainable Development, 7*(5), 240–53.

Dagoudo, B.A., Vershinina, N. and Murithi, W. (2023). Women, polygamy and family entrepreneuring in southwest Benin: The role of endogenous knowledge. *International Journal of Entrepreneurial Behavior & Research*.

Encyclopaedia Britannica (2023). Ile-Ife. Encyclopedia Britannica. https://www.britannica.com/place/Ile-Ife.

Fenske, J. (2015). African polygamy: Past and present. *Journal of Development Economics*, 117, 58–73.

Ighoshemu, B.O. and Ogidiagba, U.B. (2022). Poor governance and massive unemployment in Nigeria: As causes of brain drain in the Buhari administration (2015–2020). *Insights into Regional Development*, 4(2), 73–84.

Johnson, S. (1966). *The History of the Yorubas: From the Earliest Times to the Beginning of the British Protectorate*. Cambridge University Press.

Murithi, W., Vershinina, N. and Rodgers, P. (2020). Where less is more: Institutional voids and business families in Sub-Saharan Africa. *International Journal of Entrepreneurial Behavior & Research*, 26(1), 158–74.

Nnabuife, E.K., Nwogwugwu, N.O. and Okoli, I.E. (2019). Polygamy and family-owned business succession in Nigeria. *International Journal of Management Excellence*, 13(1), 1891–7.

Okunade, S.K. and Awosusi, O.E. (2023). The Japa syndrome and the migration of Nigerians to the United Kingdom: An empirical analysis. *Comparative Migration Studies*, 11(1). https://doi.org/10.1186/s40878-023-00351-2 27.

APPENDIX 6A: ILE-IFE, BACKGROUND AND LOCATION

The name Ile-Ife was coined from the Yoruba word "Ilẹ yi fẹ", meaning "this land is wide" and is also called Ife. It is recognized as a large historic center and probably the oldest town among the Yoruba race. The town is situated along the connection of road networks when travelling from the city of Ibadan (64 km west) to Ilesha and Ondo. Ile-Ife is often seen by core Yoruba traditionalists to be a holy city and the mythical birthplace of mankind, believed to have been founded by Oduduwa, one of the sons of a deity and was undoubtedly the capital of a well-engrained kingdom by the early eleventh century. By the late twelfth and early thirteenth century, Ife artisans were making lifelike terracotta heads and bronze pieces using the cire perdue ("lost wax") process for which the Ife kingdom was well known. At the heart of the modern Ife town is the king's palace, known as "Afin" in the Yoruba language. The king is called "Ọ̀ọ̀ni" and is regarded as the spiritual head of the Yoruba race. He takes custody of the sacred "Oranmiyan" staff, an 18-foot granite pillar made in the shape of an elephant's tusk. Ife also houses a renowned tertiary institution formerly called the University of Ife but now Obafemi Awolowo University, which was founded in 1961 and so named after the death of its founder, Chief Obafemi Awolowo. The university is one of Nigeria's foremost universities, situated north of Ife town; it has a big library and runs a teaching hospital (Encyclopaedia Britannica, 2023; Johnson, 1966).

PART II
SUCCESSION STRUGGLES (AND SUCCESSES): THE NEXT GENERATIONS

7

Schmidt Print and Media – a family business in upheaval

Christopher Khoury, Christine Keller and Nadine Kammerlander

CASE SUMMARY

This case study focuses on the print and media company Schmidt and its CEO Joachim Schmidt as the main protagonists. Mr Schmidt is currently leading the family business in the fifth generation. He is facing a difficult situation in which he needs to make the right decision to avoid conflict within the family and the firm. While Mr Schmidt yearns to retire, his daughter Katharina does not want to take over the family business and prefers to pursue her career. Although Mr Schmidt is aware that his daughter would certainly not reject him if he explicitly asked her to take over the family business, he is reluctant to follow this path because he knows about the detrimental effects on family harmony. Because none of the longtime employees is eligible for the company succession, Mr Schmidt contacts his longstanding bank advisor and inquires about sales options for the family business. The bank advisor prepares a sales exposé of the company, which is sent to potentially interested buyers, whereupon three interested buyers come forward. The three buyers differ, among other characteristics, in the number of their holdings, the focus of their investments, their strategies for Schmidt Print and Media, and their purchase price expectations. This case examines challenges that can arise in the succession process of family businesses. In this context, the case primarily addresses the tension between family–internal succession and the business sale. The readers can put themselves in the position of the M&A advisor and assist Mr Schmidt in finding the best solution for his family business.

LEARNING OUTCOMES

After reading the case material and discussing the case questions, students should be able to:

- Understand the interpersonal tension of the owner-manager, Mr Schmidt, and provide arguments:
  a. for and against passing on the family business to his daughter;
  b. for and against selling the family business to an investor.

- Evaluate from different perspectives which of the mentioned investors is the most suitable and for what reasons.
- Assess which contractual deal components might be relevant for Mr Schmidt when selling the family business.
- Structure the post-acquisition integration process by considering:
  a.   critical success factors;
  b.   the future role of family members and the effect on family dynamics;
  c.   the recruitment of a new managing director.
- Think about creative solutions where the family business remains in the hands of the family without putting family harmony at risk.

Joachim Schmidt is the managing director of Schmidt Print and Media, a family business in the printing industry currently run by the fifth generation.[1] He is standing in the gallery of the printing plant, where he has an overview of all the presses and the production processes. A few weeks ago, his only daughter, Katharina Schmidt, told him she did not want to take over and manage Schmidt Print and Media in the future. This was a real shock for Joachim, who has now started doubting the future of the family business. Katharina said she "had other plans" and wanted to follow her passion and convert her art hobby into a profession, leaving her father in an initial state of disbelief. She grew up in the family business and learned to walk in the factory. Katharina helped in the firm every vacation while she was at school and while at university studying art. She joined the sales team at the printing company after completing her master's degree. Joachim Schmidt considers his daughter an outstanding personality with great potential who knows the company better than anyone else.

Nevertheless, he tries to respect her decision to pursue her career. However, he feels trapped in a dilemma: on the one side, handing over the family firm to Katharina would ensure family business continuity and the prosperity of a business that has flourished for decades. Joachim knows that his daughter would certainly not reject him if he explicitly asked her to take over the family business and if he appealed to her sense of responsibility. Conversely, he worries about family harmony if he pressures his daughter. From several recent examples in his network, Joachim knows very well how pressure exerted on the next generation can lead to severe emotional conflicts within the family and even dysfunctional relationships. In many cases of befriended business families, such pressure encouraged the kids not only to leave the business family but also to reduce contact with their family relatives. As family harmony has always been a core value of the Schmidt family, exerting pressure on Katharina is not an option for Joachim.

Katharina loves her father deeply, and nothing breaks her heart more than rejecting his offer to take over the family firm. It has been a heart-wrenching past couple of weeks for her. While she prepared all her life to take over the family firm, her private life took its toll on Katharina. Her long-term relationship broke apart a year ago. Still, she could barely focus on work, isolating herself and focusing on her art projects, which was the only thing that kept her motivated to wake up in the morning. After her relationship ended, Katharina and her father grew closer, as he was her support system throughout the process. However, while Katharina wanted nothing more than to make her father happy, she felt she would not be able to master the stress and sacrifices that she saw her father make every day. She feared nothing more than to disappoint her father, further pushing her away from the imminent work in front of her, diverting her focus to her recent sculpture, *The Shepherd's Secret*. The daughter dedicated this sculpture to her father, showing a lonely shepherd with only one little sheep in his hands. While she focused on her project, she reflected on her inner conflict.

On the one hand, she wants to fulfill her father's wish; on the other hand, she knows she is not up for the task, potentially even risking the whole Schmidt Print and Media legacy built over the last 100 years. She wants to see the business flourish and rejects her father's request. However, to avoid a personal confrontation, she gave him her blessing to sell the business to outsiders. Deep down, Katharina knows that if her father could not let go of the business and could not sell it, she would need to step up. In general, she thinks staying involved in the firm after a sale might not be a bad idea; however, she does not entirely know how or if that would be possible. She would not like to have the full responsibility of taking over the business from her father completely.

Katharina's mother, Frieda Schmidt, never backed down from a confrontation. While Katharina and her father always sought a harmonious relationship, Frieda could not stand to see Joachim continuously spending late nights under high pressure in the company. Frieda was finally looking forward to spending some time together with her husband. When she heard that Katharina had refused to take over the business, she was understanding towards her daughter. However, before Joachim could even think about continuing to run the business beyond his retirement, she demanded he step down after endless years of working. Joachim had to look for alternatives to keep the family harmony. Mentally, Joachim was torn, but due to this disappointing news, he has been increasingly preoccupied for several weeks with what the future of the family business would look like. He turned 65 this year, and the workdays in the family business are becoming increasingly physically exhausting. Having worked day and night all his life for his own company, Joachim now feels the need to retire, travel, and spend more time with his wife, who has had his back throughout their marriage. While she has always been a supportive spouse who accepts his passion for the family business, his wife has already told him she expects him to spend substantially more time with her in the following years. He has decided that something must be done to keep the family (including himself) happy while at the same time allowing the business to prosper further. Katharina is his only child, and none of the current employees can take over the family business and manage it in the future. As such, Joachim's dreams to "keep the business as it is" begin to fade… But he needs to find a solution that satisfies the family's and the firm's needs. Therefore, Joachim Schmidt contacted his longtime bank advisor a few weeks ago and talked to him about the possibility of selling the company. After a few appointments, the account manager created a sales exposé from Schmidt Print and Media and sent it to a large group of potential prospects. Since the account manager has known the family and the family business for a long time, he has preselected three interested buyers, which he now forwards to Joachim Schmidt.

COMPANY BACKGROUND

Schmidt Print and Media (limited liability company) is a German family business with a long tradition in the print and media sector. It was founded at the end of the nineteenth century in Saxony, near Dresden, by Heinrich Schmidt as a bookbindery and has been in family ownership ever since (see Figure 7.1 for the generations of the Schmidt family). In the 1920s, the company was taken over by Joseph Schmidt, who brought in the first typograph typesetting machine, thus facilitating the production of newspaper typesetting and replacing hand-lettering. Joseph Schmidt passed the company on to his son, who in turn passed it on to his own son Heinz and his wife, Maria, only a few years later for health reasons. Keeping up the family tradition has always been important to the Schmidt family. Yet, at the same time, they are also characterized by a sense of innovation and openness to change. Heinz and Maria invested further in the modernization of the book printing business, moving to a new printing and publishing building in the same locality in 1971. In the following years, the conversion from letterpress to offset printing constituted a milestone for the company. In the subsequent years, the company was gradually transformed and innovated: in 1979, the couple purchased the first color offset press in A3 format and, two years later, in A2 format. New machines enabled more efficient and higher-quality printing, so the customer base was expanded, and printed products were exported. At the same time, the company's location was enlarged, and new printing halls with new machines were established. From the 1990s, quality management system certification and environmental management systems became increasingly relevant for business.

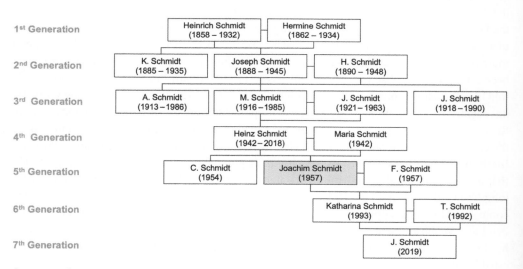

Source: Case authors.

Figure 7.1   Overview of the Schmidt family generations

In 1992, Joachim Schmidt took over the family business, proud of becoming the successor and having a great vision in mind. From the beginning, his ambition was to continue the company on a sustained basis, to ensure growth and secure jobs, and to guarantee the identity of the former bookbindery. He changed the corporate identity from Schmidt Publishing to Schmidt Print and Media (a limited liability company). In addition, he invested in new, contemporary offset presses and reformed the product range. Today's product and service portfolio encompasses media design, offset printing, digital printing, print finishing, and other offerings in the business-to-business segment. The customer segment includes large as well as small and medium-sized companies in almost every industry that uses print products for marketing purposes, for example. In this context, Schmidt Print and Media can proudly claim some long-standing customer relationships dating back over 30 years. Moreover, the 25 largest customers account for approximately 70 percent of sales.

The company currently employs about 150 people. Schmidt Print and Media generated around €20 million in annual sales in 2019, with an EBIT of €1.3 million. Despite a complex market environment, Schmidt Print and Media has positive and stable financial figures. The company has shown a growth trend over the past ten years. However, the balance sheet figures show profit stagnation over the last five years, reflecting the industry's general direction. Regarding Schmidt Print and Media's product range, the family firm has been experiencing a decrease in newspaper and magazine print jobs for several years. At the same time, the printing of advertising materials, as well as packaging materials, is expanding.

INDUSTRY OVERVIEW

The printing industry has been experiencing an increasingly complex market situation recently. First, technological disruptions, digitization, and a trend towards sustainability have caused sales in the German printing industry to decline sharply in recent years, experiencing a 15 percent decline from 2011 to 2019. Besides, the number of employees in the German printing industry is rapidly decreasing, seeing a 17 percent decline from 2011 to 2019. This development is due to increased productivity, automation, process rationalization, and necessary cost-cutting efforts. The lack of profitability in the printing industry harms investment incentives and, due to low margins in this industry, it isn't easy to find outside capital providers. Finally, significantly rising energy costs, raw material prices, and long delivery times make the industry situation even more problematic. The result is a strong consolidation trend in the industry. Whereas in 2000, there were around 15 000 print shops with 260 000 employees, there were only about 7000 print shops with about 149 000 employees in 2021 in Germany.

POTENTIAL BUYERS

Joachim is curious: what kind of investors are interested in his company? Are they beneficial to the company? To the family goals? And how about his own (financial) interests? On inquiry, the customer advisor of the local bank sends Joachim Schmidt offers from three prospective buyers for the family business. These include two private equity (PE) funds and a large, globally active printing company.

The first interested buyer is a Dutch PE fund with over 200 employees and a presence in ten European countries. The investor has completed transactions with over 800 companies and currently holds minority and majority stakes in 53 companies. Among them are already two companies in the print and media industry. Hence, the investor claims to be able to draw on existing expertise to develop synergies. Its funds are supported by leading international institutional investors that share the investment growth strategy. The investor has a fixed investment horizon of three to seven years.

Regarding Schmidt Print and Media, the PE investor reports enabling growth and increasing earnings by investing in digitization and technologies. The offered purchase price is in the medium to high range. The investor is willing to compete on the purchase price due to the prospect of significant synergies, and wants to use Schmidt Print and Media as the platform in a buy-and-build strategy.

The second interested buyer is a German mid-market PE investor with about 20 employees and a portfolio with nine companies. The investor focuses on medium-sized companies in the German-speaking region, and its current portfolio includes several family-owned companies. In addition, the investor operates with a flexible investment horizon. To continue the company values of the former owners in the long term, the investor pledges to follow the principles of a medium-sized company. In addition, the investor whose team invests a significant portion of its private capital in the portfolio companies invests with strategic partners. These co-investors are mostly well-known families and entrepreneurs who do not focus on pure profit maximization but also pay attention to the social responsibility and values of the partner companies. The investor only accepts majority shareholdings. The price offer is in the lower midrange. In the offer, the investor states it is receptive to individual contractual arrangements.

The third interested buyer is a globally active media group with US origins. The group has sites in the US and Asia. It intends to expand its presence in Europe and primarily in German-speaking countries. In this respect, the company has recently undertaken several transactions in Germany and Switzerland. According to a detailed post-merger integration report, the company aims to integrate Schmidt Print and Media into the group in the best possible way. The price offered by the group is the highest among the three interested buyers. The strategic buyer is known for its M&A activities and heavily consolidates firms in the media business. Their core business is in digital media for online shops. The idea to purchase Schmidt Print and Media supports the strategy to offer customers a vast digital portfolio of media solutions. Further, the investor wants to help online shops send out individualized offline marketing campaigns to increase average shopping card values and reduce checkout cancellations. Thus, it seeks a local player with a proven track record to fulfill its printing needs. As it sees tremendous upside potential for their clients, the investor is less price-sensitive than the two PE investors.

CONCLUSION

Standing in the gallery of the printing plant with the three proposals in his hand, Joachim Schmidt reflects on the offers from the interested buyers. It is a highly emotional decision for him that must be well thought through. On the one hand, he thinks of his mother, who still lives in an apartment adjacent to the printing factory, and his employees, whom he knows by name. He states: "It's important to me that the company gets into good hands and continues to be managed properly. An incredible amount of heart and soul went into it." Suddenly, he went silent, his eyes wandering across the production plant, the noise of the printing presses humming with a monotonous sound that feels as if it is the only thing that gives Joachim the peace of mind he needs to reflect on his decision. He spots his daughter talking to one of the employees, laughing together, as they had done for many years, since the day she was a little girl setting foot for the first time in the office building.

Joachim plucks up courage and lets his thoughts come to peace with the decision he could not live with, forcing Katharina to take over the business. Internally torn between wanting the family firm to stay in the hands of the Schmidts and hoping that his daughter would take control versus keeping the long-lasting family harmony, he reflects:

> If I push Katharina, it might lead her to despise me. My wife might even turn against me, and I want them to be happy. If they want me to sell this firm, I will do it because I have taken over the responsibility from my father so that I can provide for my family and give them a great life.

Even as he grappled with the daunting decision to let go of the business, the bond with his daughter remained one of equality and mutual respect, and disrespecting her wishes again would torpedo their relationship beyond repair. Joachim takes a deep breath and thinks,

> Don't lose your focus. Katharina has different plans, but I must decide now because my employees need me to find a suitable successor. If I make an emotional decision now, and it is wrong, I will regret that even more than letting Katharina find her path. Now... let's focus on the deal.

He has many thoughts: which buyer is best qualified for the family business, and what purchase price seems acceptable? Should the family and its family members still be able to exert influence in the company, and what should the future shareholding structure look like? What is the best solution for the business? But also: what is the best solution for himself and the family? Are they avoiding a potential conflict to keep the relationship intact but giving up the family firm in return, or is selling and finding a suitable buyer a good option to grow the business? May there even be a way to keep Katharina involved in the business beyond his exit?

Joachim Schmidt has no previous experience with family business external succession or exit, so he entirely relies on the support and advice of his advisor, whom he trusts completely...

DISCUSSION QUESTIONS

1. What are the key differences between typical M&As and those involving a family firm? What particularities must be considered in the sales process of a family business?
2. As the M&A advisor, which of the three potential buyers would you recommend to Mr Schmidt and why? How might the family business develop in each of the three cases?
3. Family side: how do you evaluate the three different options from the perspective of the family? (How) can the values of the family be reflected after sales?
4. Business side: how does Mr Schmidt evaluate the three different options from the business perspective? What contractual deal components would you recommend to Mr Schmidt (e.g., ownership structure and other guarantees)? What are the critical success factors for the post-acquisition integration process in a family business? What could Mr Schmidt's and his daughter's roles be after the sale?
5. Is there any possible and viable solution that Mr Schmidt has missed so far? Could another advisor (i.e., a most trusted advisor rather than the bank advisor) find ways to keep the business in the hands of the family without exerting pressure on Katharina and putting family harmony at risk? What might such a solution look like?
6. Looking back: Mr Schmidt takes the time extensively to look back on his past decisions. What could he have done differently to prevent such a potentially dysfunctional situation in the first place? How could he make sure to keep an eye on both firm prosperity and family harmony and make sure that both are intertwined?

EPILOGUE

Mr Schmidt sold a majority stake to a German mid-market PE investor (Investor 2 in the case). Today, this investor holds 76 percent of the shares in the family business, Katharina Schmidt 19 percent, and an external manager 5 percent. Mr Schmidt chose this investment firm primarily because of its understanding of the values and traditions of a family business and its long-term investment horizon. For Mr Schmidt, the purchase price was not the decisive criterion, but rather what other nonmonetary contractual components the investor offered. These included, for example, guarantees that the location of the family business would be maintained and that the employees would continue to be employed. Mr Schmidt has left the family business after a transition period. Besides her primary job, his daughter has an advisory role in the company. A new manager, with appropriate industry knowledge, was found after a few months through a regular recruitment process. Today, the family is very grateful to have made this step, and the family business is well positioned despite a persistently challenging market environment.

NOTE

1. This case study is based on six confidential interviews with family members and company representatives. The names of the people and the business have been anonymized.

SUGGESTED READING

McAdam, M., Brophy, M. and Harrison, R.T. (2021). Anointed or appointed? Father–daughter succession within the family business. *International Small Business Journal*, 39(6), 576–600.

Mickelson, R.E. and Worley, C. (2003). Acquiring a family firm: A case study. *Family Business Review*, 16(4), 251–68.

Worek, M. (2017). Mergers and acquisitions in family businesses: Current literature and future insights. *Journal of Family Business Management*, 7(2), 177–206.

8

Heladería Roma: challenges of succession in a climate of distrust[1]

Pablo Álamo and Unai Arzubiaga

CASE SUMMARY

This case analyzes the problems of family unity and organizational commitment that a Mexican family business must deal with when faced with the challenge of succession after the second generation has joined the business. After 45 years at the helm of ice cream company Heladería Roma, 40 of them very successful and profitable, Guadalupe, the founder, is tired and overwhelmed by the complexity that the management of the company has acquired. She considers passing leadership of the company to someone else and tries to do so by hiring an external director, who resigns as CEO a few months later. Meanwhile, the founder's two sons and her daughter work in the business at the management level. Two of them have serious problems with each other, as their relationship is characterized by a strong mutual distrust, and there are issues of serious disunity. Nicolás, who could have the skills and competencies to put the family business on the path to optimal growth, does not enjoy the confidence of his mother or his older sister, who view with distrust his propensity to be flirtatious with women, as well as not forgiving him for setting up a company in their name to whom he gave, in the name of Heladería Roma, the rights to use and manage the company's brand, without sharing with anyone the access codes to the social networks. The founder, Guadalupe, has long seen the problem, which is only growing, like a rolling snowball. She has sought the help of external consultants, experts in strategy and family businesses, to try to find a solution to her concerns. Guadalupe, seeing how two of her three children are fighting and acting on their own, does not rule out accepting one of the external purchase proposals she has received and selling the company. Or so she tells her children, who don't seem to care much about the threat of selling.

LEARNING OUTCOMES

After analyzing this case, students should be able to:

- Identify the most common barriers that arise in family businesses when it comes to the ceding of power by the founders.

- Explain the differences between operational and nonoperational problems in a successful family business, as well as the typical challenges that arise when the business grows substantially.
- Describe the challenge of thinking strategically and explain how to implement good governance practices in the family business.

On 1 July 2018, Andrés Manuel López Obrador (AMLO) swept the general elections and was proclaimed president of Mexico. It was a Sunday and the streets were crowded with people celebrating the victory of a leftist leader who, for the first time in decades, had the opportunity to challenge the dominant status quo and overturn the country's traditional political system. That same day, perhaps because of the summer heat and the joy of witnessing a historic Sunday, Heladería Roma broke its all-time sales record, news that thrilled its founder, Guadalupe García Meneses. But not everything was joyful for the Mexican businesswoman, who harbored within herself a strong concern. Like AMLO's supporters with Mexico, she felt that her family firm needed a profound change in the way of governing and felt that the time had come to retire from management of the ice cream company.

In recent years, she had shared with several people she trusted her idea of stepping aside:

I have been in charge of the business for 45 years and I am no longer the same as before, the forces are diminishing or maybe they are the same, but with a much larger company, the growth is constant and I feel that, if we do not grow more, it is my fault, because I cannot take on more work. I have to make the succession, and my wish is that one of my sons succeeds me, but their attitude shows that they are not yet ready: they respect me, but they don't obey each other or know how to work as a team.

This situation foreshadows difficulties in the succession process, because it evidences a lack of unity in the siblings and a lack of trust in the mother towards the children, facts that could lead to a separation or sale of the business in the future, depending on how the mother establishes the distribution of the property when she is gone. Thus, on some occasions she has commented discouragingly to her closest advisors: "Sometimes I think the only solution is to sell the business." In fact, at present, the second generation has entered the family business: the first to join was the eldest sibling, Susana, who has a similar personality to her mother and is her most trusted person; then comes Nicolás, who, according to his mother, "is very good at what he does, he has a special gift for winning people over, he is too much like his father"; and finally, there is Antonio, "the little one", with an unblemished career, although his introverted character does not reflect a leader's profile.

THE FOUNDATION OF THE BEST ICE CREAM IN BAJA CALIFORNIA

The history of Heladería Roma began in 1973, when Guadalupe García Meneses decided to leave her job at a bank to dedicate herself to making ice cream. Guadalupe explains her decision as follows:

> I wanted to dedicate myself to something that would make people happy, that would solve a need, and since I loved ice cream, I decided to open an ice cream parlor. Fortunately, I had a husband who supported me one hundred percent and that is why I was able to buy the basic machinery and open the business. Since Mexicali is hot almost all year round, I was convinced that it could be a good business, especially if it could be well located. That's why we were located on Reforma Avenue, which leads to the Cathedral, very close to the Curto movie theater, but on the sidewalk across the street. What better plan than to eat an ice cream before or after going to the Cathedral or the movies? The name of the company comes from the wedding trip we took to Italy, where we spent most of the time in the capital. Italians are masters of ice cream and in Rome I tasted the best ice cream, so I decided to call the ice cream Heladería Roma, a name that evoked a very happy moment that is what I want to awaken in my customers.

Guadalupe García Meneses had married Leonardo Hernández Smith, a businessman who had lived in Baja California since childhood and had held various political positions of trust in previous regional governments. From a family originally from Sonora, but with ancestors from England and Scotland, Guadalupe's husband (who passed away several years ago) was a perfectionist, a precise, correct, and formal person, but with a very sarcastic and intelligent touch of humor.

The relationship between the two was damaged over time by her husband's frequent infidelities. "Leonardo made me suffer a lot because he did not control himself and the situation became very humiliating, especially in a small town where certain social circles know almost everyone," Guadalupe says. However, Leonardo behaved loyally in the business sphere because all the shares he owned as the main investment partner went to Guadalupe once the business was already a success. "She really is the company, and the company should be hers; I only helped her to make her dream come true, and, once it was achieved, she could fly on her own," he once told a newspaper reporter.

For example, when Heladería Roma began to consolidate and grow in the market, Don Leonardo liked to say to his friends and acquaintances in the presence of his wife: "The best business I have ever done in my life was to marry Guadalupe…" Despite his ironic tone, the Baja California businessman and politician was right. In fact, only ten years after its founding, Guadalupe was the subject of a report in *La Voz de la Frontera*, the most important newspaper in Mexicali, entitled "La Reina de los Helados" [The Queen of Ice Cream], in reference to the success of the company.

The success of Heladería Roma was not limited only to Mexicali, but it won many customers in cities where it opened a branch: Tijuana, Ensenada, San Luis, and La Paz.

THE IMPORTANCE OF UNKNOWN BAJA CALIFORNIA

The state of Baja California, located in the northwestern part of the country, is one of the 31 states that, together with the capital, make up Mexico. Its capital is Mexicali, which takes its name from the conjunction of Mexico and California, and its most populated and commercially important city is Tijuana. Founded in 1903, Mexicali is the youngest state capital in Mexico and one of the northernmost cities in the country, where the executive, legislative, and judicial branches of the Baja California state government, the offices of the Federal Government, and the Mexicali City Hall are concentrated. It is nationally known for having one of the highest summer temperatures and being one of the most seismic zones, as well as having one of the lowest rates of rainfall every year. A land of hardworking migrants with a modern, conservative, and sociable character, Mexicali has an important sociocultural influence from California, which is also seen in its consumer habits.

Baja California is bordered to the north by the US state of California, to the east by the US state of Arizona and the Mexican state of Sonora, and the Gulf of California, to the south by the state of Baja California Sur, and to the west by the Pacific Ocean. It covers an area of 71 450 km² distributed along two major coastlines: the Pacific Ocean, with 740 km of coastline, and the Gulf of California, with 640 km. Although it is mostly known for its coast and valleys, Baja California has a mountain range that emerges as an extension of the Sierra Nevada of the United States and is located in the middle of the peninsula and is known by the names of Sierra de Juárez and Sierra de San Pedro Mártir.

With a population growth rate below the intergenerational replacement level, of the 3 769 200 inhabitants registered in Baja California, 49.6 percent are women and 50.4 percent are men, distributed, in order of largest population, in six municipalities: Tijuana, Mexicali, Ensenada, Tecate, Playas de Rosarito, and San Quintín. The population growth was exponential in the last century, when the United States began to reject foreigners, especially Chinese, who had come to its territory to build the railroad in the Imperial Valley to the Mexicali Valley, in what was called the Inter-California Railroad, popularly known as "El Chinero" or "El Pachuco". Many of the foreigners who were deported (or their families denied entry into the United States) decided to stay temporarily in Baja California, but eventually they were able to make a life in this region of Mexico thanks to a need for labor that the Imperial Valley and the Mexicali Valley began to demand, when this area became a strategic agricultural center in development and growth.

One of the characteristics of Baja California is the ethnic variety and its consequent cultural diversity, especially in the border cities, such as Tijuana, where the majority of the population is immigrant. Mexicali, on the other hand, is the seat of the executive, legislative, and judicial powers of the state and, at the same time, it is one of the youngest cities in Mexico, whose economic and demographic growth rates began because of the agricultural exploitation in the valley area as well as strong US and Asian investments in industrial parks. The economy is dominated by services and commerce (95 percent of economic activity with 56 percent of the labor force), although in terms of value added, the secondary manufacturing sector is the most important, generating 52.3 percent of wealth. The primary manufacturing sector, on the other hand, has the lowest percentage in terms of economic units, employment, and value added.

The climate in Baja California is very wet (69 percent humidity), although there are also dry areas (24 percent humidity), and a slightly cold temperate climate (7 percent humidity) in the mountain area, Juárez and San Pedro Mártir. This combination makes the heat and humidity not as unbearable as those who do not live in Mexicali usually imagine. In fact, the higher the relative humidity, the higher the temperature feels, and if Mexicali, in addition to high temperatures, also had very high humidity levels, it would be a place unfit for healthy human life. The average temperature is 18–19°C and the highest temperatures occur from May to September. It is a region with scarce rainfall, which rarely exceeds 200 mm of total average rainfall per year. The climate is generally temperate and dry with winter rains, which has favored the cultivation of grapes and olives, although cotton, wheat, olives, tomatoes, and sesame seeds are also grown in the region.

THE ICE CREAM PRODUCTION PROCESS

The production of Roma ice cream takes place in its factory, still located today in the east side of the Centro Cívico neighborhood, very close to the Mexicali Bullring. The ice cream production process begins with the reception, weighing, and distribution of raw materials along a chain of tanks with various functions, from temperature control, mixing, composition, and cooking. Depending on the type of ice cream, mixing is usually done at 50°C, maximum 60°C, and then the combination is heated to about 80°C, which is when the pasteurization process begins, the key to guarantee microbiological quality and avoid ice cream degradation. If there are no incidents, a high pressure is forced to make the product homogeneous and, finally, to cool it abruptly to 5°C on average. In this way, applying different temperatures and times, something fundamental for the quality of the ice cream is achieved, which is the destruction of pathogenic microorganisms, as well as most of the saprophytes present in the product.

After successful mixing, the ripening stage begins, which lasts between five and 20 hours, depending on the complexity of each product. For maturation, the pasteurized product is transferred to tanks where the contents are agitated at an average temperature of 7°C. This moment is key for the final quality of the product.

After the maturation process, comes the crystallization process: the product goes to the production machines where it is pre-frozen once the desired body and texture have been achieved. It is at this point in the process that the different flavors of the ice cream menu offered by the ice cream parlor are prepared and adhered to. After weighing the product, it is packaged and labeled, frozen at −30°C for a maximum of 24 hours, and then stored at −20°C to await distribution and sale. In other words, the ice cream crystallization process consists of a double freezing of the mixture, first partial, in order to define a crystalline structure that will ultimately determine the properties of the product, and then total, which is carried out as a preparation of the food before being marketed, which consists of a drop in temperature where 80 percent of the water contained is frozen. Consequently, crystallization is nothing more than a change of physical state of a liquid, which results in the formation of a crystallized solid phase, through a heat exchange and a mechanical means based on cylinders, tubes, and blades, which is called a Scraped Surface Heat Exchanger (SSHE), which facilitates the transformation.

Of course, there is no one way to make ice cream, and artisanal production differs from industrial production. But in both cases the process is the same in some stages:

- Step 1: mixing stage, where the solid and liquid raw materials (fluid and powdered milk, sugar or sweeteners, stabilizers, and others) are added;
- Step 2: pasteurization stage, where high temperatures are reached to eliminate pathogens, through the creative combination of temperature and time (for example 80°C for five minutes);
- Step 3: homogenization stage, by passing the product through a pump or similar device that allows to divide the fat globules of the mixture to make it homogeneous;
- Step 4: cooling and maturation stage, where the product mixture undergoes a temperature variation of 80°C to 8°C, where the product (mixture) must remain for a minimum of two hours to a maximum of 24 hours at a temperature of approximately 2°C to 5°C, through gentle but continuous agitation until solids hydration is achieved. At the end of this stage, the essence mixture and the colorant are added, in most cases, before passing the mixture through the continuous or discontinuous apparatus until the final product comes out at a temperature of −6°C to −8°C;
- Step 5: storage stage, where the product is stacked and stored in a freezing chamber at −25°C or −30°C, for a maximum of 24 hours, and then sent to the points of sale for commercialization.

According to Guadalupe, the secret of the success of the ice cream she produces is in step 1 with a secret combination, known only to her, in step 2.

THE SECOND GENERATION ENTERS THE FAMILY BUSINESS

Guadalupe (age 86) and Leonardo had three children, one girl and two boys: Susana (age 49), Nicolás (age 47), and Antonio (age 43). Leonardo had passed from the scene when the second generation entered the business. The first to join the company was Susana in 2012, upon graduating with a degree in Business Administration from CETYS University (Mexicali in Baja California, Mexico). Susana's personality is very similar to her mother's: she likes to be in positions of authority and power, likes things to be done her way, without fear of taking risks and taking the initiative, but always within her own criteria and sphere of control. During Susana's university years, Guadalupe indirectly incorporated her daughter in the tasks of assisting the general management, since she made her part of the challenges and problems of the company and asked her opinion in situations of doubt. One of the strengths that Guadalupe most appreciated in her daughter was her competitive spirit and her great ability to solve problems: Susana was a woman of action, who could not be easily manipulated or deceived. She is married and the mother of two daughters.

Guadalupe and Leonardo's second son was Nicolás, a genius for public relations, with an uncommon commercial gift, an excellent salesman. He was a talkative, optimistic, and charming man, with the ability to be funny at the right time, knowing how to be the center of attention, without being annoying or awkward. Graduating from one of the most traditional schools in the city, he had the ability to make people like him because of his spontaneity, sincerity, transparency, and deep sense of friendship. With an affable character, he became competitive and strong-willed when he felt that his decision-making sphere was being invaded, or when he felt that incomprehensible or irrational obstacles to his business objectives were being placed in his way. His mother, who recognizes in him the unique talents of a great leader, views him with mistrust: "He is ambitious and has two problems: one, he doesn't get along with his older sister, and two, he is charming with everyone, and by that, I mean with everyone… My children must set an example if they want to work in the family business: I cannot allow certain attitudes…"

Despite some misgivings, Nicolás entered the family business two years after his sister, in 2014, upon graduating with a degree in Marketing and International Business from TEC Monterrey, at the Guadalajara campus in Jalisco. Guadalupe confessed:

> I can't close the doors to a son only because of suspicions, more the result of gossip than anything else. I entrusted him with the responsibility of leading something that we were lacking, which was to have a marketing and advertising strategy, which so far had been reduced to what I did, the promotions that came to my mind, participation in significant events in the city as a sponsor, some presence on radio and press, but without a concrete plan, without knowing how to handle the internet first and even less that of social networks.

The third son, Antonio, has also joined the company, graduating in Business with an emphasis in finance from the same university as his sister. Antonio is a perfectionist and systematic character, very oriented to numbers, precision, order, and quality. According to Guadalupe,

> My youngest son is a man of few words, he tends to be introverted, but his analytical way of thinking helps us to see problems from a different point of view. I value in him that he is very realistic in his approaches, he does not like to take risks that are not well analyzed and based on numbers. As long as his work is respected, he is calm and non-confrontational, and he generally gets along well with his sister and brother. He criticizes me a lot, because I tend to make decisions based on intuition… I defend myself from his criticism by telling him that I have not done badly by being like that, but he always answers me the same thing, that we could do even better.

In August 2018, the second generation of the Hernández García family was fully involved in the family business: Susana was Guadalupe's right-hand woman in administrative management, Nicolás the marketing and commercial manager, and Antonio oversaw the financial and accounting side of the company. Heladería Roma was composed of three divisions: ice cream, with sales of $13.6 million; catering, with sales of $2 million; and wholesale, with sales of $7.2 million. Heladería Roma's operation ranged from 250 to 300 employees, with 24 stores and its estimated average gross profit could reach $10 million a year.

On Sunday, 11 August in 2018, at a family lunch, Guadalupe announced to her children the hiring of a general manager that a spiritual guide had recommended and introduced to her.

The founder was very close to a Catholic movement with strong influences from the Catholic Charismatic Renewal (CCR), which emphasizes the power of divine grace through which the Spirit of God leads us to live in an experiential way, in all areas of life. "It's a decision I've wanted to make for a long time," she said. Her children, surprised because they did not think their mother would finally decide to take this step, supported her despite not knowing the person who was going to be their new boss.

Among the new general manager's priorities was to carry out strategic planning with the entire management team and to hire an independent director for the board of directors. Until that moment the board of directors consisted of Guadalupe and her children. "We need to defamiliarize the vision of the company," Guadalupe explained. Guadalupe never retired. What she did was to hire a person to replace her in the general management functions, but she continued to go almost every day to the office, giving orders and directives. In fact, the new general manager, Selene Acosta, had to seek the founder's approval if she wanted any change or initiative to succeed. That is why Selene told Guadalupe about the need for strategic planning, who gave Selene the same answer:

> Excellent idea, for December or early next year. Now, the priority is that you adapt to the country, to this harsh climate of the Baja California desert at this time of the year, that you understand the ice cream business and see how the company is managed. Regarding your idea of hiring an independent advisor, we must wait and not incur more expenses, but it is an excellent idea for later.

Guadalupe did not like that the new general manager wanted to bring in more new people.

On 5 November, the general manager Selene Acosta resigned, citing personal matters that required her to return to her country, Argentina. In reality, Selene Acosta felt that she needed to build a team, and Guadalupe thought that she was enough. Guadalupe recalls this episode with regret, and reflected:

> It was a shame, we bet on starting the succession, we found a very capable person and when she was starting to settle in and get used to it, she had to leave us for family reasons. My desire to hand over the leadership to someone younger and prepared to manage an already medium-sized company in a complex world, is complicated. It seems as if God wanted me to continue working, because human beings, as the Bible says, were born to work.

For the founder of Heladería Roma, hiring a general manager unilaterally meant initiating succession. She was confused, because she did not understand that the complexity of the succession process, which involves not only truly handing over the baton of management, but also empowering the successor and planning the ownership structure, involving the next generation in the whole process.

A STRATEGIC PLANNING SESSION

Once Selene Acosta left, in December 2018 Guadalupe met with a Spanish consultant, an expert in strategy and family business, to tell him all her concerns, doubts, and wishes. She did it now because she felt overwhelmed again, not knowing how to manage the growth and complexity of the business, as well as the little influence she had on her children, who did not understand each other at work, and therefore she wanted to have a consultant's opinion to help her figure out what decisions to make. Record sales came mainly from the wholesale division. After more than three hours of conversation, the founder of Heladería Roma received five recommendations from the consultant: (1) Formalize the company's governing bodies and incorporate independent directors on the board of directors; (2) Update the company's organizational chart, with defined positions and functions; (3) Hire a human resources manager with the double objective of working on employee motivation and designing a productivity model adapted to each branch, with a special plan for those branches that were not being profitable; (4) Draw up a family protocol that includes some fundamental agreements on how to regulate the relations of family members with the company; and (5) Carry out a strategic planning meeting with the entire management team and hidden leaders present in the organization. "What do you think of these recommendations, Guadalupe?" the consultant asked.

> They are very pertinent, especially number 2, because as we have grown, we have not defined well the positions and functions. My daughter Susana helps me with human resources matters and we have a very capable coordinator, so I think we are fine. As for formalizing the governing bodies, an ice cream parlor is managed branch by branch, knowing how to anticipate problems, producing a quality product and taking good care of the customer. Besides, Mexicali is a small city and we all know each other in Baja California, there are no independent board members, I do not want someone outside the family to know the intimacies of the company. That is why three years ago I asked my daughter Susana to draw up a family protocol: she did a great job, but the problem we have is not to reach agreements, but to comply with them. I agree that it would be good for us to do some strategic planning, we have never done it and it could be good for us.

"I understand, Guadalupe, what you mention makes a lot of sense. The points I made to you were recommendations for Heladería Roma with the intention of improving results and reducing your level of stress and worry. I am convinced that you will know how to get it right," said the consultant empathetically, not wanting to argue with a founder.

On leaving the meeting, Guadalupe sent a voice note to the WhatsApp group she has with her children, telling them about the expert's recommendations and asking them for a date, before 15 December, to have a strategic planning session with them.

THE STRATEGY WORKSHOP

Guadalupe could only find a Saturday morning for the strategic planning workshop, which took place in a hotel in the Guadalupe Valley. An international consultant, a professor at CETYS University, acted as facilitator. The objective of the work session was to discover the necessary and high-value changes that Heladería Roma needed to make for the company to fulfill its mission, vision, and purpose of growth. Three things were essential for the success of this exercise: to get the opinions of the main stakeholders; for the participants to express themselves creatively and freely with maximum transparency, without being influenced by the past and by the charisma of the founder; and, finally, for Guadalupe to take the planning seriously and accept the consequences of it by grounding everything in a work plan with objectives, performance indicators, times, people in charge, and, above all, with everything reduced to a budget.

Previously, the consultant had sent an email to the participants asking them to respond anonymously and confidentially to four simple questions regarding actions to be taken: What things or attributes can be "eliminated" in the Heladería Roma operation? What things or attributes can be "reduced" in the Heladería Roma operation? What things or attributes can be "increased" in the Heladería Roma operation? What things or attributes can be "created" in the Heladería Roma operation?

Only three people responded to the survey, out of the seven who were invited to do so. The consultant had been told that the workshop would be attended by a minimum of five people and a maximum of nine people. On the day of the workshop, Guadalupe excused herself by saying that she was unable to answer the questions because she had to attend to some urgent business matters. With the information from the answers obtained from the respondents, the consultant created a work session in which participants had to express their degree of agreement and disagreement with each of the proposals and, finally, place the information inside three "boxes" in the form of giant cards: the first box had the name "Manage the Present more efficiently", the second "Gradually leave the Past", and the third "Create the Future". Participants filled in the contents of each of the three boxes with the information shown in Table 8.1.

At the end of the strategic planning session, Guadalupe commented that she was grateful for everyone's attitude, and pleasantly surprised by the valuable information that had come out, which, as obvious as it might seem, is forgotten or neglected because of the need to deal with day-to-day problems. Everyone was very happy, except for one person, and the consultant knew who it was and why. One person in the family in the online exercise included among his suggestions for what to eliminate and downsize, the termination of the company's current CEO and his sister Susanna. "As long as they are around, this company will not be able to innovate and grow, and it will lose more and more value." The consultant felt this suggestion was not going to help the good climate that needed to be achieved in the meeting so did not reveal it.

Table 8.1   Participant responses to Heladería Roma strategic planning survey

Manage the Present To be more efficient, we can do…	Let Go of the Past To be more competitive, we can stop doing…	Create the Future To be successful over time…
• Be excellent and have a culture of continuous improvement	• Abandon the belief that people are motivated by "carrots and sticks", by money alone	• Systematically invest in the development of international competencies, skills and experience
• We can reduce operating expenses, especially for supplies in the stores	• Sponsor social events just for friendship	• Sell part of the company to leverage international growth in legally secure markets (United States, Italy, Spain)
• Be more creative with promotions	• Buy machinery from the same suppliers all the time	• Start a line of healthy artisanal ice cream (sugar- and chemical-free)
• Improve staff motivation and empower leaders	• Set a bad example (the family) by not complying with schedules and allowed vacation days	• To produce nutritious ice cream that is a real food with minerals, etc. (with a different factory, equipment and brand)
• Treat women and all staff with respect	• Allow family members to have other businesses that demand time and energy that should be destined to the company	• Establish a new line of more commercial ice cream for supermarkets
• Punish mistakes with the same criteria and rigor regardless of whether they are made by a family member or not	• Allow a family member to have exclusive access and the right to use the brand on the Internet and social networks	• Create a branch-playground exclusively for children, which will be a space for fun and entertainment
• Train and empower middle management to lead better and thus reduce high turnover	• Despise competition and the good things they do simply because our ice cream is the best	• Opening branches in Cancun in the summers
• Hire a human resources manager	• Change decisions made without explaining or agreeing on the changes	• Opening branch in Los Mochis

Manage the Present	Let Go of the Past	Create the Future
To be more efficient, we can do…	To be more competitive, we can stop doing…	To be successful over time…
• Move the factory to a new location	• Interfere in middle management functions	• Accept one of the purchase offers that have been made to us and sell the company, in order to prioritize the family unit over the business
• Replace machines that have started to fail	• Judging and condemning people for their tastes and behaviors outside of the company	• Develop, implement and communicate a social responsibility strategy based on the Sustainable Development Goals that will have the collateral effect of improving the family's reputation and social commitment
• Manage the social networks internally, without outsourcing the service to an external company whose main shareholder is a family member	• Wasting inputs	n/a
• Have an updated real budget and review it quarterly	n/a	n/a
• Close branches that are not highly profitable and assign the best staff to branches with more traffic and potential	n/a	n/a
• Hire a CEO to bring order to the house	n/a	n/a

Manage the Present	Let Go of the Past	Create the Future
To be more efficient, we can do…	To be more competitive, we can stop doing…	To be successful over time…
• Have a family protocol that really works	n/a	n/a
• Have the board of directors meet at least once a month with an agenda, minutes and a person in charge of following up on the issues discussed and agreed upon	n/a	n/a

Source: Case authors.

While everyone was saying goodbye, Nicolás took advantage of a moment in which the consultant had been left alone gathering his belongings to approach him and ask him something: "You know perfectly well that my mother is not going to do any of the things we have worked on today, right? My mother is out of her mind and is capable of telling you something and the opposite, and the next minute she forgets she told you. And my sister supports her in everything and my brother doesn't take sides because he hates conflict. The company can't go on this way, the succession is urgent, or sell. Will you tell my mother this clearly or are you going to hide it from her like you did today? I hope you won't waste any more of our time."

To these words, the consultant replied:

"This is the first time your mother has called you together for strategic planning, and it's a good sign. In the same way, I hope that you will start implementing other good practices and recommendations. But take me out of doubt: Is it true that you set up a parallel company to which you outsourced some marketing and digital communication processes of Heladería Roma without saying that you were the owner? Your mother and sister claim you refused to give them the access codes to the social networks registered with the company's brand."

"Yes, and guess why I did it?"

"I don't know, you tell me if you want to."

"So I could work. My mother and my sister don't know anything about marketing and communications. They give their opinion, and they reverse my decisions, because they think they are not going to work, leaving me looking very bad in front of my people. I didn't lie. They didn't ask me. I didn't tell them. It was the only way I found to protect myself from these two "crazy women" and to be able to work calmly and in peace."

"I don't know if it was the only way, Nicolás. Because by acting like that you seriously damaged their trust in you."

"How would you have acted? What do you do with someone who is bipolar and unstable in their decisions?"

1. Identify the relevant facts of the case, what kind of family business it is, and list the most important problems that Heladería Roma has, which can be inferred in a special way from the results of the strategic planning mentioned.
2. Describe the leadership style of the founder, describe the behavioral profile of her two sons and her daughter as well as give an opinion as to which of them is best qualified to succeed their mother.
3. Make a flowchart of what the founder should do if she wants to pass the family business on to the next generation.
4. What are the pros and cons of picking a nonfamily member as the successor to Guadalupe? If the successor could be a relative, propose a candidate and describe the plan of action to prepare him/her, indicating the stages of the succession process.

EPILOGUE

At the end of 2023, the family business still has not finalized the succession, without having introduced major changes in family governance and without a family protocol that would help the second generation to be more united in the way the company is managed. Day-to-day operations and major strategic decisions continue to require the consent and approval of Guadalupe, who has failed to train and empower a successor, despite her age and evident health problems, which have worsened as the pressure and volume of work stress has increased along with the size of the company. The second generation is divided and, in practice, Nicolás manages the wholesale division independently, replicating his mother's pattern, without consulting with anyone with what he believes to be his strict competence, thus consolidating his mother's and his older sister's distrust of him.

The consultant who helped them with the strategic planning has tried on several occasions to motivate the family to execute the most high priority actions that affect the succession and the innovative growth of the company, without success, evidencing in this case that, on many occasions, the decisions of the owners are guided more by feelings than by rationality, making succession very difficult in a context of urgency, not importance, in management, and in a climate of distrust among the members of the entrepreneurial family, who do not manage to face the most strategic issues, perhaps disoriented, clueless, and dazzled by the current business success.

NOTE

1. This case is based on in-depth interviews with the protagonists using data collection techniques from primary sources, in a context of strict confidentiality, as well as information open to the public, media accounts, and direct observation by the authors. The characters of the business family and the events recounted are real. Some names and minor details have been changed to avoid the case being linked to a specific company or family. The four characters of the business family who are presented are real, as well as the problems of the

succession described, with some names and minor facts being changed to avoid linking the case to a specific well-known company in a Latin American country.

SUGGESTED READING

Cisneros, L., Deschamps, B., Chirita, G.M. and Geindre, S. (2022). Successful family firm succession: Transferring external social capital to a shared-leadership team of siblings. *Journal of Family Business Strategy*, 13(3), 100467.

Giménez, E.L. and Novo, J.A. (2020). A theory of succession in family firms. *Journal of Family and Economic Issues*, 41(1), 96–120.

Mahto, R.V., Cavazos, D.E., Calabrò, A. and Vanevenhoven, J.P. (2021). CEO succession game in family firms: Owners vs. advisors. *Journal of Small Business Management*, 61(6), 1–18.

9
RAJ General Supplies Limited: three daughters take over the family business

William Murithi and Karumba Kinyua

CASE SUMMARY

The case discusses the business intricacies of Raj General Supplies Limited (RGS Ltd), founded by Raj Agarwal in the 1970s after being fired from his job as a maintenance manager in a local hotel outfit. From humble beginnings, Raj grew the business and brought in his wife, daughters Uma, Shyla, and Sarika, his only son Shah, as well as his siblings and several of his nieces and nephews to work in the firm at various levels. Raj was inclined to recruit his family to create a culture of trust. The business thrived and grew exponentially through the 1980s and 1990s. However, when sickness struck, Raj settled on his cousin Pireth as managing director overlooking his three daughters who were working alongside him. Being a traditional man, Raj was unconvinced his daughters could take over the business and successfully steer it as he did. After Pireth was installed, he began to consolidate power to have control of the business, which would have meant his part of the family would eventually have direct control of the business instead of the Raj Agarwal family. Raj's three daughters were not happy with his leadership and hatched a plan to save their father's many years of hard work and investments from going down the drain. After several fights with the extended family and a legal battle, the three sisters managed to gain control, faced with strong opposition not only from the family with the emergence of their uncle, Krishna, but also from some male employees who resented being led by women. Despite the opposition, the three sisters worked hard to save their father's business, initially with little support from their father, mother, and younger brother. However, after they turned the business around and saved it from collapse, their father rejoined to serve briefly as the chairman before his death in 2019. The case exposes dysfunctionality in a family business facing succession battles, and a lack of proper governance mechanisms that enable a smooth transition from a senior dominant member to a younger generation without extended battles for control. The case also illustrates the entitlement of family members, particularly extended family, older or otherwise, unethical behaviors by successors, the effects and consequences of patriarchal cultural practices that prevent women from leading family businesses, and their experience and qualifications being overlooked because of their age or gender.

LEARNING OUTCOMES

Through analysis of this case, students can be expected to:

- Identify decisions that contribute to poor governance and control practices within family businesses.
- Explain deviant behaviors in the family business and their impact on the sustainability of the firm.
- Identify family business culture and traditions that contribute to dysfunctional behaviors.
- Describe the management of family business succession plans underpinned by patriarchal cultural and traditional contexts within developing economies.

In 2012, Raj Agarwal lay sick in bed; something that had always spelled disaster for him. He feared taking time off work and for good reason – he was fired from his job the first time he ever took sick leave. The next time he did, the company he had built for over 20 years at that point almost collapsed and he feared that this time the company would not make it. It had been 42 years since he was fired and took his first ever contract as an entrepreneur. He knew that he had given the company his all but needed to let go of the empire he had built.

The question was: To whom?

FROM JANITOR TO MAINTENANCE MANAGER – THEN THE PINK SLIP

It is 1970 in Thika Town, in the outskirts of Nairobi, the capital city of Kenya. Raj Agarwal[1] (hereafter, Raj), a typically fit man who rarely got sick, had not been feeling well lately. He assumed the bug that was troubling him would go away with time. He had a reputation to maintain as the maintenance manager of "Kings Hotels". He was a loyal employee and had seen the business grow. Under his watch, the department had received accolades. Not only for their exceptional work but also for their ability to fix broken things fast, which at times ended up functioning better than newer parts that tended to be of lower quality since the markets had been liberalized. His team worked hard to keep the facility running despite an extremely limited budget, uncooperative management, overstretched staff, and, occasionally, the unavailability of key maintenance tools and materials.

As the maintenance manager, Raj felt ashamed to take time off to attend to himself. It was a very fast-paced job, and he did not want to let his colleagues down. Everyone worked as a team, and he did not want to be the weakest link. However, his health worsened, and he was required to take time off work. During his second week away, while he was recuperating, he received the dreaded layoff notice – he had been laid off. The company was not only struggling to pay its bills to keep the doors open but struggling to pay its staff. They had decided to downsize, Raj was collateral damage, and his deteriorating health was only used as a disguise.

Although news of his firing dealt him a career blow, Raj had to think fast. He had a family of three to feed, and a fourth child was on the way. While his wife worked as a nurse in a nearby hospital, her salary was not much to fend for the family. It was the period before nurses' unions were able to lobby for better working terms and pay. With the pressure to raise an income, a light bulb moment hit him: *Why couldn't he supply construction materials, like what he had to order while he was working for his now former employer Kings Hotels, such as cement, sand, ballast, and construction stones?*

Raj did not have much formal education. He was the middle child in a family of three boys and two girls, and had seen how his parents, who were laborers on a local flower farm, struggled to make ends meet. He did not want to go down the same path. At an early age, he took the only job he could get and started as a janitor in the local hotel. Through hard work and sheer determination, he was able to rise through the ranks to become the maintenance manager.

But where and how would he start his supply firm? He did not see himself as a businessperson since all along Raj had been employed. However, his previous employment had afforded him a network of a few other construction officers, but he was unsure how working outside the framework of Kings Hotels would even kick off. Some of his previous contacts were willing to give him jobs as he had proven himself before. However, since they had existing contractual supply arrangements, there were far too many challenges to overcome before they could subcontract the work to Raj.

But as the saying goes, *fortune favors the prepared.* As he continued to seek business, a major construction site manager had a fallout with the existing supplier and without hesitation reached out to Raj, a novice in the business of providing construction supplies. He did not have the money to pay for a deposit, but he agreed to supply the materials required anyway. With the contract in hand, the network of suppliers that he had dealt with in his previous job as a maintenance manager looked like a useful resource. He had built a good reputation with them while employed and decided to use them. He called his former suppliers, but this time instructed them not to deliver materials to the Kings Hotel. Instead, he gave instructions to deliver to a new site with which he had secured a business deal.

A NEW BEGINNING: THE FOUNDING OF RAJ GENERAL SUPPLIES

After completing that first job, Raj decided to operate a sole trader business in the late 1970s when Uma, their firstborn daughter, was a toddler. In December 1979 after the general elections when Kenya became a de facto one-party state, Raj was ready to take his business to the next level. The election had brought hope to Kenyans and energized Kenyan businesses, giving renewed hope for growth. He formally registered his business under Raj General Supplies Limited (RGS Ltd). After months of planning and preparation, he found an office space in an industrial location within his small hometown of Thika. It suited his needs very well, and he was able to secure the lease.

Thika was the perfect place to work and grow his business. It was an epicenter of growth for the many companies moving to establish business in the industrial town. He was excited to be able to serve his clients in a more professional setting. From these humble beginnings, the firm grew to serve major clients, including central government and municipalities. At the height of business, the firm had almost 150 full-time workers and over 100 part-time workers engaged.

As time went on, Raj was able to build a formidable reputation among his clients and the local business community. By the end of 1981, Raj's business was thriving, and he was able to expand his office space to accommodate more clients as well as upgrade his equipment and technology to better meet their needs. He also recruited two of his brothers and a sister to work for the business in various capacities. One of his brothers, Mr Patel, was overseeing the operations of the firm, whilst Mr Vetal was the financial manager. Raj's sister, Suleya, worked as a human resource assistant at least two to three days a week as she had other family responsibilities such as taking care of their ailing parents. The siblings had joined Raj after various stints working for different businesses, some of which were extended family businesses. Several of his nephews and nieces had also been offered opportunities to work as interns or part-time in various capacities such as general supplies and field sales representatives with the rest of the junior employees.

BRINGING MORE FAMILY INTO THE BUSINESS

As RGS Ltd grew over the years, Raj managed to recruit his daughters, Uma, Shyla, and Sarika, and his last-born son, Shah, to join the business. The parents had decided while the siblings were young to involve them as much as possible so they could learn about the business. During the school holidays, Raj would tag along with his children and spend time with them in the business at least once a week. This had become a family tradition where each member of the family was required to learn the business. As they grew older Raj would allocate them to different departments where they would spend time interacting with junior staff and part-timers. Here, the children would learn key lessons on business operations. While completing their A-level studies, the siblings would work part-time in the business.

Uma, the oldest child, was first brought into the company when she was in her third year of university. Under her mother's tutelage, she was given simple tasks such as typing business letters and filing from their little home office, which had previously served as a guest room. As time passed, she was assigned increasingly challenging responsibilities such as managing fleet fueling, where she could check to see if the pump had been filled properly. Upon her graduation from United States International University Africa (USIU), a prestigious university in East Africa, she was hired as an assistant to help oversee the family business operations. Shyla and Sarika were hired as graduate trainees and later rose to oversee procurement and supplies, and human resource functions, respectively.

Shah, being the last born of four siblings and the only boy, had been lucky to be sponsored by the family to study abroad. By the time he reached university age, his parents had made lots of money and were able to pay for him to undertake his undergraduate degree in the UK. The parents had hoped their son would have access to better training and gain new skills while learning abroad to take over the business some day. They envisioned this experience as laying a foundation for him as they prepared him to take over the business. His parents were optimistic, as being the only son, he would be willing to take over the business since his father was not energetic enough to run it.

Shah spent five years abroad, with occasional visits home during school breaks, where he still would work part-time in the business. However, as the years went by, his parents noticed some reluctance in wanting to get involved in the business once he was done. He had started talking about pursuing other dreams away from the business. But his parents thought that these signs would go away once he was back after completing his studies. After completing his degree, he returned to Kenya and would occasionally accompany his father to the business. While all his siblings expressed enthusiasm and showed great interest in working in the firm some day, Shah's interest waned drastically. Raj and his wife concluded that the Western culture in which he had immersed himself while studying at the University of Birmingham in the UK must be the cause.

Shah's parents thought they would stamp their feet and require that he soon take a more permanent role in the business as time was not on their side. Shah was reluctant to heed his father's invitation to join the business. He had vehemently ranted about his ambitions to be something else and grow himself independently instead of being in the shadow of his father.

Culturally, this was a blow to Raj. Being the only boy in the family meant Shah was poised to be the heir of the business and the bearer of the family torch to the next generation. Raj had hoped his son would proudly fill his shoes and take over the business someday. Shah's refusal meant this dream was dying right in front of his eyes. He was determined not to give in to his son's ideas, thus he did not make his son's decision an easy one. If he wanted to pursue his path, he had to do it on his own. This decision just pushed his son further away from the business. Seeing this, Mrs Agarwal decided to talk to her son to at least show him the responsibility he had in the family as the only son. Despite his mother's efforts, Shah declined the offer and felt more suited to pursue his ambitions. It appeared that Shah was not prepared to be the heir that Raj and his wife were determined to make out of him.

LEADERSHIP TRANSITION: FROM RAJ TO PIRETH

In 1993, an unexpected turn of events brought about a shake-up in the company. Raj had to take time off from the business on medical grounds. With him being the sole decision maker, the business was in disarray. The company started going downhill as his absence from the business began to create a leadership vacuum. With no one to make crucial decisions, RGS Ltd failed to meet its obligations and soon began to rack up huge debts. On top of that, employees were frustrated with their salaries and working conditions and decided to go on strike. This put the company in a dire situation, as the law required them to pay the striking employees while not making any money.

Raj's illness was a huge jolt to the company, but it also served as a wake-up call to the business and family. The family realized that the business was overly reliant on their father, and they needed to create a more collaborative way of working. As it was difficult to predict when Raj would return to the business, it was decided to appoint another family member to provide leadership as he recuperated. Raj, under the guidance of his extended family, appointed his cousin Pireth to take over the business even though he had no experience in the construction or supplies business. His choice of a new leader was an epic disaster.

Upon taking over, Pireth became more concerned with consolidating the power structure than with running the business. Pireth micromanaged operations, creating a culture of fear and making a mess of things. Additionally, Pireth started embezzling funds to pay for his new lifestyle. He loved to spend time in high-end hotels, whilst also directing some of the funds to pay for his children's international school, where he had transferred them. The bureaucracy in the business increased as most of the decisions had to get approval from Pireth. He believed that this was the only way he could maintain control and stifle the rising efforts from the siblings to dethrone him. Additionally, the employees were becoming more disgruntled, and some left the company for their competitors. Some of the senior managers in the business managed not only to leave but also to take away huge amounts of business from RGS Ltd. The business suffered large losses during Pireth's reign.

The financial picture eventually became so dire it was hard to ignore. As RGS Ltd's losses mounted under the leadership of their father's cousin, the three sisters became the "Miss-keteers",[2] staging a takeover of the business through legal action against Pireth. This was of course faced with retaliation from the extended family. To begin with, they were young women going against a man, and not just any man, but someone who was considered cultur- ally as their parent. This was unprecedented in their culture and family. But the three sisters were determined not to let their father's years of hard work and investment go down the drain.

Efforts by the family to stop the legal case were futile, and through the case proceedings an independent auditing firm was brought in to review the financial statements. The audit uncov- ered the extent of the financial irregularities that were so deep that the company was on the brink of collapse. After a lengthy court proceeding, Pireth was found guilty of embezzlement and was forced to pay restitution to the family and leave the company.

With limited support from their mother, brother, and now ailing father, the three "Miss-keteers" had managed to wrestle the leadership of the company and appointed Uma, the eldest, as the acting managing director.

THE THREE MISS-KETEERS TAKEOVER AND UNCLE KRISHNA

Uma's new appointment was not without a challenge either. The deep-seated mistrust and fallout from the case with Pireth had turned many of their extended family members and friends against them, leaving the company without their support and resources. Up to this point, the girls had grown up in the business with little support from their extended family. They had only occupied junior roles and during Pireth's reign could do little. Being lone rangers in the running of affairs was not something they were used to. Further, three women were running a firm supplying construction materials. This was a male-dominated field and overcoming the hurdle of being female was not a walk in the park; everyone questioned their education and expertise. Some of the family members thought Uma was too young and inexperienced to take on the responsibility of running the company. Male colleagues resented being led by a woman. Even her mother and brother were not in favor of her taking over the business.

The situation was made worse by the arrival of their uncle on the scene, Krishna, a graduate of the famed Harvard University. Krishna, acting in concert with Raj's other brothers and sister, prevailed on Uma's father to believe he was the most suitable person to take over the affairs of the business. He was older than Uma, had experience from previous employment, and had the qualifications to prove it. Unlike Pireth, Krishna knew what he was doing. The family also loved him, and they believed he had the family's best interest at heart. RGS Ltd had delivered the Agarwal family from poverty and the importance of the business to the family was clear to him.

Raj was conflicted. Theirs was a culture that favored sons over daughters. His son wanted nothing to do with the business, and giving the business to Krishna meant that he was giving up control of the business from his family side forever. He had built it with no formal education as he had started as a janitor. He almost lost it when he let it go to an extended family member.

Not only that, but Uma was a young woman taking over a construction business. Raj was well aware of this. He wondered whether putting his daughter through the stress of having to deal with the now-frayed family business and the prejudice from the market was even worth the effort. It was clear Raj needed to let go of the empire. His poor health meant he had neither the strength nor the stamina to run the business. The question was: Who should? *He refused to decide.*

UMA, SHYLA, AND SARIKA: THE THREE MISS-KETEERS AT WORK

Their father's seeming indecisiveness was all the sisters needed. This allowed them time to prove to their dad they could lead the business. Despite strong opposition, Uma took the helm of leadership with the support of her two sisters. Shyla, the second born of the family, took the responsibility of financial and operational strategies, while Sarika stepped in to oversee corporate compliance to make sure the company was adhering to all legal and financial regulations. Uma went on to create a board of advisors and mentors to guide her and the company. With all three sisters working in sync, they began to rebuild credibility for the business.

Under Uma's leadership, Shyla, and Sarika's expertise in the financial, operational, and legal sides of the business, and the help of the board, the three sisters together worked diligently for the next few years to restore the company and its reputation. However, as the three Miss-keteers began the restoration process, they quickly realized that turning the company around after the takeover was not nearly as easy as those outside the business initially assumed. Since the trio had worked with their father in the business, many thought this would give them an advantage.

First, they had to become well versed in the art of delegation. With everything that had happened thus far, they developed a tendency to debate and consult each other on every decision. This lengthened the decision-making process, leading to delays and missed opportunities that competitors were able to capitalize on. Furthermore, they had difficulty establishing a properly constituted board due to difficulties in hiring skilled members and reaching a consensus on the number of necessary board members, given the tense relationships within the extended family. When deciding which family members to rely on, it was not clear whom they could trust or rely on to guide them, given the networked community they lived in where *everyone knew someone*. Their family members had already been working for the business before, but due to the divisive nature of the takeover they were not sure whom they could trust. Eventually, the three Miss-keteers were able to get over the initial kinks and were able to turn the company around.

In its heyday, under their father's leadership, RGS Ltd had almost 150 workers in the office and over 250 part-timers engaged. By the time Uma and her sisters took over, RGS Ltd had 30 employees in the office and fewer than 100 in the field. In addition, there was a huge reputational fallout in the family and with the firm's old customers, and the market viewed them negatively as women running a construction firm.

After the takeover, the three Miss-keteers began by rebranding the corporate headquarters of the business, something Raj fiercely resisted when he was in charge. However, their efforts began to pay off. Employees were incentivized, new business prospects arose, and the company acquired a competitive advantage in the market. They could complete projects on time, within budget, and with the best client experience. Additionally, they were able to bring the company back to profitability. Uma had effectively silenced critics who thought she was too young for the job and the family sent out a powerful message to the community that women can take on challenging roles and be just as successful as their male counterparts. The three sisters became a symbol of courage and inspiration for many young women entrepreneurs as they achieved what seemed like an impossible feat: overcoming significant prejudice and challenges to create a successful business.

WHO RUNS THE WORLD? GIRLS

The transition from Pireth to Uma became a debacle of some sort, adding salt to the wounds of an already struggling business. The firm was faced with declining business, and revolt from employees, who had collaborated well with their father over many years. Some of the older and long-serving employees were now disillusioned at being led by Uma, whom they had seen grow up over the years. The fact that they had been there long enough to see Uma grow up was impacting their willingness to accept her as the heir to the business. They could not believe that the little girl who was once running around the floor was the one who would give directions and make decisions. Several employees wanted the brother, Shah, to take over from Raj as preferred heir. Others were keen on seeing one of her uncles take over the business. Then, it went against the culture for a woman to lead other men, particularly those old enough to be her father.

At the time, Uma had become a staunch feminist. She participated in many organizations that empowered women. This had seen her take a strong stand on women's involvement in business and work. She was a self-driven believer in women's potential. At the time she was already advising women never to doubt themselves and urging them to be courageous in shattering the glass ceiling. She recalled how hard it was for her father to give her the reins of the business, yet she was able to prove him wrong. She shared, "My father, who is traditional, had to step back for me to run the business. He thought I could not do it, but I showed him I could!"

Uma was able to implement her strategies and the company's success skyrocketed. She was able to make better decisions for the company, leading it to become one of the area's most profitable businesses. Uma was also very enthusiastic about giving back to the community and so she started programs to help empower women and promote gender equality. She also took on apprentice programs to train and develop young people in the community. The stability and relationships that Uma brought back into the leadership of RGS Ltd paid off. The legacy clients who had stayed loyal were learning to trust RGS Ltd to deliver their projects as before.

The contributions made by the three daughters had been critical to the success of RGS Ltd, which had now blossomed into a construction solutions business that also offered roofing services, landscaping, and interior design. After fully recovering from his illness, which lasted close to three years, Raj was delighted to observe the progress that his firstborn daughter had achieved during his absence. When he returned, he decided to assume the role of the non-executive board member. It was an oversight role, which gave him the flexibility to take the much-needed health break but still be part of the company.

He felt an immense sense of pride in his daughter and finally accepted that she was the ideal person to lead the company. It took him over six years since the fallout with Pireth to accept that his daughters could lead the business.

THE END OF AN ERA: A SIGNAL TO RENEWED LEADERSHIP

In late 2018, Raj's health began to deteriorate once again, and he passed away the following year. The family went through a difficult period. They mourned a patriarch who had taken a significant risk to set a new path for the family. Though challenging in the beginning, it was a path that saw the family end a generational curse of struggle and poverty. Despite his lack of education, he had managed to start and build a successful business and educate his children through university. He had accumulated enough wealth to help support his extended family and enable them to acquire properties of their own.

His were big shoes to fill. Having him around in a nonexecutive capacity meant that the family, and especially Uma and her sisters, had a wealth of wisdom from which they could draw. Dad was a pillar they could all lean on in making tough decisions. Although legacy clients had remained loyal as they saw the girls in their father's shadow, a big gap was left by his death. The family vowed to steer forward and sustain his legacy. In particular, the three Miss-keteers, led by Uma, were more determined to steer the family business to greater levels from where their father had left it.

Before the passing of Raj "The Legend", his three daughters had grown RGS Ltd from 30 employees in the office and fewer than 100 casuals in the field to 67 in the office and over 237 in the field hired on a contract basis and as casual workers. Even though the company had been on an upward trajectory in terms of profitability, it had experienced phases of decline in its financial muscle due to competition from other companies. This was attributed to weak marketing strategies as there was an overreliance on legacy clients, and their limited ability to reach new clients. With their beloved father gone, would his daughters be up to the challenge of sustaining the business and keeping it in the family as their father anticipated from the start?

DISCUSSION QUESTIONS

1. What elements of Raj Agarwal's leadership and decision-making contributed to poor governance and control choices for the family business?
2. Discuss the family (both nuclear and extended) members' cultural values and preferences and how they could adversely influence the succession process within a family business.
3. Identify some of the key deviant and dysfunctional behaviors within RGS Ltd. Suggest some of the governance and control mechanisms that Raj could have considered before appointing his cousin Pireth to take over the business.
4. In your opinion, how could the transition process have been better managed to avert a fallout within the family and business context?
5. What are some of the contextual factors evident in the case that prevent women from ascending to the leadership of family businesses?

NOTES

1. This case was developed based on interviews with Raj Agarwal's three daughters (Uma, Shyla, and Sarika) who provided insights and information about the company. Their names and other names used in the case have been changed to protect the identify of the family and the business.
2. We refer to the trio of Uma, Shyla, and Sarika as the three "Miss-keteers" (after the famous French historical novel whose characters, Athos, Porthos, and Aramis, were known as the "three Musketeers") given their united, concerted, and persistent fight to take control of their father's business from Pireth. In the process, they warded off other takeover attempts, particularly from their uncle, Krishna, and the rest of the extended family. Their acts of courage, unwavering determination, and going against their father's, mother's, and brother's wishes above all societal expectations, depict them as heroes who managed to rescue the business from collapse and save their father's legacy – many years of hard work and heartbreak. Their determination paid off and spearheaded them to the top-level management of the business.

SUGGESTED READING

Murithi, W., Vershinina, N. and Rodgers, P. (2020). Where less is more: Institutional voids and business families in Sub-Saharan Africa. *International Journal of Entrepreneurial Behavior & Research*, 26(1), 158–74.

Nelson, T. and Constantinidis, C. (2017). Sex and gender in family business succession research: A review and forward agenda from a social construction perspective. *Family Business Review*, 30(3), 219–41.

Xian, H., Jiang, N. and McAdam, M. (2021). Negotiating the female successor–leader role within family business succession in China. *International Small Business Journal*, 39(2), 157–83.

10
Preventing history from repeating itself: the succession process at De Berg[1]

Astrid Kramer and Miranda Stienstra

CASE SUMMARY

The case describes the intra-family succession process of the Dutch family firm, De Berg Sensor Solutions, founded in 1920. The family has already experienced two disruptive successions in the family firm, resulting in family conflict and the dissolution of relations between family members. The current CEO, Gerard de Berg of the third generation, attempts not to let it happen again. The succession process from the second to the third generation was characterized by conflict between predecessor and successor and rivalry between Gerard and his brother. The case illustrates how lack of communication in the De Berg family about succession intentions led to severe family conflict and explains how Gerard decided to do things differently.

LEARNING OUTCOMES

By the end of this case study, the student should be able to:

- Understand the impact of family conflict on performance and continuity of family firms.
- Argue why division of ownership and control in family firms is complex.
- Articulate the process a family could choose to transform a family-owned and managed firm to a family-owned firm.

Gerard de Berg hung up the phone after a long call with his daughter. Once again, they had a conversation about one of the details of the renewal of the family constitution. His daughter would like to have her adopted child written into the family constitution and give her child an option to be part of the family firm in the future. Gerard has hesitations about this because there is no blood connection. It somehow feels different for him. He is proud because his daughter is confident to speak her mind and has good arguments. He knows that differences in opinion are healthy and even good for the family firm, but, as always, it stings a bit.

Discussions like this are standard in the De Berg family and often get heated, but Gerard is never worried. He taught his children the importance of speaking their minds to avoid problems. He had hoped to avoid some of the problems he experienced as the son of a father who tried to pass the business ownership baton to his two youngest sons. It was a long, complex, and frustrating succession process with a lot of family conflict and took a heavy toll on Gerard. Gerard promised himself that his children should not go through the same process.

A SHORT HISTORY OF DE BERG SENSOR SOLUTIONS

De Berg Sensor Solutions is a third-generation Dutch family firm in the northern part of the Netherlands, founded by Johannes de Berg in 1920. In 1952, his son Ben de Berg succeeded him. In 1977, Gerard de Berg, the current owner of De Berg Sensor Solutions and son of Ben de Berg, joined the family firm and got sole ownership in 1984. The family firm has existed for more than 100 years. Upon its founding, it produced sensors for furnaces. However, for many years now, De Berg Sensor Solutions has produced specialized sensors for cleanrooms in a business-to-business industry with only a handful of customers. A cleanroom is a controlled environment that filters pollutants like dust and airborne microbes to provide the cleanest area possible and to protect the manufacture of products like electronic devices and medical equipment. De Berg Sensor Solutions strives for continuity, reliability, and proactive partner interactions with their suppliers, customers, employees, and other stakeholders. In 1920, the company started with a handful of employees and when Gerard joined his father the company had 35 employees. By the end of 2023, it had 130 employees and most of these employees have been with the company for many years.

DE BERG FAMILY AND SUCCESSION

Gerard is the third of four sons. Due to conflict between his father and grandfather Johannes, Gerard and his brothers did not visit their grandparents often when they were young. The reason for the conflict was never discussed within the family. Gerard only knows it was related to succession in the family firm. Gerard's two older brothers were never interested in joining the family business. Although his younger brother, Theo, was very good at sales, the family agreed that he did not have the necessary capabilities to run the business. At first, Gerard did not seem interested, but during his final year in high school, he realized that he wanted to study business administration. Slowly, he began to consider joining the family firm. Gerard and his father decided that after his studies he should first gain two years of experience working at another firm in the same industry. It would enable him to gain an understanding of the industry and to gain experience outside the family firm. In 1977, Gerard started to work at another firm, but after just six months his father called and asked Gerard to quit his job and start working in the family firm. Although the request surprised Gerard, he did not ask his father why, and assumed that the request was probably because the production manager of De Berg Sensor Solutions had announced he would retire within one year. Joining the family firm now would mean that Gerard could work with this experienced production manager for a year. Gerard started work at De Berg Sensor Solutions as an assistant production manager and in subsequent years he had several positions in the company, including administration and sales, because Gerard wanted to fully understand the family business. Finally, Gerard became an assistant business manager, four years after he joined the family firm.

Then, suddenly, everything changed. Gerard's father suffered a severe stroke. Gerard stepped into his father's role where possible. Against all odds, his father recovered quite well and was back in the business only ten weeks after the stroke. However, Gerard's father was more tired and less sharp than he had been before the stroke.

TWO CAPTAINS AND ONE SHIP IS NOT A GOOD IDEA

Although the family decided that Theo, Gerard's younger brother, did not have the capabilities to run the business, Gerard's father returned to the decision that Theo could now join the family firm and did not give Gerard any explanation, and Gerard did not ask. Gerard's two older brothers still stood by their decision not to join the family business. Although Theo had not been able to hold a job, his father seemed to be confident in the capabilities of his son. With a second son joining the family firm, Gerard's father changed the ownership structure of the family firm. Gerard and Theo each bought 50 percent of the shares. The firm was valued at a high price so the two oldest sons could be financially compensated rather than take an ownership stake. According to Gerard's father this was the fairest option. This urge for fairness probably came from his own experiences when he succeeded his father, who was in his view unfair, and this perception resulted in conflict with his family, whom he never spoke with again.

Although the two youngest sons now owned the company, the decision rights remained with their father. Dutch legislation offers the legal construction of a trust office foundation that separates voting rights from the profit-sharing (ownership) rights. This construction is often used by family firms to guarantee the continuity of the firm and reduce taxes. Gerard was very dissatisfied with his brother who came in late, left early, and was not prepared for meetings. Theo officially became responsible for marketing but, according to Gerard, he did not understand the job well. Gerard decided to join Theo in important meetings with customers because he felt that the continuity of the family firm was at stake.

After two years of struggling to work with Theo, Gerard decided that his brother must leave the firm for the sake of the business. Gerard told his father, who did not agree. Although Gerard managed all day-to-day operations in the company and the employees considered him to be the CEO, his father still had all final decision rights. After one of many heated discussions between father and son, the decision was made that a team of external consultants would investigate what was best for the family firm. Gerard was confident that the advice would be in his favor. After a few weeks, the external consultants recommended that Theo should leave the company, but his father did not accept this outcome. Gerard never asked his father why he did not accept the advice but thinks that it might be due to the fact that his father felt that his youngest son would not be able to make it on his own.

Gerard was worried about the continuity of the family firm because his father did not follow the advice of the external consulting team. In addition, he was not on speaking terms with his brother and father any more. Gerard saw no other way out and decided to bring the case to the Enterprise Chamber, which has exclusive jurisdiction in corporate proceedings. After several stressful months, the court ruled in Gerard's favor. Theo had to sell his shares to Gerard and Gerard's father had to give up his decision rights.

However, the tragedy still did not come to an end, because the two brothers could not come to an agreement about the value of the company. The business valuations experts from both brothers were so far apart that the case was again escalated to court. An official validator was assigned and determined that the business valuation was only 7 percent higher than Gerard's initial offering. Theo finally capitulated and sold his shares to Gerard, who became full owner of the company. However, it all comes at a price. The relationship Gerard had with his father and his brother was severely damaged, and communication ceased. The succession crisis broke their family.

GOING OFF 'ALONE'

Gerard and his wife had two daughters a few years after Gerard bought out his brother. For more than two decades the girls were too young to have a role in the family firm. In the seven years after the buyout, and with Gerard's full focus on the firm, the firm grew quickly from 35 to 65 employees. Because Gerard was the sole owner of the third-generation family firm, he wanted to safeguard the company in case something happened to him. Not only for his wife and children, but also for the employees and their families, for whom he feels a strong responsibility. This strong sense of responsibility for the employees was Gerard's main driver not to leave the company when he had conflict with his father and brother. He feared that the company, and therefore its employees, would have suffered if his brother had taken over the family firm.

Part of safeguarding the family firm was installing a supervisory board a few years after the buyout. The role of a supervisory board is to control and advise the firm. And although Gerard did not give up his decision rights, he was aware that having a supervisory board means accepting its (binding) advice as well. He understood that managing the firm would become a delicate interplay between him, as CEO and full owner, and members of the supervisory board. Gerard selected board members with strong opinions because he believed in the power of discussion.

Meanwhile, the company had grown to 100 employees and Gerard realized he needed help in maintaining control. Gerard hired Jan de Jong as managing director, who would officially replace Gerard in case something happened to him. Jan was primarily responsible for innovation and doubled production while keeping the same number of employees. Gerard decided to give him 20 percent of the shares, which ensured that Jan could profit from his own contributions to the business.

Next to appointing a supervisory board and hiring Jan, Gerard would like to have a family constitution, which is a document that describes, for example, family values and principles and how important decisions are made by the family. The constitution of the De Berg family contains topics such as family values, ownership, control, and how to involve the next generation.

HOW TO PREPARE THE FAMILY FOR THE FUTURE

De Berg Sensor Solutions had already faced two successions resulting in family conflict. Gerard was charmed by the idea that he might be able to pass the baton to (one of) his daughters but wanted to avoid a third succession resulting in conflict. Due to his own experiences he wanted to approach a potential succession differently and believed that openness and talking with each other are the main ingredients to maintaining family harmony.

Both daughters completed a master's degree and have the capabilities to lead the family firm. After some conversations, his older daughter confirmed she is not interested in running the day-to-day operations. She is interested in engaging with the firm through an arm's length position. Gerard is relieved, because he wants to avoid the situation in which siblings together manage the firm. The younger daughter had ambitions to become involved in the day-to-day activities and joined the firm in 2018 as assistant production manager, just like her father. She rotated positions in the first four years to get to know the company inside out. According to plan, she became commercial director in 2022. In the years to come, she will be able to grow more in her position as successor of the family firm.

In 2018, when the younger daughter started working in the company, the elder daughter became a member of the supervisory board. At the same time, Gerard transferred 80 percent of his shares to his daughters, who each received 40 percent. Gerard maintained the decision rights. In 2023, Gerard believes he has given both his daughters suitable positions in the family firm. Now, his goal is to start pulling himself back from the family firm. He believes that he did a better job than his father; yet, sadly, his relationships with his father and brother were destroyed as Gerard attempted to build a thriving company under his leadership. He ponders his daughter's request that the family constitution be amended to accommodate her adopted child.

DISCUSSION QUESTIONS

1. What was the root cause of family conflict in the second succession in De Berg Sensor Solutions?
2. Gerard as well as his father chose to give their children ownership and to keep control themselves. Use agency theory to explain what problems this caused and why.
3. Which steps could Gerard have taken if none of his daughters had shown interest in leading the firm?
4. To what extent have the measures taken by Gerard helped to avoid family conflict in the third succession in the family firm?
5. Should the family constitution be amended so that Gerard's daughter's adopted child be permitted to join the family firm? Why or why not?

EPILOGUE

Gerard is succeeded by his younger daughter, who is now CEO, and soon Gerard will transfer all his shares to his daughters. The older daughter has taken on the role of involved shareholder. The company is growing, and the future looks good.

NOTE

1. The teaching case is based on two interviews with the owner of the family firm in this case and company information such as the website. Due to anonymity, identifiable elements of the company and individuals in this teaching case are pseudonymized. The request for the interviews was approved by the Institutional Review Board of Tilburg Economics and Management, Tilburg University.

SUGGESTED READING

Bettinelli, C., Mismetti, M., De Massis, A. and Del Bosco, B. (2022). A review of conflict and cohesion in social relationships in family firms. *Entrepreneurship Theory and Practice, 46*(3), 539–77.
Davis, J.H., Allen, M.R. and Hayes, H.D. (2010). Is blood thicker than water? A study of stewardship perceptions in family firms. *Entrepreneurship Theory and Practice, 34*(6), 1093–116.
Lambrechts, J. and Lievens, J. (2008). Pruning the family tree: An unexplored path to family business continuity and family harmony. *Family Business Review, 21*(4), 295–313.
Sciascia, S., Clinton, E., Nason, R.S., James, A.E. and Rivera-Algarin, J.O. (2013). Family communication and innovativeness in family firms. *Family Relations, 62*(3), 429–42.

PART III
CORPORATE GOVERNANCE – OR LACK THEREOF

11

The Johnsons unveiled: a family's clash of values, business, and philanthropy[1]

Małgorzata Smulowitz and Peter Vogel

CASE SUMMARY

This case tells the story of the Johnson family, owners of a renowned luxury brand in Western Europe, and the conflict that arose when the fourth generation joined the business. John Johnson, the eldest son, returned from the US with new ideas and strategies to improve the family business and initiate philanthropic projects. Despite facing hostility, John hired philanthropy advisors and set up a fund to help young women with genital fistulas in Africa, providing them with treatment and vocational training. His family remained unimpressed by his efforts, and his proposal to create a holding company and to establish corporate governance mechanisms was also rejected. At this point in time, John strongly felt that he was too different from his family to collaborate with them. After well over a decade of impasse, John bought out the rest of the family and became the majority shareholder. The family split and continued to stay conflicted. The case ends with John reflecting on what he could have done differently and what his next steps will be.

LEARNING OUTCOMES

After analyzing this case, students will be able to:

- Explain how conflicts affect the interplay of individuals, businesses, ownership groups, and families, and explore effective strategies to address them.
- Identify the tipping point at which family members must go their separate ways and understand the costs and benefits of striking out on their own.
- Describe a bold approach to renewing a family business that involves establishment of corporate governance mechanisms.
- Demonstrate critical thinking skills that approach succession planning from a fresh perspective.

On a chilly winter evening in 2020, John Johnson, a forward-thinking fourth-generation member of the respected Johnson family firm, sat in his office thinking about the family's history. After he joined the business, John found himself disagreeing with the family's usual ways of doing things, especially handling the aspects of philanthropy. Reflecting on the ongoing family conflict, John acknowledged he initially entered the business wearing a "rescuer's hat". Driven by youthful confidence, he believed he could "save" the family and improve the business. Now, he felt the family didn't handle its legacy well. Even though he tried hard to connect and make things better, John sensed hidden tensions and misunderstandings among family members. He learned that things were more complicated than he thought, and he wished he had understood that earlier. Amid family disagreements, John took a bold step and decided to buy out other family members from the business. As the dust settled, he found himself not just holding the majority of the shares but also steering the ship as the new captain. The thrill of owning the business was palpable, but with it came a wave of responsibility – now, every decision rested on his shoulders. It was a moment of both excitement and feeling the weight of newfound accountability.

THE JOHNSON FAMILY FIRM

The Johnson's family business was established in the late nineteenth century in the Middle East, but early on, the founder decided to move the business and its operations to Europe. For over 100 years, three generations of the Johnson family controlled and managed the business. The family built extraordinary financial and relational capital by providing luxury goods to the richest 1 percent in the world. However, family involvement in the business remained rather small, with two brothers from the third generation, Daniel and Michael, and Daniel's wife, Emily, running the business. The fourth generation, which consisted of five cousins, John, Isabelle, Julia, William, and Victoria, was slowly becoming more interested in the business (see Figure 11.1). The family defined its values as generosity, education, and hard work. However, over time, a form of competitiveness and jealousy among the family members had trumped these converging values.

In the mid-1980s, John decided to do something very different from what his father Daniel and mother Emily expected. Despite his family's assumptions that their oldest son would join the business at 19, John decided to pursue an education in the US, which led him to be far away from the business and his family in Europe for almost two decades. Indeed, the family had always demonstrated strong roots and a loyalty-based identity that could have even been perceived as "tribal". The family's excessive cohesion led them to prioritize conformity to their own set ways over adapting to a changing environment. By deciding to pursue an individualistic path rather than a communal one, John put himself on a collision course with his family.

After finishing his political science studies, John decided to continue his education in the US, and to do an MBA. After graduating, John did not immediately join the family business. Instead, he wanted to gain more external experience by working in the financial sector for around 10 years in different European countries, including France, the United Kingdom, and Switzerland.

Finally, in 2005, he joined the family business as managing director. His job was to oversee strategy and development, but the business was fully controlled and managed by his father Daniel and uncle Michael as co-CEOs. John thought his new role in the family business would give him an opportunity to do what he always desired – that is, to work *on* the business. This was in contrast with previous Johnson generations who were primarily interested in working *in* the business – specifically buying and selling. However, John really wanted to do things differently; he did not want to define himself as a person who would repeat the previous generation's actions. According to John: "My goal was to improve – to bring the 'Kaizen spirit'[2] of continuous improvement to the family business, and there were many things that needed improving."

MAKING A DIFFERENCE AS A FAMILY

Generosity was deeply rooted in the DNA of the Johnson family; Figure 11.1 shows the family's four generations. John recalled many stories about his great-grandfather, Benjamin, and grandfather, Christopher. While both men had a reputation for being "tough", they were both perceived as very generous. John's great-grandfather, Benjamin, was known for helping several poor people in the community. He would provide heaters for those in need to make sure they could survive the harsh winters. His grandfather, Christopher, was so fair and kind that he was chosen as the arbitrator for the whole industry in the Western European country where the business resided.

John knew of several more stories like these. Both the first and second generations had actively helped the less fortunate. While growing up, John noticed a similar kind of generosity from his parents, Daniel and Emily, an ad hoc generosity based on encounters and demands rather than strategic generosity. His father Daniel would usually respond to requests from individuals and religious or national groups. He did not focus on the specific causes as much as on the fact that he was being solicited by people who he felt were important to work with. John explained: "It wasn't necessarily calculating or Machiavellian, but it was something that was part of my parents' relational networking habits."

In the spirit of Kaizen, John tried to come up with a more process-based approach to the family's philanthropy. Initially, he was inspired by an *International Herald Tribune* article by Nicholas Kristof from 2004, which described how Dr Catherine Hamlin, an Australian obstetrician who migrated to Ethiopia in the 1960s, had set up a hospital to treat genital fistulas in very young Ethiopian women. Kristof painted a terrible picture of what was happening to these girls in Ethiopia and of how Dr Hamlin was trying to address their loss of dignity and humanity. Once they developed fistulas, they were often rejected by their husbands and their parents – essentially left to die. After reading the article, John was so shocked that this could still be happening in the twenty-first century, so he started to reflect: "What can I do? What can we do as a family?"

First, John gave some money to the hospital in Ethiopia. Second, he started thinking about convincing the family to support this cause and then getting the business to contribute. His philanthropic idea was to create a family foundation that would strategically address women's

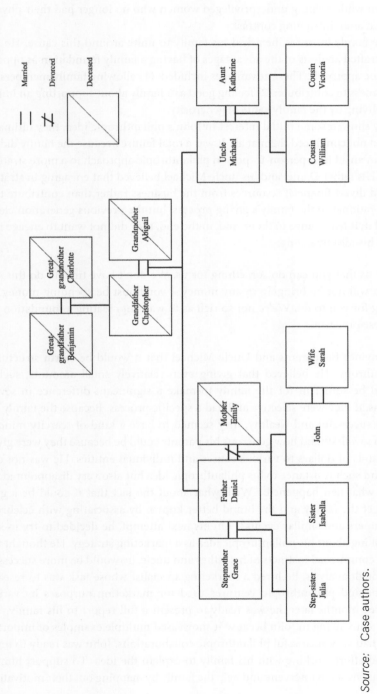

Source: Case authors.

Figure 11.1   The four generations of the Johnson family

health and education. He considered it a good fit because the family business had always sold about 98 percent of its luxury goods to women. Selling the ultimate luxury accessories to uberwealthy women while helping underprivileged women who no longer had their physical integrity struck John as an intriguing contrast.

After joining the family business, he asked his family to unite around this cause. He presented a carefully crafted analysis of the advantages of having a family foundation as opposed to the current ad hoc approach. These advantages included: (1) allowing family members not involved in the business to contribute; (2) feeling good as a family about supporting an important cause; and (3) living by the family value of generosity.

While the family showed some initial interest in John's philanthropic idea, they ultimately rejected it. John had not convinced them at all. It was a total failure because the family did not want to change from an ad hoc, person-to-person philanthropic approach to a more strategic, analytic approach. His father Daniel and his uncle Michael believed that engaging in strategic philanthropy would divert financial resources from the business rather than contribute to it. John was trying to rationalize the family's giving process, but the previous generation clearly did not understand it; it felt strange to them, and, in the end, they did not want to engage in it. They responded to his idea by saying:

> Well, first show us that you can do something for us. We don't have time to do this, and if you do it, you will not be bringing in any money – you'll just be spending money. So, not a good thing for you to do. We're not so rich as to warrant creating a foundation and rationalizing these processes.

John could not convince his parents and Uncle Michael that it would be worth structuring the family's philanthropy. He believed that giving even relatively small amounts, such as US$250 000, would be sufficient for the family to make a significant difference in several causes and locations, if they were selective and had a specific process. Because the family had not always been as successful and wealthy, they seemed to have a kind of scarcity mindset. However, John also saw firsthand how generous his parents could be because they were giving hundreds of thousands of dollars to various causes and individual entities. He was not only very surprised to find such resistance to his philanthropic idea but also very disappointed.

He reflected on what had happened: "Well, what about the fact that it could be a great marketing tool to get the family and the brand better known by associating with celebrities and having gala dinners and similar events?" On his next attempt, he decided to try to shift the family into thinking about his philanthropic idea as a marketing strategy. He thought that by appealing to the commercial instincts of his father and uncle, he would be more successful. To conduct a thorough analysis, he hired a marketing specialist whose task was to research existing foundations and philanthropic ventures used for marketing purposes by various luxury brands. Three months later, he was ready to present a full report to his family. The report seemed very convincing to John because it showcased multiple examples of important luxury groups that had very successful philanthropic collaborations. John was ready to invest substantial time and effort working with his family to explain the idea. To support him, he hired philanthropy advisors to intervene and help the family by mapping out their motivations for giving, coaching the family, and setting up workshops to think through what could become the focus of their family philanthropy.

The whole process did not get them anywhere; neither the third nor the fourth generation were swayed at all. His aunt Katherine, who at the time was also one of the business leaders, became very upset and said: "Oh, you're just doing a travesty of philanthropy for the sake of moneymaking. This is so bad. I can't believe you even proposed that." In addition, his father Daniel concluded: "You will never convince me to talk to a customer about fistulas when I'm trying to sell her our luxury goods. You're absolutely crazy."

John was amazed by the harsh feedback and the disregard of how much effort he had put into the proposal and the professional help he had hired to vet the feasibility of the project. As John's proposal was rejected harshly, he took a step back to regroup his thoughts. To his amazement, he later learned that his parents lent their house to friends to organize a philanthropic fundraiser and to support their cause. John was shocked, so he spoke to them to try to understand:

> I'm surprised by how generous and kind you are to your friends, because you even lent your house to organize parties for fundraising for their pet projects. But when I came and asked you for help for my project – and it wasn't mine alone; it would be for the whole family – you actually refused. I don't understand. What's going on?

John never understood why his parents were so much more open to their friends' – and sometimes even just acquaintances' – requests than their own son's. He was very disappointed by what he thought was a lack of imagination and vision by his family.

MAKING A DIFFERENCE ALONE

John ended up feeling like "the odd man out", asking himself: "What am I doing? What is happening in this family?" He never received a clear explanation of why the family consistently reacted so negatively to his philanthropic proposals. Later that year, his trusted advisor Eric proposed that he should create a philanthropic fund instead of a family foundation. John could then donate the money on his own to support the philanthropic projects in which he was interested. John agreed, so his advisor proposed that the newly established fund be called "John's Fund for Women". However, John still had a strong desire and hope that his family would get involved in his philanthropy; therefore, he called the fund "The Johnson's Fund for Women". In his mind, it could then be open to other family members if they wished to contribute.

At its peak, the fund had US$250 000 that John had donated. He invited everyone in the family to contribute, saying: "You don't have to do anything if you don't want to, but you can contribute any amount, from one dollar to millions of dollars if you want. My goal is to make it work." Unfortunately, nobody in the family accepted his invitation. His cousin Victoria, who he thought could have been a good participant in his philanthropic project, got upset with him and said: "If you're going to spend money on others, why don't you give the money to me first?" John was surprised by this because his cousin was not lacking wealth in any way at all.

He thought: "I don't understand – she wants more money, but she doesn't seem to be suffering in any way at all. So, it's probably coming from a psychological level rather than a financial one. Or there could be other sources, such as jealousy." John did not foresee the possibility that his philanthropic ideas could set off rivalries or resentments in the family. He did not perceive himself as wanting to dominate, be above others, or take power from others. He possibly ended up lecturing them, but he only meant to explain and convince rather than force anyone or make them feel inferior. Certainly, he was naïve about how his family would perceive his attempts at sharing, explaining, and opening up to them about his ambitions and vision.

Consequently, John acted on his own. He joined a project in collaboration with a multinational organization to support a women's hospital in Dar es Salaam, Tanzania. The hospital was just setting up a new team of doctors who could treat genital fistula. Tanzania's problem was not caused by the women being too young to give birth; rather, it was more often caused by complications at the end of the pregnancy, and the women lived too far away from well-equipped hospitals to be able to access care. John invested all his money from the fund in this project. The multinational organization chipped in a substantial amount of money as well. In the end, the project ran from 2013 to 2016 and helped 1600 women. The project was a great success because in addition to receiving help with their health, the women also received vocational training. The affected women frequently faced rejection economically because of how they smelled. The vocational training often resulted in increased confidence and new jobs, which made it possible for many of the women to achieve economic independence. John was very happy and proud of the impact that this project had achieved. He shared its results with his family members, but they still refused to support him in any way. After this experience, John realized that he was simply too different from his family to collaborate with them.

THE FALLING OUT OF THE FAMILY

The massive disagreement about family philanthropy had a negative spillover effect. In the following years, many challenging issues occurred in the Johnson family and its business. However, the family was unable to tackle them as the lack of formal governance and conflict resolution mechanisms were major weaknesses.

Around this time, John once again made a great effort to bring the family together. In 2008, he hired a US consultant in family governance to come and spend a weekend with his family. John invested about six months preparing for this weekend. During the weekend, the consultant proposed a family constitution, setting up a formal board and family council. John's father Daniel and uncle Michael once again rejected all these ideas. John reflected on this: "The irony is that the family has enough education and intelligence, social capital, and awareness that they should have been able to work on pooling resources, whether intellectual, financial, social, or educational, to do better across various dimensions."

In the early days when John joined the family business, he recalled how he pulled all the assets together and said:

> The family as a whole is the owner of probably between 200 to 250 million dollars' worth of assets, and it would be great if we were able to create forms of governance that would ensure the good-quality management of these existing assets and that we start thinking of alternative investments and businesses. It would also be great to include the 4th generation and educate them in terms of managing assets, creating future plans, participating in community work and philanthropy – something very multidimensional.

The idea was that the family could create a holding company that would invest in various new ventures, including continuing to work in the luxury goods business, have a philanthropic arm, a family council, and have a type of custom educational program for all family members so that they could develop the skills they needed to be successful. John wanted to bring everyone in the family together so that they could try new things out rather than joining the family business out of obligation. He strongly believed that, in this way, the family's talents could be catalyzed, and new interesting ideas and businesses could come into existence and be brought to fruition. The family refused his proposal again. John was appalled by the family's reluctance to improve its functioning and leverage its strengths. He concluded:

> The result today is that the family has essentially seceded; there is no affection left, or respect even, between the various members of the family, and the business has been faltering for the last 10 years because the family refused to agree on any changes, including in its own functioning.

John's dream of uniting the family and cooperating to enhance not only the way the company's assets were managed but also the consciousness and life experiences of each family member was never realized. Instead, it seemed that the third generation enjoyed bickering with each other, which obviously was not good for the business, their individual lives, or the family. John regretted this because he wanted to share the best of what he had learned from the US – the world-class education and best practices – with the family and help them benefit from it. But the family's conservative mindset was not ready for change, even when it came to the corporate governance of the business.

DISCUSSION QUESTIONS

1. What do you think went wrong between John and the rest of the family? What are the causes of the fallout between him and the rest of the family? What could have been done to avoid it or at least to manage it better?
2. Is the relationship between John and his family salvageable at this point? What would you suggest he do going forward?
3. What key takeaways can other family businesses and business families learn from

John's experience?
4. What are some of the common challenges to watch out for when managing family business succession and conflict resolution and establishing formal corporate governance mechanisms?

EPILOGUE

Since 2020, John has been in full control of the business, owning 75 percent of the shares. Ultimately, he not only obtained the majority of shares, but also, together with his wife Sarah, assumed control of the firm's management. What started with his parents Daniel and Emily, Uncle Michael and Aunt Katherine, and John and his two cousins William and Victoria working in the business, ended with just John and his wife Sarah as the managing team. John recalled that when his father and uncle took over the business, his grandfather Christopher's decision was to grant both an equal number of shares. There had been some compulsion from his grandfather that his father Daniel would accept his younger brother Michael as a 50 percent partner, even though his father had been the one to develop the business, while his uncle joined much later. This affected the business and the family in a profound way. John recalled that his father Daniel acted as if he was the leader, but his uncle Michael would often say "no". The brothers did not manage to settle many of their differences, and this affected how the family members who worked with them felt. It appears the family was dealing with a number of iceberg issues; one could only see a small portion of it, but in fact the majority of it was under water, and no one truly knew what the untold stories and challenges were.

John was relieved that he and his wife Sarah did not suffer from the kind of conflicts his father Daniel and uncle Michael experienced. Finally, he was in a position to improve the business and inject philanthropy into it if he wanted to. Obviously, if the business was not doing well, then there would be no funds for philanthropy. His initial plan was to focus the business on corporate social responsibility (CSR) – something that John had been trying to do for the last 15 years, but without success because his family did not want to do a value-chain audit or improve anything. One of the things he wanted to create was certain luxury designer goods where 10 percent of all proceeds would go toward philanthropy. Perhaps he could reactivate the fund or donate to some other basket of nongovernmental organizations (NGOs). But before he got there, the business had to be successful. John asked himself: "What should be the next steps? Where to start?"

NOTES

1. This case study was developed through direct interactions and field research with John Johnson, including two semi-structured interviews. Data were further validated using archival sources and supplemented by John's participation in a family philanthropy workshop at IMD Business School in 2020, which provided observational insights. All names have been disguised to preserve anonymity.

2.   Kaizen, a Japanese term meaning "improvement", is a business approach focused on enhancing operations involving all employees. It helps to eliminate waste and improve efficiency globally. Beyond that, it has been applied in areas such as purchasing and supply chains.

SUGGESTED READINGS

Feliu, N. and Botero, I.C. (2016). Philanthropy in family enterprises: A review of literature. *Family Business Review, 29*(1), 121–41.

Gray, L.P. (2005). How family dynamics influence the structure of the family office. *The Journal of Wealth Management, 8*(2), 9–17.

Van den Berghe, L.A. and Carchon, S. (2003). Agency relations within the family business system: An exploratory approach. *Corporate Governance: An International Review, 11*(3), 171–9.

12

The past catches up with everyone: legal failures of the previous generation threaten a family firm's future[1]

Jan Klaus Tänzler and Annegret Hauer

CASE SUMMARY

The case describes a fifth-generation family-owned supplier to the automotive industry in Germany with 1500 employees and €180 million annual turnover. The company has more than 40 family shareholders. Because fewer than 500 of the firm's employees work in Germany, it is not required to establish a supervisory board. Illegal cartels involving Meyer SE that dated back to the beginning of the 2000s were reported shortly before the end of the statute of limitations and attracted the attention of the public prosecutor's office. The subsequent penalty caused the Meyer SE family firm existential difficulties, especially as it came during a restructuring phase. As a result, the family not only struggled to save the company from failure but also had to work through the question of responsibility in the family. To make matters worse, direct responsibilities are unclear, and many family members are involved in various ways – current CEO, previous CEO and founder of advisory board, non-manager representative of one of the family factions, and so on. Due to the family's strong identification with the company, family members now fear not only loss of earnings, but also loss of reputation. All of this leads to strong tensions within the family, even though it appears to the public to be united. The case illustrates how a lack of responsibility combined with violations of the law can lead to conflicts within the family, even in later generations. This becomes particularly disruptive when the company management does not behave correctly. In this case, it became apparent that the Meyer family was not only experiencing economic difficulties due to incorrect behavior on the part of the previous generation, but that conflict had arisen in the family due to shortcomings in its corporate governance process. In addition to a loss of income, the family also feared severe damage to its reputation.

LEARNING OUTCOMES

Through analysis of this case, students should be able to:

- Explain the characteristics of family businesses, especially with regard to management and ownership.
- Describe the differences between family and nonfamily managers and the problems and opportunities for both types of managers.
- Explain the typical conflicts that can arise in family businesses. Focus in particular on the following points: succession, financial imbalances, corporate control.
- Describe how the cohesion of the family shareholders and their attachment to the company can be promoted.
- Describe the importance of a formal and effective family governance system in avoiding potential conflicts in family businesses.
- Develop a family charter for Meyer SE.

Peter Meyer, the fifth-generation CEO of Meyer SE, an automotive company founded in 1890 in Gummersbach (Germany), is sitting at his desk one fine spring day, completely caught up in the story of his family business. He realizes how much the company has developed in recent years: over the past few decades, what was originally a small metal company has become an international supplier of brake pads. Research and innovation are still deeply anchored in the corporate DNA. Metalworking characterized the first three generations of family entrepreneurs, especially during World War II, when the firm and its competitors were regulated by the state as a war-related industry.

During the years after the war – the "Wirtschaftswunder" – the company flourished and new fields of activity were explored. Heinz, CEO of the third generation to run the company, took advantage of his connections to a rubber company in South America and founded a new branch of the company, Meyer Kautschuk, which specialized in the production of brake pads. These were also in high demand as the automotive industry became more important in Germany and the sales markets were almost identical to the original business. Peter's father Walter, the fourth generation, then decisively pushed the internationalization of the company with a corresponding strategic orientation. Boosted by the good economic situation, the company was able to generate high profits during this phase. At the end of the 1990s, these profits were invested in a newly founded real estate company.

Thus, the company has operated three independent divisions since then: Meyer Metal, the original metal processing company; Meyer Kautschuk, the brake pad company; and Meyer Real Estate (see Table 12.1). For some years now, however, the effects of strategic shortfalls combined with a decline in the general economic situation have been emerging as risk factors. Peter sees himself under increasing pressure from the big players in the market, who are increasingly dictating prices. "There's still a lot to come, and it certainly won't get any easier," he thought, turning his attention to the day-to-day business.

Suddenly the door to Peter's office is flung open and several people burst in. "Senior Public Prosecutor Deller is my name, and this is my team. Mr Meyer, there is an initial suspicion of a cartel offense against your company. We have the search warrant here to seize evidence.

Table 12.1   The five generations of Meyer SE

Generation		CEO	Shareholders	Products	Employees (Year)	Sales
1.	1890–1930	Abraham	1	Blacksmith	1 (1890)	NA
2.	1930–1955	Johannes	5	Metal components Weapons (WWII)	200 (1930)	NA
3.	1955–1985	Heinz	20	Metal components Brake pads	500 (1955)	DM 50m
4.	1985–2015	Walter	34	Metal components Brake pads Real estate	1000 (1985)	DM 150m
5.	2015–now	Peter	43	Metal components Brake pads Real estate	1500 (2015)	€180m

Source: Case authors.

Please leave the premises of the company." While the prosecution start searching the offices for suspicious documents, Peter goes to his car in complete shock. On the way, he talks to the company's legal advisor, Dr Grobius, on the phone, who advises him to go home first. He cannot even imagine what it is all about in detail. Should this have happened during his still short five-year tenure? Or does the family advisory board, which his father and uncle as managing directors had initiated a few years ago, know more? And what happened at all?

On the way home, he spontaneously decides to drive to his parents. Perhaps they could shed some light on the matter for him. His father Walter, who retired five years ago at the age of 70, had been managing director for almost 30 years, and still knows his way around the company.

A TALK WITH THE PARENTS

"What happened? You've got to be kidding!" Walter Meyer is outraged. As a former CEO, he still feels very connected to the company. "Why don't you show me the letter first? What kind of cartel offense is this supposed to be?" "I thought you could tell me!" Peter replies and hands him the letter.

Somewhat exhausted, Walter sinks into a chair, takes off his glasses, and looks thoughtfully out of the window. What kind of cartel offense was this? Of course, they met with other entrepreneurs in the industry, especially since these were also mainly family businesses and people knew each other quite well in private. The market for brake pads was at that time also quite manageable. And people also talked about the business field. But that was only natural. The times were also quite different, not so anonymous. And as a company with a long tradition, it also had a certain pioneering role and its word counted for something.

"Dr Grobius has already been informed, of course," Peter interrupted his train of thought. Hans Grobius was the family's legal advisor and longtime confidant. "He will also notify the other shareholders. Hopefully this won't mean too much stress in the family."

"What stress in the family? There are no problems, I hope?" Peter's mother enters the living room. "Unfortunately, there are." Peter briefly tells his mother about the morning's events. "Oh God, how is this going to be? I don't want to have to be ashamed of us in town. After all, we have a reputation to lose too!" Father and son had not yet given this aspect any further thought but had to realize that it could well be important for many family members, particularly for those who still lived locally. Complicated meetings with the many family shareholders were in the offing. This was especially the case since views on the goals and values of the firm were quite different within various factions of the family, even if many were only interested in collecting the dividends. But that was no different from the past.

MEETING WITH LEGAL COUNSEL AND MANAGEMENT

On the same day, Peter Meyer called the entire management and Dr Grobius together for an emergency meeting. In the meantime, Hans Grobius had been given access to the files and was able to report that the accusations related to events involving price-fixing in several different markets that had occurred 18 years earlier. At that time, Walter Meyer was CEO and his brother Hubert CFO. "I have already informed the shareholders. Everyone has been invited to an extraordinary shareholders' meeting next week," Grobius said. "Of course, the work is just beginning now." Peter Meyer is worried: "What kind of penalty can we expect? We don't have any large reserves now." Unfortunately, Dr Grobius cannot reassure him: "In comparable cases, fines in the double-digit millions have already been imposed. But to be more precise, we must wait for further developments. In any case, I recommend hiring a specialized law firm. Talks with the banks are already scheduled for next week."

FIRST MEETING OF THE FAMILY SHAREHOLDERS

A week later, the special meeting of the shareholders was held at the company. Tension in the room cannot be ignored. The 43 shareholders – all of them family members – are present. Three siblings, Walter Meyer, Hubert Meyer, and Sybille Benz, who represent their respective family "tribes," demonstratively keep their distance from each other. To make matters worse, there has been a subliminal dispute between the Hubert Meyer and Sybille Benz tribes for many years, which had its beginnings in the previous generation over disputes regarding inheritance and input into selecting leaders for the company. From the third to the fifth generation, the number of family shareholders had doubled, leading to the formation of tribes of family members, each now led by the siblings of the fourth generation. Family disagreements on various matters had built up over the years. These disputes have repeatedly led to heated discussions and could now prove momentous in this existential situation for the company.

At the start of the meeting, Walter Meyer informs those present about the state of the investigation. He also points out the possible consequences of a high cartel fine: a possible sale of the company, which could not be prevented, is on the cards. This would bring a success story of more than 100 years to an abrupt end. Accordingly, nerves are on edge. Wild accusations buzz around the room among the shareholders. "How could no one have noticed?" "Who actually controls the people here?" "But I depend on the money." "What will the people in town say?" "I've never been interested in the whole business anyway." "I can understand your excitement, but let's think about it calmly," Peter urges. What follows is a very emotional discussion about guilt and responsibility.

The discussion is also triggered by the fact that family managers are fundamentally treated in a different way from nonfamily managers. "We would simply sue an external manager now! But with family managers, things are even more tricky. You don't take legal action against the family, do you?" one of the shareholders says. Most of the shareholders agree. "The advisory board seems to have been sleeping, too! Perhaps external members would have taken a better look!"

As fear for the future of the company increases, so does the fear of the shareholders for their own livelihoods. "Do you always think only of yourselves?" shouts shareholder Klaus Kurz, "Here, after all, the jobs of over 1500 people are at risk."

It goes back and forth for a while without anyone being able to elaborate on blame and consequences. Dr Grobius and Jens Schlemmer, the company's CFO, insistently point out the danger of a high cartel fine and the accompanying threat of bankruptcy. In the end, even the most optimistic shareholders cannot deny that things have never been so critical for the company and that a sale may be the best solution after all.

MEETING WITH A FORMER SECRETARY

After a sleepless night and many conversations with the family, Peter wants to jog the sketchy memory of his family members and visits Anna, his father's former secretary, in Freiburg. He hopes to find out more about what happened back then. The old lady is still very spry and is happy to see Peter again. "I should have visited you much earlier," he says, "and now it's in such a compromising situation." "Yes, I've already heard about it," says the old lady, "It's already in the news. I still have the article lying around here somewhere." "Yes, I've read that one too," Peter says dejectedly.

> We really don't come off well there. I can't believe that's all there is to it. After all, the family has survived successfully for so long. We are the fifth generation, and the company has overcome several challenges in the past. And we are truly proud of it. But now it's hard to know what to do. The whole family is at loggerheads, and I believe we are done. I'm sure everything will have to be sold now.

Anna seems very thoughtful. She has a very close relationship with Peter in particular, whom she has known since he was born just over 40 years ago and wants to get Peter out of his depressed mood.

> Don't think so negatively. I'm sure everyone always wanted the best for the company and the family. You must see that too. When I remember how your father always took care of all the employees – 1500 of them all over the world – and didn't let anyone down. Everyone still talks about that. You can't give that up so easily. I'm sure a solution can be found. If you pull out all the stops and talk to everyone sensibly, the worst can certainly be prevented. You all just have to stick together and speak with one voice to the public.

Peter needs to think about that for a while.

INTERMEZZO – PETER ATTEMPTS TO UNITE THE TRIBES

Anna's words fell on fertile soil with Peter. He sets up talks with the three spokespersons for the family tribes. His father Walter and his uncle Hubert immediately agree to pull out all the stops to maneuver the company through this severe crisis. They are still very attached to the company and, as former CEOs, also still feel a responsibility for the well-being of the employees and the family. The situation is different for Sybille Benz. She places the blame for the current misery squarely on Walter and Hubert. That is why she is convinced that both must pay for the damage that has been done. In her eyes, a sale of the entire firm would be an appropriate way to solve all financial issues and to hand over responsibility for the future. Peter tries to show Sybille that it is not only about questions of guilt, but that the company also has a social position and, as an employer in the region, bears responsibility for many employees. After hours of controversial and heated discussion, Sybille is not quite convinced yet, but she agrees to use a mediator to resolve the situation. Peter seems confident.

THE FAMILY SHAREHOLDERS AGREE TO A MEDIATOR

Meanwhile, the other family shareholders have also formed their own opinions and discussed them with each other. The range of possibilities and proposed solutions is accordingly diverse. Thus, the second shareholders' meeting gets off to a turbulent start, with many questions floating through the room. No one can yet predict exactly which opinion will succeed. Since the discussions are not only objective, but also very emotional, the decision is made to consult a mediator. Although some family members have doubts about this, most of the shareholders also want to give it a try. "Why not? After all, we have nothing to lose. We can't apparently reach a reasonable agreement on our own," argues one member of the younger generation.

Subsequently, the mediator meets several times with all the family shareholders. Acceptance of the mediator naturally varied among the family members. There were five meetings in total, which served to keep the conversation ongoing and ensure that all voices were heard. The mediator also ensured that the highly emotional discussions did not get out of hand and that the family members were still able to talk to each other. The mediator's primary task was to find a basis for discussion so that the family shareholders could agree on a strategy, which involved selling parts of the business to keep the rest of the company operating. Once the family has committed to a common strategy, the family members feel closer to each other. They drop their private differences for the moment. Everything else will be decided after the key managers meet with the bank.

MANAGEMENT MEETS WITH THE BANK

The management and legal advisor Dr Grobius make their way to Frankfurt, where an urgent meeting with the bank is scheduled. Although the gentlemen are aware that the appointment could be difficult, the discussion at the last family meeting gives them reason to be optimistic, because the family now speaks with one voice.

The bank representatives get straight to the point. The cartel fine is not only a disaster for the company for reputational reasons. The penalty also hits the company at a difficult time. One of the three divisions – metal components – has been losing money for several years and there is no future concept for the entire company. The bank representatives are unanimous: only a sale of the entire firm can be the desired goal! The family shareholders vehemently contradict this. "The family is united," says Peter Meyer, "we want to do everything to save the company. And we speak with one voice!" It is precisely with this last point that Peter Meyer tries to convince the bank representatives. The bank representatives, however, counter: "We are not willing to continue to finance this venture. We are cancelling the credit line!" says the chairman of the board of the Kreissparkasse Gummersbach. "And look on the bright side: After selling and paying the fine, there will certainly be money left over for everyone to live a good life!"

After the meeting, the management team is dejected. How can the family firm be saved?

THE FAMILY TRIBES COME TOGETHER

After the discussion with the bank representatives, Peter Meyer arranges a meeting between the three speakers of the family tribes Sybille Benz, Hubert, and Walter Meyer, and himself, representing the company. "How should we behave?" he asks his family members. "If the banks don't follow our future path, we don't need to think about our options any further!" This comment is followed by an intense discussion on how to proceed. Sybille Benz, for whom a sale was an issue shortly after the public prosecutor's investigation came to light, is still favoring this solution. "Because it is the most secure way to make safe our money without further troubles."

Walter prefers a more enterprising approach and is trying to save at least a part of the company:

> Our older division has been causing us problems for some time now, even though this division is where it all started; what do you think if we try to sell this part of the company?

I'm not a financial expert but the sale price should be enough to pay the penalty and additionally address the remaining division's investment backlog.

Peter disagrees. He is full of energy. Now he has a clear opinion of what to do: "For this, of course, we would have to get the other shareholders on our side. You know selling our original business would be very emotional for the family." "But the idea is not so bad," Hubert counters. "And maybe, we can save the total company, if we could bring a strategic investor on board." "And who knows," Peter ponders, "maybe our legal advisors will manage to reduce the penalty."

After this meeting, Peter goes home in good spirits. Even if they had not reached a decision, it was clear that the family would speak with one voice in the future negotiations. But what would the best solution be?

DISCUSSION QUESTIONS

1. How does conflict in family firms affect family cohesion?
2. How can destructive conflicts between family members be avoided or resolved constructively?
3. Why are the values and reputation of family firms more important than those in nonfamily businesses?
4. What are the differing motives of the family members in the case for dealing with the company's crisis?
5. What can families do to establish their own values and ideas in the family business?

EPILOGUE: A FAMILY CONSTITUTION

Six months later, the families meet again. In the meantime, the company has gotten off lightly. The metal components division is being prepared for sale, and the other parts of the company can continue the family business tradition. However, the turbulent period behind them has shown the shareholders that they need strategies for future issues and problems. Because of this case, changes were made both on the company side and also within the family. At the company, the internal family management has been replaced by an external one. The family is no longer involved in the direct management of the company. The corporate governance guidelines were revised, and compliance introduced. As a result, the advisory board is now composed only of nonfamily members. Furthermore, a family constitution was developed, which sets out binding guidelines for future interaction between the family and the company. The family discusses company issues in the newly established Family Council.

NOTE

1. This case is based on an actual company, its family leaders, other company officials, and family members. All names and some details have been changed. Interviews with share-

holders, managers, and employees were used to generate information. Further details were obtained from newspaper articles and internal company reports.

SUGGESTED READING

Berrone, P., Cruz, C. and Gomez-Mejia, L.R. (2012). Socioemotional wealth in family firms. *Family Business Review, 25*(3), 258–79.

Kubíček, A. and Machek, O. (2020). Intrafamily conflicts in family businesses: A systematic review of the literature and agenda for future research. *Family Business Review, 33*(2), 194–227.

Rodriguez-Garcia, P. and Menéndez-Requejo, S. (2023). Family constitution to manage family firms' agency conflicts. *BRQ Business Research Quarterly, 26*(2), 150–66.

13

Sport sponsoring at Royal Jumbo Food Group: a double-edged sword[1]

Miranda Stienstra, Astrid Kramer and Ties van Daal

CASE SUMMARY

The case discusses the colorful history of Royal Jumbo Food Group (Jumbo). Jumbo is the second largest Dutch supermarket chain, with 700 stores in the Netherlands and Belgium with annual sales of around €10 billion in 2022. In addition, it is the fourth largest family firm in the Netherlands and fully owned and managed by the Van Eerd family. In September 2022, a darker side overshadows the advantages the family has brought to the firm. Frits van Eerd, the third-generation CEO of Royal Jumbo Food Group, is taken into custody as a suspect in a police investigation involving some of the firm's sports sponsors. Besides being the CEO of the family firm, Frits displayed his need for competition and winning in his hobbies. He closed all kinds of sponsor deals for Jumbo and established its own racing team. Frits' hobby is what brings him and Jumbo into trouble. He is a suspect in an investigation concerning money laundering through real estate transactions, car dealing, unexplained cash deposits, and sponsorship contracts in motorcross sports. The investigation leads him to step down as CEO a few days later (Braaksma, 2022a). The case against Frits could go to trial, but that will probably take years. Meanwhile, how to manage this large family firm – honored by Dutch royalty due to its longevity, influence, and integrity – becomes a big question mark. What is the best way for Jumbo to move on?

LEARNING OUTCOMES

By the end of this case study, the student should be able to:

- Explain the advantages and disadvantages of family firms compared to nonfamily firms in pursuing a growth strategy.
- Describe why CEO reputation damage is more harmful for family firms compared to nonfamily firms.

- Advise on how to establish governance structures of family firms to decrease the risk of failure to control activities of their executives.

Royal Jumbo Food Group (Jumbo) is the second largest Dutch supermarket chain, with 700 stores in the Netherlands and Belgium and annual sales of about €10 billion in 2022 (Royal Jumbo Food Group, 2023a). It is the fourth largest family firm in the Netherlands and fully owned and managed by the Van Eerd family. In October 2021, Jumbo celebrated its 100th anniversary (Kooi and Koense, 2022). The Van Eerd family, consisting of Karel van Eerd, his wife Kitty, and their three children, Colette, Frits, and Monique, were all present to receive the predicate "Royal" granted by Dutch King Willem-Alexander. This honor is awarded to large, reliable companies that have existed for at least 100 years, are influential in their industries, and are governed by executives with irreproachable behavior. The predicate "Royal" symbolizes the respect, appreciation, and trust of the King and should contribute to the positioning of Dutch companies at home and abroad.[2] The Van Eerd family proudly celebrated the firm's 100th anniversary and receiving this prestigious recognition. Karel described it as "the cherry on the cake" (Parker Brady and Beernink, 2021). The future of Jumbo looked bright. However, only one year later, on 13 September 2022, Frits van Eerd, the CEO of Jumbo, was taken into custody and named a suspect in a police investigation concerning money laundering through real estate transactions, car dealing, unexplained cash deposits, and sponsorship contracts in motocross sports. To Jumbo, it came as a shock of mammoth proportions.

ROYAL JUMBO FOOD GROUP

In 1921, Johan van Eerd founded the Van Eerd Food Group, a wholesaler in food in Veghel in the southern part of the Netherlands (Royal Jumbo Food Group, n.d.). Ten years later, Frits van Eerd Sr, Johan's nephew, joined the company and in 1936 the company became a general partnership with Johan and Frits as the partners (Royal Jumbo Food Group, n.d.). In 1957, Frits van Eerd Sr handed over the day-to-day activities to his then only son, 18-year-old Karel van Eerd, because Frits Sr was advised to step down due to health issues and only in 1979 did Karel officially succeed his father and become the full owner (Royal Jumbo Food Group, n.d.). Karel was a real entrepreneur, identifying opportunities and expanding the company through several acquisitions in the southern part of the Netherlands. During a trip to the USA in 1961, Karel became fascinated by large self-service supermarkets and decided that this would be the way forward for the Van Eerd Food Group (Parker Brady and Beernink, 2021). In addition, Karel was inspired by the concept from Walmart: "Everyday low pricing." In 1983, Karel acquired a supermarket store with the name "Jumbo", the first of their now hundreds of stores.

In the early 1990s, the three children of Karel and Kitty van Eerd, Colette, Frits, and Monique, started working in the family firm (see Figure 13.1). According to their father, they first had to prove themselves in the company to be accepted (Rijlaarsdam, 2022). All three children had newly created positions in the company because Karel did not want any of his employees to be replaced by one of his children. In 2006, Karel concluded that: "They did well, which commanded respect. In the end, the company pushed the kids forward, not me" (Parker Brady and Beernink, 2021).

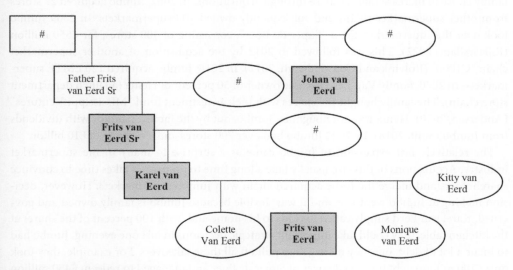

Source: Case authors.

Figure 13.1 The Van Eerd family

RAPID GROWTH THROUGH ACQUISITIONS

Between 1990 and 2002, the core activity of Jumbo slowly moved from food wholesaler to supermarkets and in 2002 the company name was changed from Van Eerd Food Group to Jumbo Supermarkets.

Around 2003, competitor Albert Heijn, the largest supermarket chain in the Netherlands, started a price war and made many price reductions. Albert Heijn wanted to change its position in the market, because it had not been successful with its strategy as a luxury supermarket and wanted to rebrand. Albert Heijn is a stock listed company and part of the multinational Ahold Delhaize. All other supermarket chains in the Netherlands felt they had to lower their prices to keep up with competition and many products were sold at a loss. The price war lasted until 2006 and several supermarket chains got in difficulties, especially because they were owned by private equity funds (Looijse and Van der Valk, 2022).

Jumbo itself did fine during the price war. On one hand, its formula already had a focus on low prices, which meant Jumbo did not have to change strategy. On the other hand, the Van Eerd family, the owners of Jumbo, did not demand short-term returns and accepted lower margins during the price war because they knew times would get better, and they were confident that Jumbo would survive. The Van Eerd family explicitly decided to take a long-term perspective.

Jumbo's strategy of a broad product assortment and a high service level in an industry where margins are razor thin, must be compensated with high sales and market share. The Van Eerd family chose to increase market share through acquisitions. In 2007, Jumbo acquired 27 stores from other supermarket chains and subsequently owned 100 supermarkets. In 2009 Jumbo took over the supermarket chain "Super de Boer", consisting of 300 stores, for €550 million (Rijlaarsdam, 2022). This was followed in 2012 by the acquisition of another supermarket chain "C1000" (Rolvink and Couwenbergh, 2011). In 2018, Jumbo acquired 120 EMTÉ supermarkets. In 2020, family Van Eerd became owner of 50 percent of Hema (a Dutch department store chain). The family bought the shares with their investment fund "Mississippi Ventures" (Andersen, 2020). Hema was not bought by Jumbo, but by the family, paid for with dividends from Jumbo (Smit, 2018). By 2022 Jumbo had over 700 stores and a revenue of €10 billion.

The relatively fast expansion of Jumbo came as a surprise to many in the supermarket industry. Acquisitions of this size usually take a long time to prepare. It takes time to convince shareholders and merge the to-be acquired chain with Jumbo supermarkets. However, decision making at Jumbo went fast, and it was flexible because Jumbo is family owned and governed. Karel van Eerd simply called his kids to his home and, with 100 percent of the shares at the kitchen table, they could take important strategic decisions in just one evening. Jumbo had to incur a lot of debt, but they managed to pull off all these takeovers. For example, they took on a €700 million debt for the takeover of Super de Boer and managed to redeem €450 million in two years, which paved the way for another debt of €900 million for the takeover of C1000 (Rijlaarsdam, 2022).

STRUCTURE AND GOVERNANCE AT JUMBO

Karel and his three children each own 25 percent of the shares, which are held in the foundation Jumbo Group. This foundation is the ultimate beneficial owner of Jumbo. In 2009, Frits became the CEO of Jumbo and, besides him, the executive board consisted of CFO Ton van Veen and Frits' sister Colette, who became responsible for safeguarding the "Jumbo formula" (Winkel, 2009). Ton van Veen was responsible for financing the ambitious growth plans of Jumbo. In the same year, a supervisory board was installed, with Karel as chair after he stepped down from the executive board.

According to Dutch legislation, companies need to have a supervisory board if: (1) the company employs more than 100 employees in the Netherlands; (2) the issued capital exceeds €16 million; and (3) the company is required by law to have a works council. All these three conditions must be met. The task of the supervisory board is to control and advise the executive board in the interest of the shareholders. Other supervisory board members included Anthony Burgmans, Harry Bruijniks, and Wilco Jiskoot. Anthony Burgmans was CEO of Unilever, Harry Bruijniks had vast experience in retail, and Wilco Jiskoot was board member of ABN AMRO, a Dutch banking group (Winkel, 2011). In 2018, Piet Coelewij became member of the supervisory board, followed by Jacqueline Hoogerbrugge in 2020, who replaced Harry Bruijniks. As the chair of the supervisory board, Karel van Eerd is ultimately responsible for Jumbo (Beijk, 2022).

In 2022, it was decided to change the governance structure by enlarging the supervisory board. Colette and Ton van Veen stepped down from their positions on the executive board and became members of the supervisory board. After this restructuring, the executive board consisted of the CEO Frits van Eerd, CFO Peter van Erp, who had worked at Jumbo since 1998, and COO Cees van Vliet, who joined Jumbo in 2020. Frits obtained a more central position within Jumbo (Braaksma and Couwenbergh, 2022).

CEO FRITS VAN EERD

In 1992, when Frits was 25 years old, he joined the family firm as category manager for Jumbo's bakery department after finishing his university degree in business, spending some of his time studying in the USA (Kosterman, 2020). Before taking up his official position, he had already helped in the supermarkets on weekends and holidays. Frits considered retail to be more dynamic and innovative than the wholesale business, which might be one of the reasons why Jumbo moved away from wholesale towards retail. Frits felt that as "the son of the boss" he was never given the benefit of the doubt and always had to prove himself.

According to his sister Colette: "Frits is entrepreneurial, very creative, constantly looking for new ideas, and always wants to win" (Van de Sande, 2019). Frits is charismatic and praised for his drive, knowledge, and understanding of the business. In 2009, he was named "Food Manager of the Year" by trade journal *Food Personality*, in 2012 readers of the journal *Management Team* elected him as "Best Executive of the Year", and in 2020 peers elected him as "Retail Executive of the Year 2021–2022" (Parker Brady and Beernink, 2021).

Besides his CEO position, Frits plays the trumpet in a Dutch carnival band and is a well-known figure in the world of motocross and auto racing (Braaksma and Van der Linden, 2020). In 2006, Frits won the Rallyclinic Dutch Open and became Dutch rally champion. He competed multiple times in the Dakar Rally, drove the 24 hours of Le Mans in a Jumbo-sponsored car, and collects vintage cars, mostly Formula 1 cars. Furthermore, Frits owns two Spitfires, a British single-seat fighter aircraft that was used in the Second World War (Bartol, 2018).

JUMBO'S LONG HISTORY OF SPORT SPONSORING

Jumbo has a long history of sponsoring sports teams. Karel van Eerd loves cycling and speed ice-skating, whereas, as noted, his son is fond of motorsports. Due to the rapid expansion of Jumbo's stores and sales, the budget for sponsoring and marketing grew as well. Currently, Jumbo sponsors Formula 1 driver Max Verstappen, motocross world champion Jeffrey Herlings, a few motorsport teams, a cycling team, and a speed ice-skating team (Tuenter, 2022).

For years, Frits was responsible for Jumbo's marketing and sponsoring activities, in addition to his CEO position. Jumbo's formula is based on low prices for customers, which means that it makes money by demanding low prices from its suppliers. Jumbo is a powerful party because of its size, and negotiates hard with suppliers on price. Suppliers of Jumbo seemed willing to sponsor Frits' racing team because it gave them the possibility to interact with Frits during matches (Been et al., 2023a). Jumbo's annual report of 2022 revealed that several of Jumbo's suppliers directly sponsored Frits' teams for €3.8 million, whereas Jumbo's total sponsoring budget was around €20 million (Been et al., 2023b). The entanglement of formal and informal relations of suppliers, sponsors, and friends turned out to have some downsides. Sport sponsoring has been of great value for Jumbo's public relations; however, by now, the shadowy sides of Frits' activities dampened the positive light that those sponsoring activities delivered.

Through his activities in motocross, Frits became acquainted with Theo Eggens, the main suspect in the police investigation for which Frits was taken into custody on 13 September 2022 (Meeus, 2022). Theo Eggens was the manager of a motocross team. As early as 2014, Jumbo had decided to withdraw from a sponsoring contract with this team's manager because he was a suspect in another investigation concerning money laundering and tax fraud and eventually in 2018 sentenced to prison for 15 months for money laundering activities. However, Frits did not end their relationship and just a couple of months after the restructuring of Jumbo's supervisory and executive boards, Frits was taken into custody due to his contacts with Theo Eggens.

Jumbo's supervisory board commissioned an independent investigation to examine Jumbo's sponsorship contracts in auto racing and motocross after the arrest of Frits. Also, their in-house accountant investigated whether the supermarket chain was at criminal risk. No criminal offenses or irregularities were found; however, "a number of vulnerabilities" were revealed by independent investigations (Smit, 2023).

Based on these vulnerabilities Jumbo established stricter internal rules now that Frits had been discredited for involvement in a sizeable money laundering case. The tightened processes and procedures are designed to prevent the probability of repetition. For many years, Frits was personally responsible for sponsorship contracts and there were no checks and balances when Frits signed a sponsor deal.

SEPTEMBER 2022

On 13 September, the Dutch Fiscal Information and Investigation Service (FIOD) raided Frits' home because of suspicion of fraud, and more than €176 000 in cash was found in a safe hidden behind the doors of his bedroom closet (Been et al., 2023c). In another bedroom and in a bag in his car, investigators then found several more bundles of banknotes totaling €19 000. In the workshop of Frits' personal racing team RTN, in the grounds of the Jumbo headquarters in Veghel, the FIOD found another sum of more than €250 000 in cash (Been et al., 2023c). Furthermore, 104 banknotes of €500 and 253 banknotes of €200 were found.

Ten days later, on Friday 23 September, Jumbo sent out a press release with the following statement:

> After careful consultation with his family and the supervisory board, Frits van Eerd has decided to temporarily step down as CEO of Jumbo. This is in the best interests of Jumbo and allows Frits to concentrate fully on his personal situation. The Van Eerd family, the

supervisory board, and the management team respect this courageous decision and wish him every support in the coming period. Naturally, this will have consequences for the management of Jumbo. We expect to be able to announce more about this in the near future. Until that time, the daily operations of Jumbo are fully guaranteed by the management team. We would like to thank all customers, colleagues, franchisees, suppliers, and other relations for the support received for the family and Jumbo during this difficult period. (Royal Jumbo Food Group, 2022a)

On 4 October, Jumbo (Royal Jumbo Food Group, 2022b) announced "temporary adjustments to management of the company." Ton (van Veen), former CFO of Jumbo, will temporarily lead Jumbo's executive board as delegated supervisory director, and Colette fulfills the liaison role between Jumbo, the supervisory board, and the Van Eerd family (Braaksma, 2022b; Royal Jumbo Food Group, 2022b). In addition, she is temporarily appointed vice chair of the supervisory board of Jumbo (Royal Jumbo Food Group, 2022b). At the beginning of 2023, Jumbo announced immediate withdrawal from all sponsoring activities involving motorsport and to stop sponsoring the cycling and speed ice-skating teams by 2024 (Van Lakerveld, 2023).

DISCUSSION QUESTIONS

1. Jumbo is fully family owned and managed by the Van Eerd family and is therefore labeled as a family firm. Mention three advantages of family firms compared to non-family firms that explain the success of Jumbo over the past years.
2. What are the strengths and weaknesses of the leadership of Frits van Eerd?
3. To what extent did the governance structure of Jumbo contribute to the current situation in which Frits' hobbies have endangered Jumbo's reputation?
4. Advise the supervisory board of Jumbo what to do with the current CEO position.
5. What can a family firm structurally do to avoid a family firm CEO getting too much power?

EPILOGUE

Two years after Jumbo's 100th anniversary a drama unfolded for the family and the firm. At the time of writing, Frits van Eerd had not returned as CEO of Jumbo (Braaksma, 2023). However, as shareholder of the foundation Jumbo Group he is involved in strategic developments. Karel van Eerd died in December 2022 at the age of 84. His three children inherited his shares and now each have one-third of the shares.

Ton van Veen took over the role of CEO, being the first external CEO to take on this position. Van Veen had worked alongside Frits van Eerd for 18 years (Pijpker, 2023). Colette van Eerd, now chairman of the supervisory board, stated on the website of Jumbo: "He [Ton van Veen] knows our family values like no other and understands how Jumbo was originally intended" (Royal Jumbo Food Group, 2023b). Besides ceasing their sponsoring activities in motor sports, speed ice-skating, and cycling, management also decided not to renew its sponsorship with Formula 1 driver Max Verstappen and the Formula 1 Grand Prix at Zandvoort in the Netherlands. It seems that all those sport sponsoring activities are too closely linked to Frits van Eerd and his impending court case. To distance the company from this disgrace, the once great marketing tactic has come to an end. Frits van Eerd has not been charged officially, but nobody expects him back as CEO for the foreseeable future.

NOTES

1. The case was prepared after the authors read and analyzed many news articles published in Dutch high quality newspapers *NRC Handelsblad*, *Volkskrant*, *Het Financieele Dagblad*, and *Telegraaf* and the magazine *EW*. All articles were accessible via the database Nexus Uni. We used "Frits van Eerd" as a keyword in this database. In addition, the authors listened to a podcast series about Jumbo, read a book about Jumbo, searched for additional information on national and regional news websites, read press releases and annual reports of Jumbo, and looked at its website.
2. See: https://www.royal-house.nl/topics/decorations-and-honours/royal-warrants-and-honours -for-businesses-institutions-or-associations.

SUGGESTED READINGS

Hambrick, D.C. and Mason, P.A. (1984). Upper echelons: The organization as a reflection of its top managers. *Academy of Management Review*, 9(2), 193–206.
Rondi, E., Benedetti, C., Bettinelli, C. and De Massis, A. (2023). Falling from grace: Family-based brands amidst scandals. *Journal of Business Research*, 157, 113637.
Sageder, M., Mitter, C. and Feldbauer-Durstmüller, B. (2018). Image and reputation of family firms: A systematic literature review of the state of research. *Review of Managerial Science*, 12, 335–77.

REFERENCES

Andersen, R. (2020). Overname Hema door Jumbo is voor alle partijen een win-win-situatie. *De Volkskrant*, 22 October.
Bartol, R. (2018). Jumbo-topman Frits van Eerd heeft twee gevechtsvliegtuigen gekocht: "Een historische gebeurtenis". *Omroep Brabant*, 24 December. https://www.omroepbrabant.nl/nieuws/2906919/ jumbo-topman-frits-van-eerd-heeft-twee-gevechtsvliegtuigen-gekocht-een-historische-gebeurtenis.
Been, J., Braaksma, J. and Mos, B. (2023a). Jumbo-leveranciers sponsorden raceteam Frits van Eerd: "Voor wat hoort wat". *Het Financieele Dagblad*, 3 February.
Been, J., Braaksma, J. and Mos, B. (2023b). Leveranciers sponsorden raceteam van Frits van Eerd vorig jaar met bijna 4 mln. *Het Financieele Dagblad*, 19 March.
Been, J., Braaksma, J. and Mos, B. (2023c). Fiod vond cash in slaapkamer Frits van Eerd en op Jumbo-terrein. *Het Financieele Dagblad*, 13 September.
Beijk, C. (2022). Deze mensen beslissen over de toekomst van Frits van Eerd bij Jumbo. *Omroep Brabant*, 22 September. https://www.omroepbrabant.nl/nieuws/4153014/deze-mensen-beslissen-over-de -toekomst-van-frits-van-eerd-bij-jumbo.
Braaksma, J. (2022a). Frits van Eerd treedt tijdelijk terug als topman van Jumbo. *Het Financieele Dagblad*, 23 September.
Braaksma, J. (2022b). Jumbo benoemt voormalig CFO Ton van Veen tijdelijk tot opvolger van CEO Frits van Eerd. *Het Financieele Dagblad*, 4 October.
Braaksma, J. (2023). Frits van Eerd keert niet meer terug in directie van Jumbo. *Het Financieele Dagblad*, 7 March.

Braaksma, J. and Couwenbergh, P. (2022). Hoelang kan Jumbo het stellen zonder Frits van Eerd? *Het Financieele Dagblad*, 27 September.

Braaksma, J. and Van der Linden, L. (2020). Hamsteren, huilen, Hema: Dit was het jaar van Jumbo-baas Frits van Eerd. *Het Financieele Dagblad*, 19 December.

Kooi, R. (Producer) and Koense, M. (Producer) (2022). *Elke dag beter*. MRK2.

Kosterman, R. (2020). Frits van Eerd: "Ik heb het gevoel dat ik lekker ben ingewerkt". *Elsevier Weekblad*, 17 October.

Looijse, B. and Van der Valk, T. (Hosts) (2022 – today). Jumbo, van supermarkt naar supermacht (Audiopodcast). *Hoge Bomen*. https://www.bnr.nl/podcast/hoge-bomen.

Meeus, J. (2022). Hoe Frits van Eerd terecht kwam in een wereld van louche autohandelaar Theo Eggens. *NRC*, 31 December.

Parker Brady, R. and Beernink, M. (2021). Jumbo wil altijd winnen: De 7 gouden ondernemersregels van kruidenier Karel van Eerd. *Het Boekenschap*.

Pijpker, J (2023). Na dik honderd jaar geen Van Eerd meer die besluit bij Jumbo. *NRC*, 10 March.

Rijlaarsdam, B. (2022). Karel van Eerd laat Jumbo in een roerige tijd achter. *NRC*, 15 December.

Rolvink, F. and Couwenbergh, P. (2011). Jumbo zette CVC onder druk: Supermarktketen moest C1000 wel overnemen om inkoopmacht veilig te stellen. *Het Financieele Dagblad*, 25 November.

Royal Jumbo Food Group (2022a). Frits van Eerd treedt tijdelijk terug als algemeen directeur van Jumbo (Press release). 23 September. https://nieuws.jumbo.com/frits-van-eerd-treedt-tijdelijk-terug -als-algemeen-directeur-van-jumbo/.

Royal Jumbo Food Group (2022b). Jumbo voert tijdelijke aanpassingen door in aansturing onderneming (Press release). 4 October. https://nieuws.jumbo.com/jumbo-voert-tijdelijke-aanpassingen-door-in -aansturing-onderneming.

Royal Jumbo Food Group (2023a). *Annual Report 2022*. https://www.jumborapportage.com/downloads/.

Royal Jumbo Food Group (2023b). Jumbo benoemt Ton van Veen tot CEO en Colette Cloostermand-van Eerd tot president-commissaris (Press release). 7 March. https://www.jumbo.com/nieuws/jumbo -benoemt-ton-van-veen-tot-ceo-en-colette-cloosterman-van-eerd-tot-president-commissaris/.

Royal Jumbo Food Group (n.d.). Een kleurrijke historie. https://www.jumbo.com/service/het-bedrijf -jumbo/historie.

Smit, M. (2018). Familie van Eerd vist 40 miljoen uit supermarktketen Jumbo. *RTL Nieuws*.

Smit, R. (2023). Jumbo-onderzoek brengt geen strafbare feiten aan het licht. *Het Financieele Dagblad*, 3 January.

Tuenter, G. (2022). Sport hoort bij Jumbo, ook nu de topman verdachte is. *NRC*, 16 November.

Van de Sande, M. (2019). "Frits will altijd winnen". *Het Financieele Dagblad*, 6 February.

Van Lakerveld, E. (2023). Jumbo stopt na 2024 met sponsoring wieler- en schaatsploeg. *De Volkskrant*, 29 March.

Winkel, R. (2009). Supermarkttycoons uit het Brabantse Bentonville. *Het Financieele Dagblad*, 21 September.

Winkel, R. (2011). Ton van Veen, de man van 900 miljoen. *Het Financieele Dagblad*, 25 November.

14
The enemy at home: diversification and professionalization at BOMBE[1]

María Jesús Hernández-Ortiz, Manuel Carlos Vallejo-Martos, Myriam Cano-Rubio and Francisca Panadés-Zamora

CASE SUMMARY

This case describes the creation, growth, and diversification of BOMBE, a second-generation family business whose development was motivated by the growth of the owning family as well as the need for economic growth in the province in Spain where it is located. The case shows the paradoxes faced by family businesses by highlighting, on the one hand, the need to professionalize the firm's management to improve business performance and, on the other, how too much trust in nonfamily members can lead to opportunistic behaviors that, due to the lack of oversight by family members, almost destroyed the family business and the family itself. The case details how an ill-informed decision to hire an outsider based on trust and business relationships ended with the group of companies almost reduced to ashes, legal proceedings, and police protection for the owners and their family. Now, family leaders admit they made mistakes, but they still do not know when it started and, even worse, how they arrived at the current situation.

LEARNING OUTCOMES

After analyzing this case, students will be able to:

- Identify and explain some of the paradoxes of family businesses.
- Diagnose the main elements of socioemotional wealth (SEW) of this company.
- Identify and explain suitable governance mechanisms for family businesses.
- Describe the dark sides of professionalizing family firms.
- Analyze the role played by management control systems in family businesses.
- Explain the role of succession protocol in avoiding dysfunctional behavior in family firms.

"How could we have been so blind and not realize what was happening?" Miguel asked his wife, Belén.

We have ignored the opinions of professionals of great value, internal and external, of trusted friends who tried to remove the blindfold to prevent us from falling into the hands of this network of fraudsters! Fortunately, we have hired this famous consultant in Seville to solve the file that the tax agency had opened against us, and he has alerted us that we are being swindled and we are in the hands of an extortion network led by Fernando. We are in serious danger, we could lose everything forever, the future of our children is at risk, everything has been lies to weave the spider's web that can ruin us completely, we must react as soon as possible and try to get out of this situation, the worst we have lived since we became entrepreneurs.

Belén replied, "Miguel, I am very afraid of what may happen from now on, Fernando has no limits."

COMPANY ORIGINS

The BOMBE Business Group was created by the López family in 1997 as a temporary employment agency to provide labor intermediation services to other companies. The company is in Jaén (Spain), a Spanish province with a low per capita income ratio, 642 174 inhabitants, and limited business fabric.

Manuel López, by profession an industrial engineer, founded the group with his son Miguel, who at that time combined his work with his undergraduate studies in Business Administration and Management. In 2000, his girlfriend, Belén, joined the company and combined her work with undergraduate studies in labor relations. In 2004, Miguel and Belén married and became an integral part of the family business.

The López business family is characterized by its great concern for development in the province. This has led the family to want to continue investing in Jaén, create employment, and, thus, contribute to greater economic and social development – apart from continuing the company in the hands of a growing family. The third generation numbers six siblings. Additionally, the business has required substantial lines of credit for insurance: credit policies and discounted promissory notes and invoices.

FAMILY BUSINESS DEVELOPMENT

Sparked more by the family's entrepreneurial spirit than their viability, the López family opened some smaller businesses such as a consultancy service and telephone sales in 1997, which disappeared over time. Notwithstanding these setbacks, the labor intermediation business providing services to other companies was growing. BOMBE's business activity focused on the center and south of Spain. Since the company's launch, the firm has placed customers at the center of the company, offering the products and services that they require. Company flexibility was of paramount importance for meeting new customer demands.

Temporary employment agencies seek out and hire people and assign them to other companies where they will provide services temporarily. The agency oversees the recruitment and selection process as well as hiring and payroll, and then invoices the client. The temporary employment agency is responsible for managing all the paperwork related to the temporary worker's salary. This includes withholding taxes, social security payments, and any other relevant deductions, all of which are made monthly and are advanced by the agency. Agencies can also offer additional services such as worker training, advice on labor legislation, or even comprehensive human resources management.

However, the temporary work sector is a mature sector, with small margins, very rigid legislation, and little opportunity for credit. Therefore, to offer competitive prices and build a sustainable business over time, these companies must have an efficient cost structure. In addition, large lines of financing are required: credit policies and discount policies for promissory notes or invoices to be able to meet cash flow needs. Despite these difficulties, BOMBE developed this business for many years with good results.

The main suppliers were workers, the social security system, and public finances, who charged cash, which made it important to always seek a very efficient cost structure to offer a competitive price and build a sustainable business over time.

ECONOMIC PROBLEMS AND NEW FAMILY ADDITIONS TO THE FIRM

The 2008–2010 economic crisis affected the López family, as it did many other Spanish companies. Important steps were taken to move the company forward: to structure the governing bodies well with the inclusion of external professionals and to try to define business–family relations by preparing a family protocol led by an external advisor. Miguel commented on the measures:

> We changed our operations processes. We analyzed the markets and types of companies that were least affected by the crisis. We set up a Management committee. Our work was results-based. An action protocol was implemented to avoid any management mistakes. In short, the company was professionalized. We moved on from being a company that did things the way we wanted to, to one that did things professionally. I think this helped us to improve a lot because it made us all work toward the same objective. As for the protocol, we tried to get one done, but my father and sister didn't see eye to eye when it came to limiting certain actions and controlling others, so in the end, we worked out a minimal arrangement to be able to work together in peace.

In 2010, Miguel's only sister, María, joined the company. She had finished her university degree in technical architecture and had begun working in a construction company. However, she lost her job because of the 2008 financial crisis and joined the family business. When she joined, she had no experience in business management and showed a lack of responsibility when dealing with administrative tasks. Her husband did not work for the company and was self-employed. María had little initiative or business knowledge, but her involvement as a company owner was on a par with her brother's, and the express wish of her parents was that her salary should be the same as that of her brother and sister-in-law. Over time, this changed and Miguel's pay increased due to the greater responsibility that he took on.

BANKRUPTCY OF A CLIENT

At the beginning of 2018, the family had managed to partially get through the economic crisis and achieved an annual turnover of between €15 and 18 million, with a workforce of 70. On 11 June of that year, their first serious problem arose: the company's main client, who they invoiced for about €1 million per month, went bankrupt, resulting in the client defaulting on payment of €4 million. This involved most of the recent invoices and the remainder in discounted promissory notes. These were returned to the banks, who then blocked company operations. BOMBE also had to pay dues, taxes, and payroll of the preceding month to the social security institutions and public finance, which, as they were no longer collecting from the client, resulted in a debt that amounted to €7 million. This default, together with the high level of debt caused by investments made to expand the company, triggered a situation that was difficult to resolve.

Faced with this situation, Miguel, who was already the visible head of the company as his father had gradually ceded responsibility to him, said: "There were two alternatives. One was to say we close down and go into receivership. We bring down the shutters and shut up the shop. Or we try to renegotiate everything, refinance everything, and go on working." They made the decision to refinance all their debts.

Recovery from customer bankruptcy and diversification

The second part of 2018 and all of 2019 was a very complex time for the López business family, as Miguel related:

> There were meetings with banks, with financial institutions … you had to have everything very well balanced, everything under total control, and at the same time, you had to rene-gotiate and refinance with Social Security Institutions, refinance with the tax authorities, workers … In short, we had to deal with a lot of staff and internal personnel had to be dismissed … Anyway, it was very, very complex. We had to struggle with a lot of trips, a lot of upsets, we didn't spend any time with our children. It was really hard, but it turned out well. We were able to rearrange our financial situation with all the banks, the Social Security Institutions, and the tax authorities, and we managed to move forward despite the problem.

Most of the responsibility fell to Miguel and Belén, while María only dedicated the required hours to the company since she devoted most of her time to caring for her new family. Miguel said,

> My wife and I have always been very close, and I think we have been able to transmit that to all our workers and our customers. We brought peace to the company. We are not 1 + 1 = 2 but possibly 1 + 1 = 4 because we work in different areas. I can calmly manage the commercial and financial area while I know that the internal and labor part is 100% covered. But there was one part of my family that did not add up to everything it should: because I wanted more shares, a higher salary, and yet ..., although I love her to death, my sister has never been seriously involved with her job or given her whole life to the company ... so ... this was, of course, a very serious problem.

The family problems transcended the company. A company with great financial difficulties had to move forward, and this required absolute commitment from the people in managerial positions. But one family member took home a high salary while working part-time and not being fully engaged with the future success of the company. So, grievances arose, especially among the managers.

Once the debts had been restructured, Belén and Miguel thought it was time to diversify the company. The temporary employment sector was increasingly competitive and provided smaller profit margins, and they did not want the previous problem to arise again. Their temp work provided in-depth knowledge of many sectors and the business fabric of each sector. For this reason, it was not difficult to detect underexploited or fast-growing businesses to try to diversify the company and provide strong growth potential. So, Belén and Miguel put forward a proposal to the family: diversify the business. At first, the father, Manuel, was uncertain. He said they had dedicated their whole lives to one sector and thus the family business would be sapping strength from that activity. Also, María was extremely concerned about what her involvement in the diversified firm might be. Eventually, they agreed on a solution with her and their parents that was mediated by a highly respected external advisor who specialized in family business issues. Thus, began the diversification of the company.

The negotiation with other family members about their holdings in the business was conflictive. As Miguel says,

> Getting the entire family to reach an agreement was very hard, sometimes even unpleasant, not only for us [Miguel and Belén], but also for the advisors who were met by my sister and my father who showed utter contempt for anyone who told the truth about her work and attitude, or that didn't think the same way about María's work as they did. In the end, a hard-worked agreement was negotiated on a protocol that was, in part, very biased. A distinction was made between the shares in the companies whose activity was temporary work, shares in undertakings with new activities, and shares in companies in which equity had been generated and reinvested in the company for many years. Unfortunately, the onset of the COVID-19 pandemic and subsequent events have invalidated this protocol. Now, the family is timidly beginning to talk about these issues again.

BOMBE DIVERSIFIES ITS OPERATIONS

From that moment on, BOMBE began to invest. In June 2019, the firm bought a vegetable canning factory in the province. They thought that the agri-food sector would grow and be a safe investment. The owner wanted to give up the business and so BOMBE paid him the sum of €1 million for the entire company, including its assets and debts. However, after only a year, some additional liabilities emerged to an amount equal to what they paid for the company, and this raised their own level of indebtedness to over a €1 million.

Public institutions in the province supported their investment to refloat a company that was going to close and leave many people out of work. They encouraged the initiative, promoted BOMBE's image in recognition of its social work, and even endorsed its arrangements with financial institutions.

BOMBE obtained some very advantageous loans from the Spanish Official Credit Institute (ICO) for an amount exceeding €1.5 million and received subsidies that allowed them to make more investments. The firm launched a project related to plastic injection and an assembly factory together with a partner, a conglomerate of companies in the plastics sector. This industry is of paramount importance in Jaén and one of the most innovative.

BOMBE then went into the booming home delivery market triggered by the increase in online shopping. Package distribution and take-out food delivery became more flexible and required only a small investment. A call center was launched, which did not require much investment either, as the firm outsourced tele-operators. BOMBE started a new textile business with a partner who was working in large-format printing and adapted the old factory to the new work.

At that time, it was decided to change the name of the group to something more commercial that also identified its origins. The old name, BOMBE, was only retained for the temporary division of labor and outsourcing, and the entire group was renamed The Andalusian Group, and the logo is an animal that can be found in drawings at an archeological site in Jaén. The group's portfolio of activities now included:

- Canned foods;
- Plastic injection and assembly;
- Home delivery;
- Temporary labor and outsourcing (the original BOMBE).

State of alarm: Covid-19

On 14 March 2020, a state of alarm was decreed in Spain as a result of the coronavirus pandemic, and this brought all the group's activities to a halt. A few days before, the López family had begun to prepare their company and their family for the looming crisis. Confined to their houses, they began to remodel their company for the post-Covid-19 era by creating a committee to oversee the future of the company. The committee was formed of first-level managers, factory managers, and the senior management team. The first decision they made was to furnish essential company personnel with computer equipment, internet connections, and other hardware in their homes so they could start to work remotely. Thus, when the state of alarm was decreed, they gradually grew accustomed to living with uncertainty. Once they were in lockdown, they had more time to think and take the actions that they felt could be very beneficial for the future. The lockdown lasted more than two months.

The team always remained in contact with customers and some important demands arose due to the circumstances. They received a proposal from their branch manager in Madrid that they should set up an online agency as many companies found themselves without any advisors to deal with the urgent problems caused by the crisis. They launched the agency within a day or two and so were able to continue giving help and advice to multiple companies on how to manage their immediate issues with personnel during the Covid-19 crisis. This was a business activity they were already conducting and only the way it was being done changed. Moving it online also opened it up to other geographic areas.

They received an unusual proposal during this time: the Santa Maria religious order asked them to distribute the food products made by its nuns as they could not do it themselves and needed the distribution to survive. Thus, the company embarked on the free distribution of the religious order's food products under the name of "tele convento" and added several of its own products from the agri-food division. This enabled promotion of its own products while taking responsibility for a social issue. The nuns were able to sell all their produce, and the firm continues to sell its agri-food products online today.

As a result of the fortuitous distribution of these foodstuffs, the firm rented motorcycles in collaboration with a car dealer to distribute the products sold by small shops in the city of Jaén, as these shops found it very difficult and expensive to fulfill their customers' orders. BOMBE helped SMEs by efficiently distributing their products and also helped with their marketing. Small stores were responsible for contacting their customers and offering them good products. They saw that their businesses can move forward, they trust in them, and this new business activity has expanded greatly.

A new textile activity was started in the industrial division before the crisis. The facilities were all prepared and everything was ready to start when the pandemic broke out, and it all came to a standstill. However, a new need also emerged: the use of face masks. Spain lacked a good supply, so the idea arose of making face masks in the new factory facilities. BOMBE rented sewing machines that their partner was not using. At first, the face masks were made by hand, using the staff they had in the town of Guardia, where the factory was located. They also received help from the village authorities to obtain the necessary material to make the face masks since supply was very difficult and the material had to comply with government standards. Thus, BOMBE began the manufacture of face masks using 100 percent Spanish cotton. Then they purchased a machine capable of making 1000 masks an hour as well as an embroidery machine to make the business activity more productive. These industrial machines were also capable of making other products when face masks were less of a social requirement. This was yet another opportunity that kept the company from going under.

BOMBE had a functional structure with marketing, production, financing, and human resources departments. After a month in lockdown, Belén and Miguel realized that they could not work as they had up until then with such a rigid structure. Teleworking, close observation of the market and customers in real time, the new needs of workers with work and family at home did not fit with the old organizational structure that led them to form an organic organ-izational structure of six circles: Strategy, Legal Issues, Marketing, Finance and Accounting, Manufacturing and Supply Chain, and Internal Control.

For each project, a temporary group was created comprising staff from each of the circles to carry out the project and a person appointed to lead the group. When the project was completed, the staff returned to their own permanent groups. The intention behind this was to make each of the divisions autonomous, eliminate bureaucracy and rigidities, and set clear objectives for all the people involved in the company. Under full lockdown, it was not easy to change the structure and mentality of the staff. Many hours were devoted to informing and training personnel about the new way of working. Some workers could not get used to it and left the company, but, even so, they believed that it was the best way to develop the company strategy.

A steering committee was formed, led by Belén and Miguel, and divided into two blocks. Belén coordinated labor, legal, and external human resources issues, while Miguel oversaw commercial issues, clients, institutional relations, and internal human resources. Financial, accounting, and control issues were the responsibility of two very trusted managers. Thus, a diversified group was formed, with four divisions: outsourcing and human resources, agri-food, industry, and business services. A consolidated workforce was established of about 70–80 workers. Their sales rose and reached over €10 million a year, and profit margins were also higher than in the previous stage.

A NEW HIRE

With so much uncertainty and extra work at that time, Belén and Miguel thought that, despite having brought the business under control, it was necessary to incorporate someone new into senior management in addition to external advisors who assisted in their decision-making. This would be a kind of operations manager, someone to whom they could delegate general management tasks. During the pandemic, the founder, Manuel López, stopped going into the office and relinquished his responsibilities. The work he did was purely symbolic. As María had not taken the trouble to keep abreast of affairs or stay up-to-date with her work training or the company's day-to-day business, she was on the margins and her position in the company was rather unclear at that time. Additionally, the Department of Accounting, Control, and Finance was led by two very trusted managers and some new people had been brought in.

As a result, a new managerial position was needed, and Fernando was brought in as a full-time external advisor. Belén and Miguel had previously met Fernando when he had been doing the paperwork for a company they were intending to purchase. When the sale was about to close, Fernando told them the company had some problems that had not been disclosed. He sent them some files and documents and informed them there was an ongoing tax audit, and that the family who owned the company did not get along. Considering the information that he provided, BOMBE did not go ahead with the purchase.

Thus, when they needed to hire a new manager, the marketing director suggested Fernando. Miguel considered him to be an honest person because of what had transpired during the purchase operation, apart from which he was also a teacher at their children's school and, so, in May 2020, during the pandemic, they took him on as a full-time external advisor to the company by videoconference – and without consulting anyone else.

LOSING CONTROL OF THE BUSINESS

During the first three months, the newly hired Fernando fulfilled all the expectations they had of him, and he was seen to be deeply involved in the business. After that, Belén and Miguel do not know when exactly they lost control of the company. They thought everything was going fine, but they were living in a parallel world as far as what was going on in the business was concerned. In March 2022, the realization suddenly hit them: practically all the companies had disappeared, they had 5–6 employees on their payrolls, a monthly turnover of €50 000, and several tax audits were being launched. Despondent and utterly distraught psychologically, Belén and Miguel had no family support as everything had occurred without their knowledge.

Over a year after those events, they can recount some of the experiences of the time, albeit with many gaps, mostly thanks to what they gathered from the accounts of company workers and managers in court.

Now they know that everything about the company's downfall was intentional, and the same thing had been done previously to several companies and institutions. An example of this was the company (Regal Menu) that provided catering services for schools that they had wanted to buy shortly before the pandemic. BOMBE thought the company would be a good purchase because it would enable them to introduce their own food products to schools. However, Fernando contacted them before the sale, suggesting that they not buy the company because it had hidden debts, several tax inspections in process, and that the partners were a married couple who were in the process of separating and would have a lot of difficulty in transferring company ownership. Because of this information, the López family did not purchase Regal Menu, and it ended up in liquidation. This resulted in the hiring of Fernando by BOMBE based on the loyalty he had shown by providing Miguel with that insider information. Subsequently, Miguel discovered that the Regal Menu tax inspector was the same one who was inspecting BOMBE, that Fernando was Regal Menu's company's advisor, and that he was acting in the same way he had with them.

Miguel and his wife were able to reconstruct what happened after the fact. It appears that after he had been working at BOMBE for three months, Fernando began to embezzle money from the business, strip it of its assets, and to fire all the people who were standing in his way. One of the first departments that he annulled was accounting and control where he fired a director, Helena, who had been with the company for 20 years. Fernando justified this by saying, "Helena doesn't want to work. I've told her what the conditions are, and she doesn't want to … And I've told her that she's wrong, but she won't listen to me." He also subjected this manager to some appalling bullying, as Helena testified later in court: "He came to me every day, sat in front of me and said, 'What, haven't you brought the gloves yet? Haven't you left the company yet? Tomorrow, you'd better bring gloves because I'm going to make you clean the toilets.'"

Fernando dismissed all the most trusted people one by one, and others left. He told Miguel: "You should devote your time to institutional work, to building up brands. Don't worry, I'll take care of the company."

When the top managers had all gone, he began to discredit the company by talking to customers and telling them that the company was doing badly, that there was a tax inspector after the owners, and that the inspector had in fact visited some of them. He forced the canning company suppliers not to deliver any raw materials to the factory. There were no accounts for 2022. They had disappeared.

This is how he ruined all the companies and kept their assets. Fernando's answer was always: "This has to be done like this because it's the only way to stop the tax inspector sticking his nose in" or "Look, this is very simple. The inspector is a friend of mine, and if I don't do this, the inspector will …" Eventually, the tax audit came and Belén and Miguel were thrown into the depths of despair.

As the judge declared in the first statement he made when the matter came to court: it was really a process to isolate the couple from the reality of the company and their trusted staff, and to totally undermine and demoralize them through coercion, extortion, and blackmail with the sole purpose of appropriating the business's assets and then destroying it.

FERNANDO EXITS, THE POLICE ENTER

In April 2022, when faced with the bizarre situation of the business and the inspection report, in a moment of clear-mindedness, Belén decided to talk to an advisor from outside the city. The advisor suggested that it was the "person inside the company" who had caused the situation. Belén immediately returned to Jaén and dismissed Fernando. When she fired him, he threatened her and even tried to attack her physically: "With everything I've done for the company. You know what I've done. You'd better be prepared because you're going to end up in jail."

A few days later they received a WhatsApp message: "Either you put your apartment in my name, or you better be prepared because on Monday I'm going write a report and I'm going to go to the prosecutor's office and I'm going to go to the tax office and I'm going to destroy you."

At that point, the couple went to the police. They were driven there by a high-ranking person in the provincial administration whom they trusted, someone who has subsequently given them a great deal of help to extricate themselves from this grave situation.

When they explained the case, the police informed them they knew all about Fernando and the extortion network in which he was involved. The police insinuated that there were other cases but that their case was rare, in as much as Fernando had not been able to use marital troubles or hidden business issues to extort Miguel and Belén, and that is why his extortion ring had ended up being more aggressive. In addition, none of the previous companies had been able to find a way out of the situation.

The case moved from the police to the investigating court and a long judicial process began that has not yet ended. Miguel was given police protection, and a forensic psychologist also supported him and Belén and their four children in the judicial process. Fernando was arrested, then released, but he was served with a restraining order forbidding him from coming within 500 meters of the López family. However, when he breached the order, he was removed from the province and forbidden to return.

The family's situation had changed. His parents had delegated full responsibility to Miguel, who was the only one who could have suspicions. However, as other people spoke so highly of Fernando, Miguel trusted him completely. When he began to realize the situation, he tried to solve the problems by himself, without communicating them to anyone in the family to avoid worries.

DISCUSSION QUESTIONS

1. What elements of BOMBE's history, culture, and policies contributed to its downfall and will contribute to a subsequent recovery?
2. How does instituting order, discipline, and formality in the workplace not only foster trust, confidence, predictability, and success in the enterprise but also have a favorable effect on emotional trust within the family?
3. What kind of governance mechanisms could be developed in the family and in the family business to mitigate the negative effects of excessive trust? Family firms use formal (control-based) and informal (trust-based) governance mechanisms to manage the internal organization and govern collaborations. The trust-based governance mechanisms mitigate relational/performance risks.
4. What role could psychological ownership play in the behavior of a nonfamily CEO?
5. How do higher levels of social capital increase something negatively valued, such as free-riding or extortion?
6. What role have external relationships played in the growth and survival of the business group? How could they have avoided the negative effect of these relationships?

EPILOGUE

Several immediate problems had to be solved in the business. First, was to deal with the tax audit. They were able to settle that debt thanks to a relative lending them some money. Second, they had to tell the family about the situation since they had not informed them previously because, among other reasons, the police had forbidden them to do so.

Third, they had to drive up company activity to overcome the family's and the business's precarious economic situation. They remembered some friends from Murcia who they had lent some money to many years previously to enable them to keep their company afloat and who were now doing very well. Their friends gave them their support, based on trust, their track record, and their knowledge.

They prepared a business plan to develop their temporary work services as a franchise of their friends' company and an agreement was reached between the two businesses to rebuild BOMBE's temporary work activity. The business has continued to operate despite multiple problems, especially due to debts acquired during the diversification process; they have kept the logistics company and the call center. They have sold the textile company machinery and assets online to put some money in the company account and cover substantial outstanding loans. They are selling the canning factory, although they are going to remain as minority partners at the wish of the buyer. Lastly, they will be involved in legal proceedings for a few years to come.

And so, little by little, they are getting over the fraud they were subjected to. They keep asking why. Overconfidence ... Excessive initiative ... Not having the advice and external advisors ...? The question remains in the air.

Their psychological recovery is also on track. Miguel says:

Now we live, now we smile, and especially since last Wednesday when confidentiality restrictions were lifted. We can talk and tell everyone everything ... and we can do so many things with peace of mind. We have already paid off a lot of things. It is true that we are invoicing €150.000 monthly, which compared to what we had been invoicing isn't much, but it isn't bad.

NOTE

1. This case is based on several in-depth interviews conducted by the authors of the case. The results of this analysis were sent to the interviewees to verify the veracity of the data and eliminate inaccuracies. The identities of those involved and the company have been anonymized for their privacy.

SUGGESTED READING

Baycan, T. and Öner, Ö. (2023). The dark side of social capital: A contextual perspective. *The Annals of Regional Science, 70*, 779–98.

Eddleston, K.A., Chrisman, J.J., Steier, L.P. and Chua, J.H. (2010). Governance and trust in family firms: An introduction. *Entrepreneurship Theory and Practice, 34*(6), 1043–56.

Stewart, A. and Hitt, M.A. (2012). Why can't a family business be more like a nonfamily business? Modes of professionalization in family firms. *Family Business Review, 25*(1), 58–86.

PART IV
BAD BEHAVIOR IN THE FAMILY BUSINESS

15
Landscape Plus[1]

Steve Gaklis

CASE SUMMARY

Peter Henley is the founder of Landscape Plus, but his foundation in agricultural distribution came from his father, Paul, who operated in the green industry most of his life. Both of Paul's sons, Peter and Chris, gravitated to the industry but believed bigger and better opportunities existed in large-scale distribution of agricultural products. Both sons were successful individually and in partnership with their father in candy production in Michigan. Peter grew Landscape Plus into a six-division company tied to horticulture, but his children – Lee, Jenny, and George – didn't subscribe to their father's sales culture and arguably disjointed strategy for growth. The younger generation wanted systems and controls to improve or eliminate perennial problems in theft, waste, margins, and growth, which not only plagued the family business but also plagued local banks. The younger generation also wanted to stop expansion, believing it was better to turn existing divisions profitable than "Rob Peter to pay Paul" and use high levels of debt to maintain operations at all six divisions. But as the case recounts, George and Jenny resisted Lee's attempts at systems and controls, believing they knew better. Both Jenny and George often expressed resentment toward their brother in company meetings and behind his back. However, each sibling agreed with Lee's overall assessment of the organization that Peter didn't have any systems in place, and there were too many different things going on, with competing needs of resources and cash and everything else. The case ends as local officials and bank regulators knock on Peter's door to seize the business and personal assets that he had pledged to secure loans for Landscape Plus. It appeared his quarreling family and his family business were coming to a disastrous end.

LEARNING OUTCOMES

After analyzing this case, students will be able to:

- Explain dysfunctional behavior in a family firm in terms of conflicts, problems, and challenges that arise in a family-owned and operated business.
- Describe the causes of dysfunction in a family firm such as:
  - a lack of clear boundaries where family business participants attempt to take on issues that do not relate to their roles or responsibilities within the organization;

- a communication breakdown involving ineffective and/or nonexistent communication and failure to open an honest dialogue in decision-making;
- ambiguity involving succession planning, that leaves the next generation and external managers to guess who might lead the organization in the future;
- role conflicts in which differences among family managers in expectations, skill sets, education, and level of commitment lead to disputes over authority and responsibility;
- emotional dynamics and personal relationships that may play a large role in a family business and sometimes interfere with business operations.
- Explain the importance of professionalization at the family firm in operational practices, governance structures, and external expertise.
- Describe the differences between a sales culture and an operations culture and how a clash between the two can lead to conflict and dysfunction.

Head in hands and exasperated after a company meeting, Peter Henley sat quietly at his desk at the headquarters of Landscape Plus in Michigan. Once again, his son had undermined his authority; as always, his daughter had espoused all the answers but refused to lead, and his youngest son had disengaged and left the family firm eight months earlier. Dysfunction arguably raged at the family firm, with each of his children expressing their intent to lead the organization while they battled each other for power and authority. Peter trusted his children and he believed in their abilities, but he also understood they did not work well together. Peter was unwilling and/or unable to stop infighting among his children. He was also unable to stop the business he started from sliding into oblivion.

Meanwhile, banks were once again outside the company door, eager to pounce on the assets of the family firm after multiple years of lackluster performance and decreasing valuations. Five years earlier, Peter had got his son, Lee, to negotiate with banks, but now he knew the time had come for a very difficult decision about the future of the family business. Times had changed, and banks were more selective in their lending practices in 2018, and Landscape Plus was not a star performer, with many divisions of the family firm underperforming or not performing at all. Banks were frustrated yet again by the lackluster performance of several divisions, and they had started to call the shots at Landscape Plus with requests for revaluations and repayment of debt. It was only a matter of time before they called all Landscape Plus loans, forcing Peter to scramble for cash yet again or close the doors.

THE CONTEXT

Landscape Plus was in the business of horticultural wholesale distribution, and Peter understood too well that wholesale distribution was all about sales. If you could sell it, you could usually make money selling it. That was the formula for more than 40 years since he started in agricultural/horticultural distribution as a spin-off from his father's agricultural distribution businesses. Yes, the business was about reducing expenses, costs, waste, and theft, but he always understood that he or anyone of his sales staff could "pull a rabbit out of the hat and book a big sale and keep things going" when things got difficult. He had arguably engineered the business culture around sales and selling.

In 2018, the US experienced a relatively positive economic performance. The country's gross domestic product (GDP) grew by around 2.2 percent, reflecting a steady expansion. Unemployment remained low, hovering around 3.3 percent throughout the year, indicating a strong labor market. Additionally, consumer spending remained relatively robust, supported by wage growth and low inflation. Overall, the US economy demonstrated resilience and maintained a positive trajectory in 2018. The building and housing market, which is directly tied to Landscape Plus sales and profitability, showed mixed trends. On one hand, there was continued growth in construction activity and home sales, and the construction sector saw steady expansion, with new residential construction reaching its highest level in over a decade. Low mortgage rates and a strong demand for housing contributed to increased home sales, particularly in the first half of the year. On the other hand, there were challenges in the housing market. Housing affordability remained a concern in the Midwest US, as home prices continued to rise faster than real wages. This led to a shortage of affordable housing options, particularly for first-time home buyers. Adding fuel to the fire, there was a shortage of available homes for sale, which increased competition among buyers.

By most accounts and indicators, the economy and building sector in the Midwest US was good, but Landscape Plus was unraveling, with continual family infighting, dissent among managers, physical fights among sales staff, and general discontent at the family business. Yet again, banks were becoming restless with the performance and profitability of the organization. In interviews, Peter's son, Lee, remembered,

A shit show, but it was always a bit of a shit show and at this point, when our cash flow situation started getting really tight, we're literally promising people that the check was in the mail as they're loading the truck for spring for product that we had bought maybe the previous fall or the previous spring!

The situation was dire, and Peter was at a loss to stem the tide and tame his unruly family and staff.

THE ORGANIZATION

To develop Landscape Plus, Peter drew on his father's entrepreneurial legacy, entrepreneurial orientation, and financial capital to develop his innovative ideas on wholesale distribution. With the introduction of lower gas prices, innovative logistics, and effective distribution models in the early 1980s, Peter recognized endless opportunities for wholesale distribution of agricultural products including horticultural green goods such as Christmas trees, wreaths, shrubs, trees, and other horticultural products. Both Peter and his brother Chris had effectively transitioned their father's business from small, local distribution to truckload distribution to many parts of the US and beyond, but Peter understood he could leverage the power of distribution in horticultural wholesale centers, growing operations, retail centers, and direct distribution. By 1992 Peter had established horticulture distribution centers (HDC) to provide a local outlet for his Christmas trees and wreaths from Canada while also providing one-stop shopping for landscape contractors and developers in Michigan during spring, summer, and fall. By all accounts, it was a sound strategy because area homeowners were moving to the suburbs and building bigger homes with bigger yards requiring ever more landscape material. In short order, Peter realized more opportunities in sod farms and ornamental tree farms which might also supply his existing HDCs.

In 2002, Peter acquired a large tract of land outside Detroit, Michigan to relocate his largest HDC and established a new venture in outdoor furniture and outdoor living for an affluent local community. He reasoned that the 20 acres he purchased were perfectly suited to horticultural distribution while the structure on the land was perfectly suited to retail furniture sales. It was of little concern that he knew nothing about buying or selling outdoor furniture to retail homeowners. In short order, he expanded retail operations to three locations while he expanded wholesale distribution operations to three locations throughout Michigan. With more affluent people moving to the suburbs in and around Detroit, Landscape Plus supplied all their outdoor living and landscaping needs at the wholesale and retail level. By all accounts it was a sound strategy of vertical integration, given limited competition and plenty of interest. Appendix 15A provides specific information about each division.

On paper, anyone might argue that the lineup of Landscape Plus divisions was impressive. Peter had arguably satisfied supply and distribution for his HDCs with a vertical integration of divisions that could supply them. *The Farm* supplied sod and shade trees; *Canada* supplied wholesale Christmas trees; *The Upper Peninsula* supplied wholesale wreaths; *Direct* filled out tractor trailers heading to each HDC; and *Retail* provided off-season cash flows. By most accounts, it was an impressive lineup of businesses, but Peter's son, Lee, disagreed, and in interviews he vociferously commented, "The six different profit centers so to speak were not strategic creations. They were, you know, Peter as an entrepreneur going, 'Oh, here's an opportunity; oh, here's an opportunity; oh, here's another opportunity,' but not really knowing what you're getting into – just looking to fill a need."

There was some truth in what Lee said, as fewer than half the divisions were making money, and family members often debated the need for divisions that were perennial losers. George, Peter's other son, also weighed in on the scattered model of growing, distributing, and expanding horticultural distribution that was Landscape Plus: "So, the model was broken. It was really clear. There were certain parts of the business where the business model was just broken."

THE FAMILY

Over three generations, the Henley family had built upon a strong legacy in agricultural distribution as distributors of fruit, vegetables, and horticultural green goods in Christmas trees, wreaths, and landscape material throughout Michigan in the US and Ontario in Canada. From the beginning, when Paul Henley emigrated to the US from Greece, business and entrepreneurship had been a family tradition. Paul always encouraged his sons, Peter and Chris, to start their own businesses, albeit with his help and support.

Paul Henley came to the US from Greece to escape a lack of opportunity and general government unrest. With support from family living in the US, he envisioned his goal to build a successful family business and create a family legacy in agricultural distribution. In short order, he
married and had two sons who would soon join his expanding business. Long involved in agriculture and entrepreneurship at a young age, Paul began with only a pushcart selling fruit and
produce to an affluent population outside Detroit, Michigan. Before long, Paul owned multiple carts and then a distribution center where Detroit area restaurants and markets would buy
their fruit, produce, and meats. His business grew rapidly, gaining a reputation for reliability,
frugality, and quality. Paul also ventured into meat markets and a grocery store for local retail
customers in nearby Birmingham, Michigan where he lived with his family. However, Paul
moved slowly to build his network of businesses; he avoided debt and only started new ventures after careful consideration. Paul also prioritized his growers and suppliers, a philosophy
that he tried to instill in both sons. In separate interviews, Peter and Chris remembered, "It
was no coincidence that Paul selected locations that catered to growers, truckers, distributors,
and customers; he believed that business should be a partnership among those who grew the
product, those who shipped the product, those who distributed the product and those who
bought the product."

According to his sons, Paul was known for his ability to create partnerships and help others
in business, believing what was good for others would be good for him. Paul went further
than most in his ability to partner with growers by partially financing their operations and/
or supplying them with what they needed to get their product to market. Peter recalled: "He
helped finance the growers by getting their fertilizer, supplying them with plants, and he also
would supply them with the baskets and the crates for all that. He was a real organizer – a great
planner." Both sons confirmed: "And it was good for [Paul's] business, because the growers
and the farmers that shipped him merchandise depended on him to get the right market price
and get a good return on their merchandise, whatever they were growing."

Peter showed little interest in his father's limited and local distribution business, and he
recounted:

> There was no interest in me going into his business. And I think he understood that, and he
> didn't ever talk about taking over his business as he aged because it was difficult – a difficult
> business. It was a hard business. It required all your time and all your energy … We didn't
> want to play around with quarts and small quantities at Paul's business … We wanted to
> move truckloads.

True to their word and with Paul's support and encouragement, Peter and Chris pursued
wholesale distribution of blueberries and Christmas trees from their individual operations
out of Canada. By all accounts Paul and his sons enjoyed the dynamic of their individual
businesses, supporting each other while they considered additional opportunities together.
According to his sons, Paul was eager for them to join him in agricultural distribution with
their own ventures. He was eager to partner with them, and he communicated partnership
opportunities. Peter's older brother, Chris, believed there was a plan with every communica-

tion: "Well, I suppose his major thought was to get Peter established – you know, Paul wanted Peter to be in business. Yeah, probably to look after his own business."

Peter also assumed his father had a very clear plan to partner in the success of his sons:

> Well, he invested in his two sons. He thought they knew what the heck they were doing [laughter] … He didn't want his sons to take over the fruit and produce. Well, he saw the future in the produce business as not something profitable and a very difficult lifestyle.

But Peter and Chris understood that Paul harbored distrust, whether from his upbringing or experiences in business, and Chris noted in interviews,

> Yeah, no, it was hard for him, you know, that you couldn't trust people, that they steal from you. Lack of trust around money and theft or lack of trust in terms of commitment and managing skills. It's just not trusting that you can trust people, either to be honest with you or to do what you would do or to do a good job, etc., etc.

In the early 1970s, Paul partnered with his sons to manufacture candy. Candy production required a significant investment on Paul's part. Peter, who had just finished college, remembered that Paul invested at least $100 000 in the joint venture that Peter and his brother pursued. Paul saw it as a good opportunity for his sons to get into a different kind of business and assumed he was trying to set up a business for his two boys, the brothers recalled. Candy production represented an off-season opportunity for both sons while they simultaneously developed individual ventures with Paul's help in wholesale blueberry distribution and wholesale Christmas tree distribution out of Canada. While Chris harvested blueberries in Canada during summer months, Peter ran the candy factory. In winter, the situation reversed, with Chris running the candy factory. Peter and Chris recalled that Paul provided them with these business opportunities, and both were making good incomes from them.

Peter Henley soon developed additional ventures by establishing HDC, believing the centers could supply local landscape contractors and real estate developers in and around Michigan with landscape material. To supply his HDCs as they expanded throughout Michigan, Peter started sod farms and shade tree nurseries to supply his centers. In 2002 he opened retail centers and ventured in outdoor furniture and garden centers, and in 2002 he purchased a large tract of land in Detroit, Michigan for his largest HDC and the headquarters of Landscape Plus.

Like his father, Peter also believed that business should be a partnership among those who grew the product, those who shipped the product, those who distributed the product, and those who bought the product, and he cultivated relationships, but his relations with partners were always secondary to sales, and he arguably harbored distrust for employees within the organization and suppliers and customers outside the organization. His son, Lee, commented: "I think [Peter] was troubled by trusting people. He had never seen that model, and I think that was part of the issue. It was crystal clear to me that, you know, I don't know if he was capable of trusting. I just don't think it was in his vocabulary."

However, he was eager to expand his own businesses with production operations, shipping operations, additional distributors, and retail operations. Unlike his father, Peter was eager to finance his various operations and commented, "One business paid the bills for the other business … We kept pyramiding, and they weren't all profitable all at the same time, and we'd rob Peter to pay Paul. Yeah, we were cash poor all the time!"

The purchase of land in Detroit for his largest wholesale distribution site was a big leap and a large investment requiring significant debt. Additional ventures and investments for Landscape Plus would require more debt financing, yet Peter recalled his eagerness to always start more businesses that could leverage and vertically integrate his other businesses.

Throughout the rise of Landscape Plus, while Peter would "Rob Peter to pay Paul", he would hire managers like Tom Woole and many others in his mold – supreme salesmen but arguably poor operators and relatively poor managers. Lee gave his own impression:

> Well in all areas of the business, you ended up with, you know, unmanageable salesmen – big egos, questionable honesty. And that was what Peter wanted – somebody who could produce the sales at any cost, and they did not know how to manage gross margin, manage inventory, or how to manage people very well … Peter loved to start things but really was not a manager. He was a salesman. He sold his way out of every problem. He hired people kind of like him; he hated the details of business. It was kind of comical watching him, you know.

Tom Woole, under Peter's close supervision, had been leading sales at Landscape Plus since 1996. Upon his release from the Marine Corps, Tom began his ten-year tenure at Landscape Plus under Peter's close supervision, and he quickly developed into a leader at the organization with expectations to lead it someday. Over ten years, he was a valued employee for Peter, working as sales manager and general manager in both wholesale and retail operations. By all accounts, Tom was a strong leader and excellent salesman, and he admired Peter, and Peter reciprocated with guidance and responsibility. Tom arguably set the standard for sales among salesmen at the organization, and he pursued sales at all costs, at times not knowing where the product would come from or when it would deliver. His aggressive sales set a tone at Landscape Plus.

Lee Henley joined the business in 2002, and Tom trained Lee in sales and ushered him into the organization. Lee remembered that Tom was a very good salesman who learned from Peter and had great relationships with people in the industry. That same year, Landscape Plus began operations at its largest distribution center, *Detroit Wholesale*, to attract sales from more and bigger building and landscape contractors, garden centers, and big box stores. To that end, Lee assumed responsibility for getting more sales, and he remembered that Peter and Tom told him he needed to, "blow the doors off your area of responsibility."

Lee lamented the close relationship between Peter and Tom, and over the ensuing years, there was quiet competition between them as Lee increased his sales responsibilities at Landscape Plus while Tom took stock of his future at the family firm. Lee remembered,

> Peter really took [Tom] under his wing, and Tom kind of felt like he was Peter's son or heir or whatever. Tom was really hoping that he could step into something, and you know, I had

to bear that, but at the same time it had nothing to do with me. It had everything to do with Tom.

Lee recalled the move to establish *Detroit Wholesale* with more sales wherever he could find them added to his own uncertainty and insecurity about the direction of the organization. "It was so scattered. It was like, we have stuff we'll sell it to anybody and, you know, you'd be making up your product offering as you walk in the door." His analysis of the situation at Landscape Plus was a lack of restraint, organization, and resources in every division of the company. As Lee remembered it, systems arguably didn't exist. "I mean Peter didn't have the systems in place. So, my initial assessment of the company was that there were too many different things going on with competing needs for resources and cash and everything else."

Yet from the start, Lee threw himself into sales by studying books on sales and listening to blogs and tapes on sales as he drove hours to sales meetings. "Honestly, when you come straight out of college and you go right into the family business, your perspective is lacking. You don't know how it looks when you're doing it right." Lee was committed and persistent in his efforts to produce sales for the family business, but his frustration was palpable as he remembered his inability to connect with other Landscape Plus salesmen from the beginning. "I mean I was resented as the son of the boss; who's kidding who – totally resented."

By 2006, understanding that Peter prioritized his family in the business, Tom chose to exit from Landscape Plus. It was a disappointment for Peter, and a pivotal moment for the future of the family firm. By 2009, Peter elevated Lee to sales manager, but Lee continually expressed his frustration with the position, that is managing well-established but unruly salesmen at the family business.

> So, it's trying to make me into something Peter thought I should be versus who you are and where your skills and talents are, and where would it be best to use them. Instead, it was always about toughening me up and turning me into the super salesman or whatever! … I'm NOT the person who's going to go and beat the person up for the sale. I'm the person who's going to show them what's going on in the numbers and enroll them in doing something better. That's my style, but that's not Peter's style.

Jenny Henley, Peter's daughter, did not join the family business out of college like her brother, Lee. She joined in 2009 after a successful ten-year term in administration at Cannon Corp. outside Detroit, Michigan. In administration she oversaw contract paperwork from several hundred salespeople within the corporation while managing 15–20 people. By all accounts, Jenny was a particularly organized and competent manager at Cannon, and she thrived within the corporate culture. She was reluctant to leave that corporate culture, but in 2009, at 32 years old, she joined Landscape Plus at the request of her father, who hoped she might bring professional accounting, organization, and administrative skills to the scattered family businesses. Peter also hoped she might introduce a stable and productive environment within the organization.

She immediately got to work within the administrative group at Landscape Plus to organize controls and accounting of the disjointed divisions within the family business. But, almost as quickly as Jenny began to streamline administration, she began to disagree and argue with her brother. Lee recounted, "Well, Jenny was impossible to manage, and she knew how to do everything better than everybody else but didn't want to do it. She just wanted to sit back and tell me everything I was doing wrong. I had to bear that."

In short order, the division between Jenny and Lee became untenable, with Peter unable and/or unwilling to manage conflicts and disagreements among his two oldest children. Lee remembered that "At one point, we got into this argument in a meeting, and I said, 'Jenny, you want to run this?' I said, 'You want to take this over?' And she looked like a deer in headlights."

While Lee believed he deserved leadership authority to bring the six divisions of Landscape Plus together, Jenny believed she was more capable to handle leadership roles in all aspects of the organization, and she voiced her dissatisfaction often during company meetings, believing she should run the business straight away. Peter now had two children demanding more authority and leadership responsibilities at the family firm.

George Henley joined the family business in 2012 at the urgent request of his father and brother just as banks were demanding debt repayment. George knew he was entering an uncertain and unstable environment at the family firm, but with his horticultural knowledge after attending Cornell University's School of Agriculture, and his sales skills after three years at Cannon Corp., he believed he was perfectly positioned to help calm banks and lead the company. What he didn't perceive was the high level of disorganization, dissension, and dysfunction between his brother and father, along with infighting between his sister and brother. George did not join the family firm until after some success at Cannon Corp. where he understood that corporate was simply a stop along the way to a leadership role at Landscape Plus. Yet upon entering the family business, Peter and Lee positioned George to purchase for all the companies, believing his horticultural knowledge and organization skills were a perfect fit. George disagreed and demanded to negotiate with banks and manage more divisions at Landscape Plus. He also believed he could sell after sales training and success at Cannon Corp. It was a complete affront to his brother, and it introduced more infighting and dysfunction at the family firm. However, George committed to the purchasing duties, and his business principles harkened back to his grandfather, Paul, who professed a partnership among growers, shippers, buyers, and customers.

BAD RELATIONS

By 2012, banks were stalking company assets, demanding new valuations, cost cutting, and more assets of family members to offset debt. Given lackluster financial performance after the effects of the Great Recession of 2009, one midsized lender to Landscape Plus decided to call outstanding loans for repayment. US Trust demanded a $3 million cash paydown of debt in 48 hours and an immediate revaluation of all Landscape Plus' assets. It was a daunting challenge that immediately threatened the future of the family business and the financial security of every member of the Henley family. Lee had to bear the responsibility of working with uncooperative banks to convince them he could bring the divisions together into a profitable whole.

"I called it basically six dysfunctional businesses all hoping that if we smash them all together, somehow some magic will happen. Of course, I didn't tell the banks that at the time."

By 2014, in response to leadership challenges from his brother and sister, Lee demanded more authority and the title of president of Landscape Plus. He complained:

> After the loans got called, I sat down with [Peter] and I said, "This is enough. If I'm going to be the one who's putting my neck on the chopping block all the time, I need the authority … So, [Peter] would always dangle the carrot and then yank it away. My hands were tied, and yeah, I kept pushing him into it. That's the only way he would [make me President] of Landscape Plus.

Yet Peter refused to hand complete control of the family business to Lee, and he continued to maintain much of the everyday authority, overseeing employees, approving expenditures, overseeing budgets, and many other day-to-day operations. Lee recalled that "it was crystal clear to me that … I don't know if he was capable of trusting. I just don't think it was in his vocabulary."

As president of Landscape Plus by 2014, Lee effectively negotiated with the banks and restructured loans which were somewhat more favorable to the family firm. However, Lee would continue to struggle with his father and sister to implement his own vision of systems and controls while he also struggled with an unruly management team and unmanageable and arguably dishonest staff. Yet, between 2014 and 2018, sales and margins improved somewhat with an improving economy, a building boom, and more management systems and organization in place at all Landscape Plus divisions, but dysfunction and infighting increased exponentially within and outside the family. George recalled, "I would enter family offices every day with acid in my stomach. The relationship between me and my brother at the time was toxic. Anything he did, I would counteract, and anything he said, I would contradict."

It was a toxic relationship, like the dynamics playing out between Lee and Jenny, but George frequently voiced his dissatisfaction with the way his brother was running the firm: "In my mind, he could do nothing right at the family business, and I watched as phones went unanswered, theft increased exponentially, and staff went rogue. I believed Lee wasn't capable of leading six disparate divisions at Landscape Plus. He was tearing them apart."

Meanwhile, Jenny continued to contradict and correct Lee in meetings and in front of employees. For Lee, it was a constant challenge to his authority and ability to maintain control of managers and employees, who began to take sides and play family members off against each other. However, Jenny could clearly show profit and cash flows from her *Retail* division, profits that supported several unprofitable Landscape Plus divisions including *The Farm*, *Canada*, and *The Upper Peninsula*. While George and Jenny could clearly show organizational improvements and profitability in every area they operated, Lee could not. As 2018 approached, *Detroit Wholesale*, *The Farm*, *Canada*, and *The Upper Peninsula* began to struggle, with poor sales and poor operating margins. Once again, banks began taking notice.

By 2018, George's frustration with his brother made him even more unmanageable. With the blessing of Peter and Lee, he chose to spin off *Direct* and exit the family business to independently pursue his own entrepreneurial ventures in the horticulture industry. George recalled, "By 2018, I made up my mind that I wouldn't go down with a sinking ship!" While Peter was disappointed with his son's decision, he understood that the dynamic between George and Lee was splitting the family and family business apart. By all measures, George was very difficult to manage, believing he was educated and trained to be in a position of authority inside Landscape Plus. He often said as much to Peter over frequent lunches and dinners. Like his sister, George believed he was in a better position to lead the company and usher the divisions toward profitability. While Lee labored to calm banks and repay debt, both George and Jenny schemed to remove Lee from his leadership position at the family business. George believed that he and his sister should lead the organization together, and he believed that Lee should take full ownership of *Canada* and *The Upper Peninsula* and separate both divisions from the core. Peter neither agreed nor disagreed, arguably believing that if he hedged his bets among family members, something would work out, and the infighting would stop. Instead, his inability or unwillingness to act decisively increased divisions and divisiveness in the family and in the organization.

CONCLUSION

Peter believed there was no way out when local officials and bank regulators knocked on his door the morning of 17 April 2019 to seize his business and personal assets which he had pledged in order to secure loans for all Landscape Plus divisions. It appeared his family and family business were coming to a disastrous end. In past times, he could always count on the next sale to get him out of financial trouble, but time had run out, and his son was now formally calling the shots and negotiating with banks. He had few options since he had relegated negotiating power to Lee five years earlier when he named him president of all Landscape Plus divisions. He had to trust his son to find an equitable solution, and find it fast.

Lee and Peter quickly convened with their lawyers to determine a payout strategy that might satisfy the banks. Unfortunately, banks were not in a bargaining mood. They arguably saw the writing on the wall at Landscape Plus and refused to extend loans another five years for a family business in continual crisis operating only to "Rob Peter to pay Paul." His son was right; it had become a "shit show" at Landscape Plus, and it looked as if the show was about to end.

DISCUSSION QUESTIONS

1. Identify elements of Landscape Plus' history, culture, and policies that contributed to both the success and ultimate downfall of the Henley family.
2. At what point in Landscape Plus' history did things start to go wrong? Why?
3. What were other options to elevating Lee as president of Landscape Plus? What options could be considered better or worse? Why?
4. What would you have done if you were (a) Peter, (b) Lee?

EPILOGUE

The demise of the *Detroit Wholesale* division came in its sale to the competition. It was arguably a fire sale that rescued personal homes and property of the Henley family from banks but paid all the outstanding debt and secured a lease of the land from the new owners. Sale of *The Farm* went to an aspiring cattle farmer, Lee sold *Canada* and *The Upper Peninsula* to employees, and Jenny was given full control of *Retail* by Peter. By all accounts, 2019 was a personally and financially traumatic year for the family, with very heated discussions between Lee and Peter. With Lee as president of Landscape Plus, he had full authority to sell assets of the company, and upon counsel he did, much to the consternation of Peter. Peter was devastated by the sale and severed all contact and communication with his elder son. While many might argue that the sale was a necessity with banks and competition closing in, it was a devastating blow to the family who had worked so hard for so many years to build a legacy in the green industry. Reflecting on his tattered relationship with his father, Lee reflected in interviews,

> Well, I think the reason why he was so bitter when I sold [Landscape Plus] was because to him, it was like a confirmation that I couldn't be trusted, even though he tried and tried and tried to be trusting, you know, both in business and in life. Yeah, I just don't know that he was capable of it.

NOTE

1. Over a period of 36 months, the author conducted nine semi-structured interviews with Landscape Plus family owners, family members, employees, and industry experts. To organize and analyze the qualitative data, create case histories and tables and link data, he used NVivo software. He collected additional data from archival publications, documentation, and personal histories to ensure the consistency and quality of the data. Names of the company and the individuals involved as well as locations have been disguised to preserve anonymity.

SUGGESTED READING

Cater III, J.J. and Kidwell, R.E. (2014). Function, governance, and trust in successor leadership groups in family firms. *Journal of Family Business Strategy*, 5(3), 217–28.
Gordon, G. and Nicholson, N. (2010). *Family Wars: Stories and Insights from Famous Family Business Feuds*. Kogan Page Publishers.
Steier, L. (2001). Family firms, plural forms of governance, and the evolving role of trust. *Family Business Review*, 14(4), 353–68.

APPENDIX 15A

The following paragraphs provide details regarding the six divisions of Landscape Plus.

Detroit Wholesale referred to the Detroit HDC at which contractors, landscapers, architects, and others with wholesale accounts could purchase live horticultural material and hard goods in fertilizers, stone, and mulch in bulk. From its inception in 2002, *Detroit Wholesale* had been a critical contributor to the overall success at Landscape Plus, and it arguably became the sales backbone of the family business, but to purchase the property and transform it, Peter had taken on significant debt. At its peak there were three HDCs located throughout Michigan similar to *Detroit Wholesale* but typically smaller in size. Each center inventoried landscape grade coniferous evergreens along with deciduous and ornamental trees and shrubs above ground on 5–20-acre land parcels. Wholesale customers could request pickup or delivery of horticultural material the same day. Before HDCs a request to any horticultural grower could take days or weeks. Given a strong economy which transferred wealth and building out to city suburbs, there was a need for speed and economy in all aspects of building and contracting throughout the late 1990s and early 2000s.

The Farm, as it was known, grew ornamental turf, shade trees, and ornamental trees for wholesale distributors and landscape contractors in the green industry in Michigan for more than 20 years. Situated upon fertile river bottom land adjacent to the Merrimack River, it was an idyllic site not only for a family compound for weekend getaways, but it was also a favorite site to host green industry events and company outings of more than 200 employees on more than 600 acres of perfectly manicured grass. However, always the poor stepchild to other divisions within the family business at Landscape Plus, it necessitated continual cash injections from whichever division and/or whichever bank offered them.

The *Retail* division had always been a stalwart moneymaker since its inception in the early 2000s. At its peak, *Retail* boasted three locations in the Detroit area, each selling the very best outdoor furniture in the spring and summer months then live and artificial Christmas trees, wreaths, and ornaments during the winter months. Displays were a source of competitive pride at each store, with customers queuing for hours to see the animatronics and various displays built to attract them. Not just an outdoor living store, *Retail* was also a destination for many families on an outing.

Canada referred to the Christmas tree distribution division at Landscape Plus, and it was the first division of the company. Founded in the early 1980s, *Canada* was an early pioneer of live Christmas trees and wreaths with the advent of more effective logistics and cheaper freight in the US. At its peak, *Canada* was selling more than 300 000 live Christmas trees to Midwest US home centers, garden centers, and box stores including Home Depot, Lowes, Costco, and Walmart. *Canada* shipped trees as far as Saudi Arabia and Bermuda.

The Upper Peninsula referred to wreath factories located in Northern Michigan in the US and in Canada. At its peak in 2012, *The Upper Peninsula* produced approximately 300 000 live wreaths for sale at Midwest US home centers, garden centers, and box stores, including Home Depot, Lowes, Costco, and Walmart. Between the US and Canadian factories, *The Upper Peninsula* employed about 60 people.

Direct referred to the distribution of live horticultural material direct from the grower to a customer location or jobsite. Somewhat a neglected child of all Landscape Plus, it would later burgeon to become the effective heir to the family business by offering customers more efficient and cost-effective logistics of green material.

16
Jacobson Hardware Store: overcoming conflict, dysfunction, and death in a family business[1]

John James Cater III

CASE SUMMARY

Following the burgeoning oil and gas industry, Harry Jacobson opened a new business, Jacobson Hardware Store, in Shreveport, LA in 1940. The store has stayed in the Jacobson family through three generations of ownership and management. Harry's son, Thomas Jacobson, grew up at the hardware store and then assumed the leadership of the business upon Harry's death in 1977. Joined by his wife, Martha, Thomas expanded the business, opening a much larger store in 1993. Upon Thomas' passing in 1996, Martha Jacobson took over the leadership of the company and was joined in the family business by her two sons, T.J. and Richard.

Unfortunately, the two sons did not get along with each other, and conflict and the dysfunctional behavior of the younger brother, Richard, led to a split in the family. The older brother, T.J., moved to Alexandria, LA to open another family hardware store but at the last minute, his mother, Martha, and brother, Richard, withdrew their support and refused to help T.J. in the new store. Despite the lack of family support, T.J. opened the new store in Alexandria. However, after ten years, T.J. had to close the store due to low sales volume and the ensuing financial problems. T.J. then began a successful career as a life insurance agent. Then, tragically, Richard Jacobson is gunned down on the doorstep of his home by an unknown assailant. Stepping into the turmoil, Martha Jacobson must decide what to do with the family business. Should she close the family legacy, invite an outsider to help her run the business, or persuade her son, T.J., to return to the hardware store?

LEARNING OUTCOMES

Through analysis of this case, students can be expected to:

- Explain the consequences of relationship conflict and dysfunctional behavior from the perspective of family business leaders, both incumbents and successors.

- Describe the consequences of the sudden death of a family business leader for the family and the business.
- Evaluate alternative courses of action for an incumbent family business leader for the future of the business, such as:
  - selling the business to outsiders;
  - bringing in outsiders to manage the business;
  - or persuading a willing and able family member to join the family business to assume the leadership of the company.
- Demonstrate an understanding of the pride family members possess regarding the legacy of a multigenerational family firm and their desire to see the business through to the next generation.
- Explain the strategies that a small family business may use to defend itself from external threats in a declining industry.
- Evaluate the financial position of a small family firm and estimate its sales price to potential outside buyers.

The hot Louisiana sun was beginning to set, and the Jacobson family had just settled inside their home at the dining table to enjoy a Memorial Day dinner consisting of hamburgers and hot dogs still sizzling from the barbeque grill with all the extras – potato salad, baked beans, pickles, and chips to be followed by apple pie, pecan pie, and vanilla ice cream. Richard and Louise Jacobson and their five children, all under the age of 18, were gathered to celebrate the holiday when the doorbell rang. Richard Jacobson, the 54-year-old co-owner of Jacobson Hardware Store, an independent hardware store business, rose to answer the door. The Jacobson home was on the outskirts of Shreveport in a neighborhood of homes with acre lots, so the neighbors were present but not too close. Richard opened the door and faced a gunman. Michael Patterson, a neighbor who lived across the street from the Jacobsons, was outside at about 7 pm on Monday when he heard "two rapid shots followed by a third and then screams of 'Oh, no.' and a car screech."

Another neighbor, Jack McConnell, and his family had just returned from a Memorial Day trip. Jack heard the shots and immediately drove to the Jacobson house, where he tried to help Richard's daughter, Amy, resuscitate Richard before the police arrived. "It was not good, hearing his kids yelling 'Help!' and screaming," McConnell said. "We pray for them because I can only imagine how hard it would be. It's concerning because you don't know who's lurking in your neighborhood. … But it wasn't a random deal from what I can think."

Anna Carter was visiting her grandparents the night of the shooting at their home across the street from the Jacobson home. She stated,

It was crazy. At the time, I didn't know what it was because – I mean, around here, it's the country – so you hear a bunch of random things anyway. So that night it happened, we didn't know what was happening until we saw the police cars, and then they closed the whole street down.

State troopers, sheriff's deputies, and rescue workers arrived within ten minutes of the shooting, but Richard Jacobson was declared dead upon arrival at the Shreveport hospital. The sheriff's department issued a statement that the hardware store owner's death was not a random act of violence and that community residents were not at risk.

INDUSTRY, COMPANY, AND FAMILY BACKGROUND

The hardware store industry

Independent hardware stores, such as Jacobson Hardware, have been a part of the fabric of American lives dating back to the time of the Revolutionary War. Shopkeepers ran old-fashioned hardware stores that were like storerooms (Dipman, 1929) with home repair and maintenance items such as wires and cables, pipes and elbows, hinges, washers, nuts, and springs; slotted, Phillips, hex, and Torx screws; roofing nails and framing nails and finishing nails (NP Gallery, n.d.). The oldest known store was founded in Worcester, MA, in 1782 by Daniel Waldo, Sr. The business remained in the Waldo family until 1821 when Henry Miller purchased the hardware store. Miller sold the business in 1886 to Elwood Adams, who gave the business the name Elwood Adams Hardware. The Adams family operated the company until its closing in 2017 (Carmody, 2018).

In recent years, two trends have greatly influenced the hardware store industry: (1) a movement toward retailers' cooperative companies and wholesalers, and (2) the emergence of home center stores. Ace Hardware and True Value Hardware fueled the first trend. Ace, a cooperative company, began in 1924 and has grown from a small chain of stores in the Chicago, IL area to over 4600 stores in all 50 US states and more than 70 countries. Ace Hardware's revenues are growing, reaching a record high of $8.6 billion in 2022, an increase of 10.7 percent over the previous year, with same-store sales rising 6.9 percent (Ace, 2022). In 1948, John Cotter founded Cotter & Company with 25 independent member hardware stores, also in the Chicago, IL area. In 1963, Cotter acquired the True Value trademark. Today, True Value is a leading wholesaler serving more than 4500 independent stores worldwide with annual revenue of $1.5 billion in 2021 (Zippia, n.d.).

The second significant trend affecting independent hardware store companies has been the rise of big box retailers – known as home center stores, primarily Home Depot and Lowe's. Recognizing a consumer trend toward do-it-yourself home projects, Bernie Marcus and Arthur Blank conceptualized home centers and started Home Depot in Atlanta, GA, in 1978. From the original two stores in Atlanta, the company has grown to 2321 stores in the US, Canada, and Mexico. Home Depot's annual revenue for 2022 was $151.157 billion, a 14.42 percent increase from 2021. The company's annual revenue for 2021 was $132.11 billion, a 19.85 percent increase from 2020.

Meanwhile, L.S. Lowe opened a general hardware store in North Wilkesboro, NC, in 1921. Lowe's did not expand until 1949, when Jim Lowe, L.S. Lowe's son, opened a second store in Sparta, NC. In 1952, Carl Buchan became the sole owner of Lowe's but retained the name of the company. Buchan led an explosive growth period for the company, going public in 1961.

Lowe's reached $1 billion in annual sales in 1982 and then $22 billion in 2002, joining the Fortune 100 largest US companies. Lowe's has spread across the US and entered Canada in 2007 and India in 2015. Now, with over 100 years of operations, the Lowe's revenue for fiscal 2022 was $96.25 billion, a 7.43 percent increase from 2021. The Lowe's annual revenue for 2021 was $89.597 billion, a 24.19 percent increase from 2020 (Lowe's, n.d.).

Given the above trends, US independent hardware stores have declined from 24 000 in 1991 to 19 900 in 2013 to 10 646 in 2022 (IBISWorld, n.d.). In the five years from 2017 to 2022, the number of businesses in the hardware stores industry has declined 5.1 percent per year. Home center stores now dominate the industry, with 13 000 stores in the US and over 63 percent of the market share. The average annual sales for a typical hardware store is $1 439 052, and the average annual sales volume per high-profit store is $1 695 647 (Profile America, 2013).

Shreveport and North Louisiana

Shreveport rests in the northwest corner of Louisiana and is the educational, commercial, and cultural center of the three-state Ark-La-Tex region (Southwest Arkansas, Northwest Louisiana, and Northeast Texas). The city is the third most populous in Louisiana after New Orleans and Baton Rouge, with a population of 393 406 in 2020 (US Census Bureau, 2021). On Interstate 20, Shreveport is only five miles east of the Texas state line and 188 miles east of Dallas. Alexandria is 125 miles south of Shreveport on Interstate 49 (TRIPinfo, 2016). The Shreve Town Company founded Shreveport in 1836 to connect the Red River, which had recently been made fit for navigation, and the Texas Trail. Throughout the twentieth century, Shreveport served as a center for the oil industry. In the 1990s, the oil and gas industry suffered a downturn, and Shreveport transitioned to a service economy. The gaming industry with riverboat gambling casinos has grown rapidly in the Shreveport area. Casinos include Sam's Town, Bally's, Horseshoe, Boomtown, and Margaritaville (Brock, 2008).

Jacobson family and company history

Harry Jacobson, an immigrant to the US from Syria, arrived in Gladewater, TX, in 1930, attracted by the oil boom. According to his grandson, Thomas James Jacobson, known as T.J.,

> From 1930 to 1940, he lived in Gladewater or Wichita Falls. We have relatives in Wichita Falls. He went back and forth between the two cities. Finally, in 1940, he settled in Shreveport, LA, and started the hardware store. Then my grandfather's brother-in-law worked with him. My grandfather bought the brother-in-law out after a few years. My dad, Thomas Jacobson, was five years old when my grandfather started the business.

Harry and Thomas Jacobson worked together and built the family business. See Figure 16.1 for a partial Jacobson family genogram (showing the direct line of business owners). Thomas

Jacobson stated, "I was there from the beginning. I'd walk to the store from grade school to help my daddy. He was there every day, doing what he needed to." Thomas further recalled,

My daddy was a tough, hard man. Like anyone in those days, he did what he had to do to survive. But I remember seeing poor people walk into our store hungry, needing help. He never let anyone know, but I saw him reach in his pocket and give them what he could.

Harry owned and operated the business until his death in 1977.

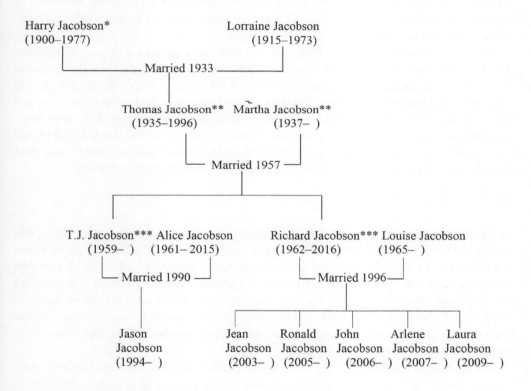

*First Generation Owner of Jacobson Hardware
**Second Generation Owner of Jacobson Hardware
*** Third Generation Owner of Jacobson Hardware

Source: Case author.

Figure 16.1 Partial Jacobson family tree (showing the direct line of business owners)

Second generation leadership

Then, Harry's son, Thomas Jacobson, took over the family business. "My father was Thomas, yes, like I am, but I am not a junior. My father did not have a middle name for some reason.

That is why I am not a junior," explained T.J. Jacobson. Thomas' wife, Martha, joined her husband in the second generation of the family business. Together, they managed and grew the business, most notably building a new store in 1993. A fire destroyed a nearby competitor, so Thomas knew it was time to move. He recalled, "The next morning after the fire, I said we're moving the whole thing. All that old wood made our place nothing but a matchbox waiting to go up. My daddy's store had been there 53 years, and I was not going to see it burn." The couple led the company until Thomas died in 1996. Subsequently, Martha took the reins and managed the hardware business with the help of her two sons, T.J. and Richard. Martha retained 51 percent of the ownership of the company and gave the remaining 49 percent to her two sons, divided equally. See Table 16.1 for Jacobson Hardware Company's income statements from 2014 to 2016.

The stores sold seeds and animal feed, wire, and all things associated with creating a garden. The Jacobson Hardware Store sold wrought iron furniture and carried a variety of high-end pet food such as Diamond Naturals, a well-known US brand. "Half of the bird feeders in Shreveport use Jacobson's bird seed," Martha claimed. The store had a loyal following, and people would drive from miles around to shop there. Mrs Jacobson loved the customers. Another reason for their success was that Jacobson had extensive knowledge of feed and seed and helped their customers, unlike a big box store. The Jacobson Hardware Store won a prize from Baylor University in 2007 as an outstanding small family business in the region.

Third generation conflict

In the third generation, the older son, T.J., worked in the family business after school and during the summers until his graduation from a nearby community college. Then, he joined the business on a full-time basis and formed a strong bond with his father. By all accounts, T.J. was a good and faithful worker. However, his brother, Richard Jacobson, did not share the same work ethic. On multiple occasions, Richard left the family business and worked with relatives and friends in other states. T.J. recalled, "He just came and went. The year my dad passed away; he had just come back home. He got married in January 1996. Dad passed away in June of 1996. He has not left since then."

During Martha's ownership, the relationship conflict between the two brothers grew. Seeking family unity and harmony, Martha made concessions to keep Richard involved in the family business. However, as the prodigal son's behavior worsened, his mother tried even harder to keep him in the fold, and the older brother did not enjoy this display of favoritism. T.J. recalled:

As the years went by, my mother became very partial to my brother because he was always the one leaving. She wanted him to be in the store, and he did not want to be in the store. She was determined that he would be in the store. Everyone else told her to leave him alone. She kind of made him come back in 1995. We had a good month, or so, and then everything went back to the way it had always been. It is hard to work with your family. It can be good if you can get along. After we were together for a short time, my brother and I were at each other's throats.

Table 16.1 Jacobson Hardware Store Corporation financial information / income statements for the fiscal year ending 31 December 2016

	31 Dec. 2016 ($)	31 Dec. 2015 ($)	31 Dec. 2014 ($)
Net Revenues	2,237,000	1,980,000	1,840,000
Cost of Goods Sold	1,203,000	1,045,000	968,000
Gross Profit	1,034,000	935,000	872,000
Operating Expenses			
Officers' salaries	250,000	240,000	230,000
Employees' salaries	200,000	185,000	180,000
Health insurance	100,000	95,000	90,000
Interest expense	36,000	36,000	36,000
Depreciation	75,000	75,000	75,000
Advertising	100,000	80,000	70,000
Equipment	50,000	50,000	50,000
Utilities	24,000	23,000	22,000
Property insurance	25,000	20,000	19,000
Property tax	25,000	23,000	22,000
Office supplies	13,000	12,000	12,000
Total operating expenses	898,000	839,000	806,000
Net Income Before Taxes	136,000	96,000	66,000
Provision For Income Taxes	40,800	28,800	19,800
Net Income After Taxes	$95,200	$67,200	$46,200

Note: Martha Jacobson was the CEO and majority owner of the company. She also owned the company's building. The company consistently earned a small profit each year, and the above years were typical of the profits of Jacobson Hardware. After-tax profits in the three years of the income statement were primarily saved rather than distributed to the owners to invest in new computer equipment for the company, with a small portion going to employee bonuses.
Source: Case author.

Martha understood that her sons did not get along and viewed this as having "different ideas about operating the business." Although she wanted them to work together in the business, it did not work out.

According to T.J.,

I had a poor relationship with my brother. That was a lot of the problem, and that was why I moved to Alexandria. Originally, the store was going to be store #2, and I was going to run it. My brother and I just needed a little space. We were in each other's hair all the time. We all agreed that we would open store #2. So, we moved to Alexandria and got settled in. Three months later, my mother and brother decided that they were not going to participate in store #2. They did not consult me or ask and did not really care. So, I said that I would do it by myself. I was not going back then. We had sold everything we had in Shreveport.

Meanwhile, Richard's work habits did not improve, making life difficult in the family hardware store in Shreveport.

T.J. opens his own store

T.J. relocated to Alexandria, LA, in the middle of the state, to open another Jacobson Hardware Store. After initially agreeing to this plan, Martha opposed the move and refused to allow T.J. to use the Jacobson Hardware Store name. Thus, her son named the business T. J. Jacobson Hardware Company. He remarked, "I wanted Jacobson in there because everybody knew that name. The only way I could do that was to use my whole name – T.J. Jacobson. That was not what I really wanted to call it." After starting with a bang, for the first two years T.J.'s business began to struggle as revenues dropped dramatically. T.J. continued,

> The sales revenue did not pay the bills. I was using my personal money, and then we finally ran out of that too. I did not want to close because of my customers and my friends. We sold a lot of stuff that was unique, unlike the big stores. People did not know us quite as well in Alexandria, but we were working on that. Our reputation was that we had a lot of unique and hard-to-find items and that we had a lot of knowledge and personal service. I did not want to inconvenience our customers by closing. I still see people almost every day that ask me, "where did I go" or they say that we miss you and that you had such unique stuff.

Life became very difficult for T.J.:

> We were open for ten and a half years but should have closed after five. I just kept trying to make it work. The prices of feed rose steeply, and the economy worsened. We built the store in Alexandria, so we had a lot of overhead. We just kept struggling with it until we ran out of money.

T.J. closed the Alexandria store at the end of the year and began a new career selling New York Life Insurance. Then, tragedy struck repeatedly as T.J.'s wife, Alice, died of Lou Gehrig's disease, and Richard Jacobson was murdered the following year.

DECIDING THE FUTURE FOR JACOBSON HARDWARE STORE

Martha Jacobson was devastated by her son's death. At 78 years old, Martha had shared the management of the hardware store business with her son, Richard. But now, Richard was gone, and the full weight of responsibility fell on Martha. Mrs Jacobson realized that without Richard serving as a family presence, however flawed he may have been, it would be difficult to manage the store by herself. However, she settled in to do just that.

About a year later, Martha thought of her son, T.J., as she often had done since his brother's death,

T.J. has the knowledge and ability to step back in and run this business, but I have offended him by not supporting the store in Alexandria. I was just trying to keep the peace and make the whole family happy. Now, he is doing very well selling life insurance. Why should he come back and help me? I am approaching 80 years old, and it has been difficult to run the store by myself.

Martha picked up her cell phone and called her son, T.J., "Hello, son, how are you doing?"

T.J. answered the phone, "Hello, Mother. I am doing well. How are you?"

"Son, I am not feeling well. I just cannot get rid of this nasty cough," Martha replied. "I have been thinking about our family and our business, and I want you to know that I am sorry for how things turned out with the store in Alexandria. I should have supported you better."

"Yes, it hurts that you sided so much with Richard, but I understand that you were trying to keep him in line for the family. You know that Richard and I just did not get along. That is the reason I left and the reason why I could not come back. He was the instigator in everything, unfortunately," T.J. responded.

"The situation with Richard has been very hurtful all around, and now I have to admit that things are a bit of a mess here at the store," explained Martha.

I know you are busy selling life insurance and taking care of your mother-in-law, but I need some help. As far as the family goes, there really is no one else but you who can help. Richard's children are all very young and still in school. None of them has shown any interest in the hardware store. In fact, they have never worked here in the summers or after school. Richard's wife, Louise, certainly has no interest in helping me here. After the police cleared all the family members in Richard's killing, Louise has the money from the keyman insurance policy. She has her own job, and I understand she has taken up with another man. She does not want to be involved with the family business. Your son, Jason, is the oldest of the grandchildren. How is he doing now?

T.J. replied,

Jason is working, but his health is not strong. He does not want to take on the physical labor involved in the hardware store. As you know, he never worked in the store after school or during the summers and has shown no interest in the business. Mother, you may need to hire a non-family manager to help you with the business.

Martha reminded her son, "You know we have never trusted an outsider to make the decisions and handle the money at the store, T.J. I might as well sell the business to an outsider as hire one. The store is our family legacy. Do you want that to go away?"

"Yes, I understand about the Jacobson Hardware legacy, but there are some issues that need to be addressed," stated T.J.

Summoning her best motherly charm, Martha requested, "Please, at least, come back to the store and help me for a few days so I can get over this cough and we can talk about everything."

DISCUSSION QUESTIONS

1. A family member employee may perform so poorly, whether intentionally or not, that they damage the operation or reputation of the family firm. This condition has been described as the "Fredo effect," recalling the inept and ineffectual middle brother from *The Godfather* movies and books (Kidwell et al., 2013). Ultimately, Michael Corleone ordered the murder of Fredo, his own brother, to protect the family and himself from Fredo's multiple betrayals. Does Richard Jacobson fit this description of Fredo? Explain why he does or does not.
2. As the case ends, discuss the alternatives facing Martha Jacobson in her leadership of Jacobson Hardware Store. Should Martha hire an outside person to help her manage the hardware store? Should Martha sell the family business to outsiders? Or should Martha try to fully persuade her son, T.J., to return to the family business? Choose the best alternative and defend your choice.
3. Provide evidence that T.J. Jacobson will return to the family business, Jacobson Hardware Store, in Shreveport, LA. Explain your reasoning.
4. Jacobson Hardware Store is a small family firm operating in the hardware store industry, which has been threatened by big box retailers, such as Home Depot and Lowe's. According to the case, how has Jacobson Hardware been able to survive in this industry? Which of Porter's generic strategies does the company use – Product Differentiation, Low-Cost Leadership, Focused Product Differentiation, or Focused Low-Cost leadership? Explain why you chose the generic strategy.
5. Estimate the value of Jacobson Hardware Store if Martha Jacobson decides to sell the family business to outsiders.

EPILOGUE

Martha Jacobson is a very persuasive individual. T.J. Jacobson described the situation in which his mother asked him to return to the family business,

> I rocked along with New York Life for about a year after my wife died. Then the next year, my brother died. About a year later, my mother needed some help. I did not have the intention of coming back full-time. Then, she was sick for three weeks. There were things about the store that was a mess. So, I said, "why don't you let me come in on Saturdays, and I will start cleaning the warehouse to get you ready for springtime?" That was my intention. That turned into a Friday, Saturday, and Monday. I still worked for New York Life on Tuesday, Wednesday, and Thursday. Then, she needed me on a Wednesday, and she needed me on a Thursday. It evolved into, okay, I am back. So, I moved back to Shreveport, so I am here.

T.J. has taken the high road of forgiveness and reconciliation with his mother. The two are back working together, although the case of the murder of Richard Jacobson remains unsolved. T.J.

explained, "My goal now when I came back was to run the store until I am 81. Then, the store will be 100 years old. That is my goal. Then, we will decide what to do at that point."

NOTE

1. This case is based on real events, but the names of people, places, and details were changed to protect the family's privacy. The author performed in-depth interviews with family members of the second and third generations of Jacobson Hardware Store. The tape-recorded interviews followed a formal list of questions but were semi-structured in nature. The Jacobsons answered follow-up questions as needed. The author transcribed approximately three hours of interviews, which totaled 30 pages of transcripts. Independently, the author gathered journal, magazine, and newspaper accounts.

SUGGESTED READING

Cater, J.J., Kidwell, R. and Camp, K. (2016). Successor team dynamics in family firms. *Family Business Review*, 29(3), 301–26.
Kidwell, R.E., Eddleston, K.A., Cater, J.J. and Kellermanns, F.W. (2013). How one bad family member can undermine a family firm: Preventing the Fredo effect. *Business Horizons*, 56(1), 5–12.
Santarelli, E. and Lotti, F. (2015). The survival of family firms: The importance of control and family ties. *International Journal of the Economics of Business*, 12(2), 183–92.

REFERENCES

Ace (2022). Ace Hardware reports fourth quarter and full year 2021 results. Accessed 31 December 2022 at https://newsroom.acehardware.com/ace-hardware-reports-fourth-quarter-and-full-year-2021-results/.
Brock, E.J. (2008). Shreveport history. Greater Shreveport Chamber of Commerce. Archived from the original on 19 February 2008. Accessed 3 January 2023.
Carmody, T. (2018). The history and future of the hardware store. Accessed 29 December 2022 at https://kottke.org/18/08/the-history-and-future-of-the-hardware-store.
Dipman, C.W. (1929). *The Modern Hardware Store*. New York: Good Hardware/The National Magazine of the Hardware Trade/The Butterick Publishing Company.
IBISWorld (n.d.). Hardware stores in the U.S. – Number of businesses 2003–2028. Accessed 30 December 2022 at https://www.ibisworld.com/industry-statistics/number-of-businesses/hardware-stores-united-states/#:~:text=There%20are%2010%2C646%20Hardware%20Stores,of%20%2D5.1%25%20from%202021.
Kidwell, R.E., Eddleston, K.A., Cater, J.J. and Kellermanns, F.W. (2013). How one bad family member can undermine a family firm: Preventing the Fredo effect. *Business Horizons*, 56(1), 5–12.
Lowe's (n.d.). Lowe's – who we are – our history. Accessed 30 December 2022 at https://corporate.lowes.com/who-we-are/our-history.
NP Gallery (n.d.). National register of historic places. Accessed 29 December 2022 at https://npgallery.nps.gov/NRHP.
Profile America (2013). Quick-Learn Report – Hardware Stores. Accessed 30 December 2022 at https://pattyplundy.com/wp-content/uploads/2015/05/Hardware-Stores.pdf.
TRIPinfo (2016). Interstate 20 in Louisiana. Louisiana Department of Transportation and Development, Highway Inventory Unit. Accessed 3 January 2023 at https://www.tripinfo.com/maps/la.
US Census Bureau (2021). Shreveport. Accessed 3 January 2023 at 2020 Population and Housing State Data. *US Census Bureau*.
Zippia (n.d.). True Value revenue. Accessed 30 December 2022 at https://www.zippia.com/true-value-careers-1122243/revenue/.

17
Lost in transitions?[1]

Cristina Alvarado-Alvarez and Martin C. Euwema

CASE SUMMARY

This case addresses the quandary faced by Laurent and Anne Garnier, founders and owners of Tech Inc., a successful European-based company providing support services for companies in systems infrastructure. The problem they face involves potential succession and the role of their only son, Luc. Luc works in Tech Inc.; however, he shows problematic behaviors, which call for action, perhaps intervention or even an exit from the firm. This occurs at a time when Laurent and Anne have decided to transfer shares to Luc and his sister Sophie. Sophie is married to Paul, who is managing director of Tech Inc. The relationship between Paul and Luc has become tense at work.

LEARNING OUTCOMES

Through analysis of this case, students can be expected to:

- Explain how business family dynamics are entangled in the interaction between family and business systems.
- Describe how dysfunctional behaviors at work are influenced and sustained by business family dynamics.
- Identify ways to prevent dysfunctional behaviors in the workplace.
- Explain decision-making structures in the business family that can prevent escalation of negative behaviors.

Another sleepless night. In the last weeks, Laurent, owner and CEO of Tech Inc., has been experiencing severe sleep problems. Tech Inc. is a flourishing business. It's family issues that keep him awake. Luc, his son, far from being a good employee for the family business, has been creating a lot of problems lately. Luc does not attend meetings on time, shouts at other people, and spends money without control.

Laurent knows that Luc would be out of a job if he were not Laurent's son. However, taking Luc out of the company would be the end of the family relationship with his son and spark an intense conflict with his wife, Anne. He thinks that his son could be a good leader for the company because of his bravery and charisma. Luc reminds Laurent of his own younger years, when the family firm was at its beginnings and only a small group of family members and nonfamily employees worked together to conquer the world. Nevertheless, he realizes the company has reached a top level of professionalization and the nonfamily managers are not pleased with Luc's behavior. Moreover, Laurent's son-in-law (Paul) has proven to be a highly competent manager and hopefully would make a great successor when Laurent retires in five years.

Anne and Laurent Garnier own 100 percent of the shares of the company (each 50 percent); however, they have decided recently to start a transfer to their two children, Sophie and Luc. At the New Year family party, they announced that they will do a first tranche of 20 percent of the shares to each sibling, with the intention to transfer more shares in the future. In the coming years, Sophie and Luc will become major shareholders. Laurent and Anne will hold, at least for the next ten years, a golden share, giving them veto rights on key decisions.

Sophie and Paul met on the 30th anniversary of the company when Paul had just been hired as operations analyst. Now, Sophie and Paul both worry about the problems that Luc has created recently. Sophie picked up a basic knowledge of psychology as she trained for her current post as a pediatric oncologist; she believes that Luc could be dealing with some mental and behavioral disorders. She is determined to call a friend who is a psychologist to ask for advice. Sophie and Paul think Luc should leave the company (at least temporarily) to get therapy or go on a retreat and find his moral compass. Sophie fears that her parents think this would not be a good idea, and only offend Luc.

THE FAMILY BUSINESS AND THE BUSINESS FAMILY

Anne and Laurent met at university when they were doing their bachelor's studies in business administration and engineering, respectively. After finishing their studies in 1978, with the financial support of Anne's father, Renaud (a former entrepreneur in real estate), they founded Tech Inc., a European-based company that provides support services for companies in systems infrastructure. At the beginning, they divided their tasks as an entrepreneurial couple; Laurent was focused on developing the business model, searching for new clients, and managing operations, and Anne was responsible for managing human resources and finances.

Family and business were growing together; three years after they started the company, Jean, their first son, was born. Both Anne's and Laurent's families were looking forward to Jean, the first grandchild. This was especially true for Renaud, Anne's father, because after three daughters, he longed for a grandson. Sadly, Jean died at age 9 due to childhood leukemia, devastating the family.

Sophie and Luc were born in 1982 and 1991, respectively (see Figure 17.1). Luc was born some months after the death of Jean, while the family was in deep mourning. Anne and Laurent dealt with their loss by working many hours in the nascent company, while Anne's parents cared for Sophie and Luc.

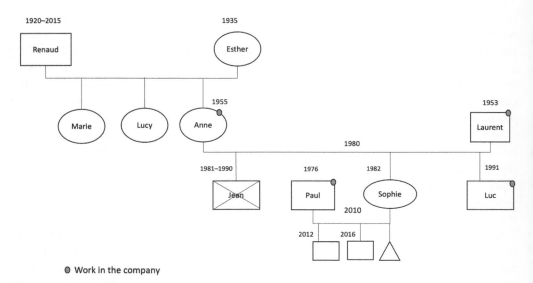

Source: Case authors.

Figure 17.1   Garnier family genogram

Sophie was determined to study medicine to help children and families. Inspired by the family's history, she decided to do graduate studies in pediatric oncology, and she is now a renowned specialist in this area. She is sensible and empathetic.

Luc grew up in the care of his grandparents while his parents were recovering from the sadness of the loss of his elder brother. His grandfather, Renaud, looked after him with indulgence to the point of spoiling him. Renaud thought that Luc deserved all the gifts and attention for being his only grandson. Luc brought companionship to Renaud and enjoyed his expensive lifestyle. After Renaud's death, Luc inherited a large amount of money.

PROBLEMS WITH LUC

From an early age, Luc dealt with behavior problems and learning difficulties at school, which were not managed effectively before he went to college. After two failed years in college, he left and tried to enroll in some professional courses in business, but he did not complete them. His parents decided he should join Tech Inc. to prevent him from too much partying and leisure travels with friends. From 2011 until the present, he has been working in several areas of the company without much success. Other colleagues frequently complain about his lack of responsibility or rude behavior. He neither respects time schedules nor meets deadlines. What he enjoys most is going to foreign countries to do commercial missions with his father. He delights in meeting new clients, wining and dining them, and representing the business family. He feels proud of what the family has accomplished in the industry. Paradoxically, he would like to achieve more and be recognized by other family members, especially by his father, who seems disappointed and feels hopeless about his behavior. Although Luc would like to talk with Laurent and make some commitments to change, it is hard to find a moment to have a quiet conversation that doesn't end without screams and insults.

Luc's absenteeism has escalated in the last year and, for this reason, he does not have specific roles and duties in the company. Also, the relationship with Paul has deteriorated after Paul has been given more responsibilities in the company. Paul was first an employee, and then became a family member. He was hired by the founders to fill a vacancy in operations of a highly trusted employee who retired soon after Paul arrived. Paul gained the trust of Anne and Laurent through hard work, loyalty, and professionalism. When Paul and Sophie met at the 30th anniversary of the company, it was love at first sight. Anne and Laurent were pleased with this relationship. Two years later in 2010, Sophie and Paul married.

After making a steady and fast career in the company, Paul was recently appointed as the managing director, leading the business with success and according to the family's values. However, the last six months have not been easy because Luc has started to behave rudely towards him, challenging his authority in front of other employees. Moreover, Paul has rejected expense reports presented by Luc because they did not comply with the organization's guidelines. Luc has been overspending, especially in commercial missions with his father. Laurent has permitted these expenses, but he knows it is not permissible for this to happen again. The straw that broke the camel's back was a quarrel between Paul and Luc about his absences from work and other employees' complaints about his mismanagement of international clients. Laurent was present in the room, feeling ashamed and guilty about Luc's misbehavior, which had remained unchallenged until this point.

WHAT TO DO ABOUT LUC?

The evening after this meeting, Laurent received a call from Sophie, who was very concerned about this last quarrel between Paul and Luc. She shared with Laurent that ultimately Paul needed medication to calm his anxiety. Sophie suggested that considering these events, Luc should leave the company, at least temporarily, if they wanted to prevent Paul's burnout. She suspects that Luc is involved in some other problems, such as drug abuse, which are the main causes of his misbehavior.

Anne also started to think that Luc is crossing some boundaries that are not acceptable. However, she believes that Luc cannot leave the company, and he will change his behavior when he feels more recognized by Laurent. Luc wants attention and recognition as future leader of the company and successor to Laurent. His father just doesn't know what to do – he loves his son, but he wonders about the future of the firm if this behavior is allowed to continue, and whether Luc can ever ascend to the leadership.

DISCUSSION QUESTIONS

1. Should Luc leave the company due to misbehavior? Why?
2. How have the problems of Luc got to this point? What contributed to the escalation of Luc's behaviors?
3. Why were effective measures not taken earlier, and what could such measures be?
4. What are the main determinants of family dynamics promoting and reinforcing Luc's dysfunctional behavior?
5. How do you assess the career path followed by Luc and Paul? Should being an in-law be a relevant factor in leadership succession?
6. How should the business family decide Luc's situation? Should this decision only be made by the parents? Should other family members participate? Or even outsiders?

EPILOGUE

Luc continued working in the company after making a development plan with the support of an external mental health professional and a career mentor inside the company. Moreover, the family engaged in a healing process of relationships to improve family communication and manage dissent constructively. This new family landscape allowed monitoring and provided feedback and support to Luc in this journey. At the same time, family members, including Paul, have worked together in succession planning, discussing their concerns and expectations about succession and defining a long-term vision of the family business with the support of a family business advisor.

NOTE

1. The story, all names, characters, and incidents portrayed in this case are fictitious. No identification with actual persons is intended or should be inferred. The case is based on the extensive experience with a multitude of cases in the practice of the authors, and other expert psychologists who were interviewed. All cases showed patterns of destructive entitlement of successors linked to family dynamics. Authors and the interviewees act as advisors from a psychological perspective.

SUGGESTED READING

Cooper, J.T., Kidwell, R.E. and Eddleston, K.A. (2013). Boss and parent, employee and child: Work-family roles and deviant behavior in the family firm. *Family Relations*, *62*(3), 457–71.

Mussolino, D. and Calabrò, A. (2014). Paternalistic leadership in family firms: Types and implications for intergenerational succession. *Journal of Family Business Strategy*, *5*(2), 197–210.

Shanine, K.K., Madison, K., Combs, J.G. and Eddleston, K.A. (2023). Parenting the successor: It starts at home and leaves an enduring impact on the family business. *Entrepreneurship Theory and Practice*, *47*(4), 1093–131.

APPENDIX 17A: BUSINESS FAMILY TIMELINE

- 1978: Foundation of Tech Inc.
- 1990: Death of Jean due to leukemia when he was 9 years old.
- 2008: Paul hired as operations analyst.
- 2010: Sophie and Paul's marriage.
- 2011: Luc leaves college and joins the family business in the operations area.
- 2015: Renaud's death.
- 2023: Paul's appointment as managing director.

18

Frutas y Verduras San Miguel: gambling with the future of the family firm[1]

Pablo Álamo and Unai Arzubiaga

CASE SUMMARY

This case analyzes the dilemma faced by the CEO of a Paraguayan family business who must decide whether to leave the family business, due to irreconcilable differences with his father, or continue running the company while accepting some bad corporate practices that affect the profitability of the business and the family's reputation. The moment of maximum tension occurs when the CEO, Demetrio Fernández, wants to dismiss his brother Xavier as director of the company, and prevent him from entering the company offices. The reason given by the CEO of Frutas y Verduras San Miguel is that Xavier has withdrawn money from the company to spend it on gambling in the city's largest casino. The case raises the question of how to act in extreme situations where the family unit is at stake due to a difference of criteria when dealing with the addiction of a family member that negatively affects both the reputation of the family and the profitability of the business.

LEARNING OUTCOMES

Through analysis of this case, students can be expected to:

- Explain why generational differences are accentuated when there is not the same vision, or the same values shared among the members of the owner family.
- Describe what happens when ownership and management are not aligned in the strategic vision of the company and in the fulfillment of their respective roles, as well as to debate whether, in situations of conflict, priority should be given to family unity or to good business practices.
- Explain why family firm leaders need emotional intelligence and assertive communication tools to manage relationship conflicts adequately.

Demetrio Fernández, CEO of Frutas y Verduras San Miguel, went to bed visibly worried. He could not stop thinking about the possible repercussions that the news of the day, which had shocked the entire Paraguayan society, would have on his business. The US Treasury Department had sanctioned Horacio Manuel Cartes Jara, former president of Paraguay, and Hugo Adalberto Velázquez Moreno, the current vice president, for their participation in rampant corruption that undermined democratic institutions in Paraguay. Additionally, the Office of Foreign Assets Control (OFAC) sanctioned Tabacos USA Inc, Bebidas USA Inc, Dominicana Acquisition S.A. and Frigorífico Chajha S.A.E., for being owned or controlled by Cartes.

Demetrio Fernández's concern was based not only on a long-standing business relationship with some of the Group's companies, but also on the key role that one of the men closest to Horacio Cartes had played in the growth of Frutas y Verduras San Miguel, a third-generation family business. However, this was not the only concern of Demetrio, the founder's grandson. At Sunday lunch at his parents' house, the CEO of Frutas y Verduras San Miguel had suggested dismissing his brother Xavier as a director of the family firm. However, his father, majority shareholder of the company, and his mother, with 10 percent of the company, had rejected his proposal, ending the discussion in the worst possible way, on the verge of a total rupture between father and son.

DEMETRIO'S PROBLEMS WITH XAVIER

Demetrio Fernández, 38, was an engineer from the Catholic University of Asunción, the youngest of three siblings. He was married to Susana, 35, but even though they had sought professional help at a renowned fertility clinic in Asunción, they were unable to have children. His sister, María Beatriz, 42, a dentist by profession but not currently practicing, was devoted to the home, to the care of her two teenage children and to various social activities typical of the mothers of the American School of Asunción. Demetrio had a good relationship with his sister, although he did not share her total disconnection from the family business, except when he sought some kind of "help." On the other hand, Demetrio maintained important differences with his older brother, Xavier, 45, a lawyer at the National University of Asunción and president of a well-known charitable association in the country. These differences had increased in recent years. Xavier had been married and divorced twice, and had three children (20, 18, and 10), who did not live with him, but whom he saw periodically.

Engineer Fernández's motive for proposing the dismissal of his brother as director of Frutas y Verduras San Miguel was mainly professional: he had to fire his brother for having done what would lead to the dismissal of any other employee who had done the same in the company. According to Demetrio, his brother Xavier, for the third time so far in a year, had withdrawn money from the company and spent it, once again, on gambling. Demetrio was furious with his brother, and frustrated with his parents, negatively influencing the creativity and proactivity required by the position and the situation. Specifically, Demetrio was certain that there were only three alternatives to consider:

1. Try to convince his parents that his brother should not set foot in the company again and should get professional help to overcome his gambling addiction.
2. To go along with his parents, majority partners in the company, and leave everything as it was, because the company's profitability could financially absorb this loss of cash.
3. To resign himself and start a business on his own, as had already happened in the family, precisely with his brother Xavier.

This last option was the one that had gained the most strength in Demetrio's mind, due to a phrase that his father had said to him at Sunday lunch and that had stuck in his mind: "I will never support you in abandoning your older brother in this way. We are a family before we are a company." It was not the first time the CEO of Frutas y Verduras San Miguel had experienced strong differences with his father, and in the last hours he had not been able to get a constant thought out of his head: "Maybe the time has come to embark on a new course," he kept repeating to himself.

Demetrio's differences with his brother Xavier went back a long way, to when Don Javier (Don is a prefix that expresses respect) supported his son Xavier in starting his own business, very similar to the family firm. Demetrio felt that, on his brother's part, it was mean and unethical to abandon the family business, precisely when it was in a phase of active growth with the need to evolve towards a stage of organizational development, in which the family business should optimize the structure and establish formal processes. Demetrio did not understand why Xavier was able to leave the company as a worker, but not as a director, continuing to receive a salary while working on setting up his own business, in the same sector. Demetrio did not agree with his brother's behavior, much less with his father allowing it.

Demetrio also did not agree that Xavier would go to his father to use money from the company to incur expenses that should have been paid with his own salary, such as trips abroad with some of his girlfriends, expenses associated with his children's studies, and the purchase of several cars to compete in the Trans-Chacho Rally, a traditional event in the country, a speed and endurance competition that has been held since 1971.

When Demetrio expressed his opinion on the matter in meetings and family gatherings, Xavier's attitude was that of an older brother who "scorns" the childish complaints of his younger brother. Xavier was sure he was doing well, convinced that what differentiates a family business from a nonfamily business is precisely that the business helps the family in its needs. "There must be some advantage to being a family business…," Xavier would say to his brother. "I don't do anything that others don't do," he would say, peacefully. "Besides, it's good for the company to participate in the Rally, because we make a brand, it's the best marketing platform in the country." To which Demetrio replied: "It's a decision that can be made, and in any case, it's not up to you or Dad to make it."

The relationship between the two brothers worsened when Demetrio assumed the position of general manager and began to implement management practices and to establish processes that he had learned at a prestigious business school based in Costa Rica. This international academic experience was of great value to Demetrio, but it caused a real and progressive distancing between the brothers in how they viewed the company.

Succession in management of the family business was made at the insistence of Don Javier's wife, Marité, who saw that her husband, at age 69, no longer had the strength to manage the day-to-day running of the company. Marité was not far wrong. She saw how her husband had suffered a significant physical decline after a motorcycle accident from which, miraculously, he had emerged without serious injury, although with strong bruises and pain that took him months to overcome. The accident, which caused Don Javier to be unable to go to work for months, accelerated the succession, which was made to the younger son, not only because he was the ideal person, in terms of preparation and experience, but because the older son was committed to his personal projects and undertakings, and because their sister María Beatriz had no interest in working in the company. In the end, the succession took place without major conflicts, and everyone agreed, although Xavier, in practice, did not recognize his brother's leadership, as he acted according to his own rules and went to his father when he wanted to achieve something, bypassing his younger brother's authority.

PARAGUAY: THAT ODD COUNTRY IN THE HEART OF SOUTH AMERICA

Frutas y Verduras San Miguel was founded during the military dictatorship of General Alfredo Stroessner, who ruled for 35 years until his fall in February 1989. After a golden era in the 1970s and 1980s, Paraguay dragged along a structural political weakness that prevented it from developing to its full potential. At the end of the 1990s, fiscal accounts began to deteriorate, but since 2003 economic activity had been growing, showing good performance in terms of fiscal deficit, structuring of public debt, supervision of the national financial system, and, above all, a firm commitment to agro-industrial development, which is one of the greatest strengths of the country's economy.

Paraguay is known for being a "different" country in the region. Being the only country in Latin America, along with Bolivia, that is landlocked, has made it a more isolated country than the others, with a strong influence of agriculture on the economy. Paraguay's big businessmen have always been in the agricultural and commercial sectors, taking advantage of the country's strategic location between the two giants of Brazil and Argentina. With reduced consumption due to the size of its population (6.8 million in 2023), Paraguay has always had an agro-exporting vocation, boosted since the 1990s by the cultivation and export of soybeans, taking advantage of the fertile lands on the left bank of the Paraná River, the advances in genetic engineering and government facilities, which are not usually demanding when it comes to creating companies, and using fertilizers and phytosanitary products, sometimes with negative effects on the environment. With more than 40 percent of the population living in rural areas, Paraguay is possibly the only country in Latin America with an economy based on agriculture and livestock.

Another significant characteristic of Paraguay is the precarious labor market insertion of the rural population, both young people and women, with commercial activity accounting for

45 percent of new jobs, generally in small businesses with low productivity and innovation. The agro-industrial sector, being highly technified due to its export vocation, does not employ a significant percentage of workers, despite the impact it has on the economy. In any case, fewer than 20 percent of workers belong to companies with more than 20 workers.

But of all the particularities of the Paraguayan nation, possibly one of the most striking at world level is the preponderant role that women have had and still have in the development of the country when the War of the Triple Alliance wiped out the male population of Paraguay in the nineteenth century. Paraguayan women are known for their tenacity, courage, and love of their country, as demonstrated during the tragic wars, close to genocide, that Paraguay experienced. In the educational field, for example, it was women who organized the country's educational system: the sisters Adela and Celsa Speratti, and Serafina Dávalos, among others. Paraguayan society, which is markedly patriarchal, recognizes the value of Paraguayan women, and acknowledges their historical role as "head of household" and "head and rebuilder of the nation," sometimes falling into a symbolism of praise, but not of power distribution. A good part of Paraguayan society, sexist and macho, falls into the symbolism of praise for women, but without renouncing intolerant attitudes towards diversity and the role that modernity has given to women, also in the field of business.

FRUTAS Y VERDURAS SAN MIGUEL

The origin of Frutas y Verduras San Miguel dates to 1957, when Javier Fernández, together with his wife María Ramona Fuster, decided to open a small fruit and simple breakfast store in the Central Market of Asunción. It was a service offered to the workers of the market, which meant that the business had to open at 5:00 am. During the dictatorship, some of its customers had no money, but the founders did not stop providing the service: "fruit, in a country where fruit is surplus and rots in the fields, and a breakfast, nobody can be denied," the grandmother used to say, as she remembered how in the beginning she had accepted the barter of goods as a means of payment.

The Paraguayan breakfast offered by Don Javier and Doña María Ramona was influenced, like all Paraguayan gastronomy, by other cultures. There were two breakfast options: (1) a hot drink – coffee or cocido (a kind of mate cooked with yerba mate) – accompanied by some kind of baked goods (cookies, coquitos, bread with butter and jam) or the famous Paraguayan chipa; (2) coffee, juices, and mix of natural fruits. In wintertime, in the proximity of the festival of San Juan, 23 June, the star breakfast was the mbeju (pronounced mbeyú), a kind of pancake, inherited from the mestizo Guaraní-Spanish cuisine. Don Javier says:

> My father did well and we grew up fast because, although he had no studies, he always knew that with hard work, sacrifice and dedication, results come. Besides, something that few dare to say is that my grandfather's business was favored by Stroessner. With him we were able to work well, there were no robberies or delinquency, nobody bothered you as long as you did not criticize the General and his circle of trust.

Founders Javier Fernández and María Ramona Fuster had five children: Fernando, Néstor, Belén, Demetrio, and Javier Junior. Eventually, Javier inherited the family business because two of his brothers became priests, Belén married a wealthy man with business in Bolivia, where she lived for many years, and Demetrio died in a road accident on a trip to the countryside. In turn, Javier Fernández Jr had three children: Xavier, María Beatriz, and Demetrio, named in memory of the deceased brother and now the CEO of the company. Xavier had worked with his father from when he was a young teenager, until he became independent. Demetrio joined the family business in 2006. Figure 18.1 displays the Fernández family tree across four generations.

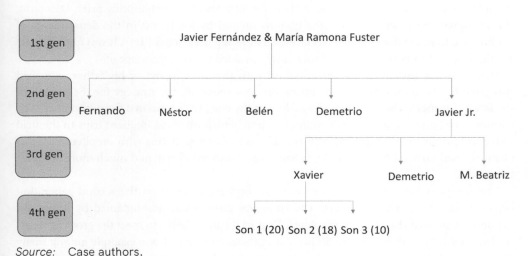

Source: Case authors.

Figure 18.1   Fernández family tree

GRUPO CARTES RELATIONSHIP AND RAPID GROWTH OF THE FIRM

During the management of Javier Fernández Jr, second generation, Frutas y Verduras San Miguel grew exponentially. In the first generation, the business moved from a stall on the street in the Central Market to having its own building for wholesale supermarket functions. In the second generation, with his son Javier Jr, the company grew radically: from selling fruits and vegetables it went on to produce them. In effect, the company leased land in one of the most fertile areas of the world, forever changing the business model and the nature of the company.

This milestone in the company was made possible thanks to Javier Jr's friendship with his close friend "Sebas," a school classmate of one of the most important men of the Cartes Group, a very powerful economic group in Paraguay, following in the footsteps of the two giants: Vierci and Zuccolillo. His friend offered Javier a chance to rent him some land that one of the Group's companies had bought: "We are not interested in producing on the land, but in the capital gain that the value of this land will have in the future," explained Sebas to Javier. That

Table 18.1   Evolution of Fernández family firm in the third generation

	2014	2022
Employees	67	325
Ownership (assets)	570,000 USD	3,042,000 USD
Liabilities	280,000 USD	1,320,000 USD
Income before taxes	165,000 USD	1,810,000 USD

Source: Case authors.

is why the Group was willing to lease the land for 50 years at a very tempting price. Demetrio, the young engineer, went to visit the options offered by his friend in the departments of Canindeyú, Itapúa, Misiones, and Ñeembucú, bordering the Paraná River. It was undoubtedly a unique opportunity that the Fernández family decided to take advantage of.

Demetrio was leading this transformation with the full support of his father, who had delegated to his son the bulk of the operation and, above all, the strategy for the growth of the family business. The company was no longer the one Javier inherited from his father. The complexity of managing the production operation, which involved frequent trips to the field to control processes and expected performance, as well as negotiating with suppliers and sales channels, had turned Frutas y Verduras San Miguel into a different and much more complex business.

The company went from two employees at the start to 15 when the second generation began, to the current 325 workers. The employee growth was accompanied by important profits that allowed the main shareholders, Don Javier and Marité, to meet the growing needs of their children, with hardly any limits. All of them, to give just one example among many others, had their own house in their own name bought with the money generated by the operation of the business. This quality of life of the Fernández family was largely the result of the evolution that the business had experienced during Demetrio's management since he took over the leadership of the company in 2014, as shown in Table 18.1.

A CLASH OF VISIONS WITH NO SOLUTIONS

If the management succession came naturally to the most prepared and committed son, his father continued to go to the company every day to have breakfast with his wife: "we have the chef who prepares the best breakfasts in the city," he used to say, or to have lunch with his friends in the company's private dining room, all at the company's expense. Don Javier was a very good host and his friends, most of them pensioners, liked those generous, long and relaxed gastronomic encounters.

One of the things that began to cause division in the business family was the difference of views between Demetrio and his parents regarding some situations that arose in the family. For example, on one occasion, Demetrio's sister María Beatriz came to the company requesting an advance on dividends because she wanted to renovate her house – a house built by her chosen architect and financed by the company without restrictions of any kind – and to get her a son a new car. The son had wrecked his current vehicle a few days earlier when leaving a discotheque, fortunately without fatal consequences. The CEO of Frutas y Verduras San Miguel was against this type of assistance to family members using the company's money, but the parents, in general, always ended up giving in to their children's requests. The usual dynamic was to go to the mother first, perhaps to validate that they would not have greater resistance, but she always used to tell her children: "It's fine with me, but whatever your father says."

Demetrio used to confront his parents: "We are setting a very bad example; people look at what we do and compare their salaries with the use we make of the money. We must maintain grandfather's austere and industrious style." But his father, even when he agreed with his son's arguments, gave in to his children's requests, with the following reasoning: "What's the money for, son? As long as the money is enough, I want to help my children in everything they need. You worry about a macanada [local expression, meaning that something is not very important], I can't take the money to the next world, I'd better spend it here."

Demetrio tried to convince his parents with arguments, without success, to the point that eventually he stopped putting up a fight, starting a process of demotivation and great stress for himself. The company was growing at an accelerated pace, and the management level had become very complex, with many daily fires to be fought, especially in the field, in which most of his family was not involved.

Another particularly difficult time was when his brother Xavier decided to set up his company in the same line of business, and to do so he turned to his father to finance the costs associated with it, but without signing subsequent obligations or recognition of a percentage of the profits in the future. When he learned of this, Demetrio exploded at his parents:

> You are not obliged to help your children in everything they ask of you! But don't you realize that what Xavier is asking of you is wrong? How is it possible that you don't realize it?! It's wrong for him to set up a company that is going to be a competitor and ... it's even worse that he wants to do it with the company's money without any kind of consideration! I can't believe that you have accepted! I can't believe it ... it's crazy!

Demetrio's "unloading" always met with the same response in more or less the same words:

Don Javier: Money is there to help others, starting with the family. How can I not help a son who asks me for help, if I can do it? Put yourself in my place and you will see that it is not so hard to believe. I want your brother to succeed, to do well, and I want to prove it to him with facts: there is room for everyone in the market.

Demetrio: Dad, anyone you ask will tell you that the money must be reinvested in the company, we can buy more land to increase production, we can make the leap to international exports, we must hire more qualified and expensive

	personnel, pay the most productive collaborators better… the money is not worth wasting!
Don Javier:	It's decided, son. I have said yes to your brother and I will keep my word. I want to help him. It's my money and I decide how to use it.
Demetrio:	It's not just your money! Besides, deep down you're not helping him because you're setting a bad example, Dad. He doesn't respect you, what he is asking you for is disrespectful, and he will never respect you … no matter how much you help him, because you don't demand it, neither from him nor from María Beatriz, who gets paid good money for doing absolutely nothing.

At these words of his son, Don Javier reacted, deeply hurt, cutting the conversation short and withdrawing in a tense silence. Father and son did not speak to each other for more than a month, except for the usual greetings at meetings where they had to interact. The relationship between father and son was seriously damaged by a difference of criteria between the ownership and the management of the company.

THE STRAW THAT BROKE THE CAMEL'S BACK

On 30 April 2023, Don Javier received a photo on his cellphone with a brief message from a cousin: "He has been here for more than 3 hours. Awaiting instructions." The photo showed Xavier playing the machines of the city's main casino, when he had informed his family that he was going to Club Centenario, one of the most famous social clubs of the capital, to play tennis. It was the third time in a week that he had gone to play. On one of these occasions a cousin, warned by a mutual friend who was a member of the casino, had tried to get him to leave in a subtle way, but Xavier reacted violently, pushing his cousin with force.

Later, at a family lunch at his parents' house, the traditional Sunday barbecue to which the children and their families were always invited, Demetrio asked to speak to his parents alone about Xavier's gambling problem, and they both agreed to go to the studio.

Demetrio:	We must find a solution to this: this is the third time Xavier has withdrawn cash from the company, taking advantage of one of my trips to the country. No one dares to say no to him, except me. As CEO, I cannot allow this to happen again, so I am requesting your permission to remove Xavier from his duties as company director and prohibit his access to the company's premises in the future.
Don Javier:	Is this how you plan to solve the problem, son? That's no way to treat a brother. Your brother needs professional help, not to be fired, which will aggravate the situation.
Demetrio:	Dad, the company has acquired such a size and complexity that it is only possible to handle it with professional management criteria, without exceptions because it is a family member. We can only help those who allow

themselves to be helped, and my brother doesn't want to. His attitude is very clear, he has repeated a behavior that we cannot accept and he deserves to be fired. Why don't you dare to make difficult decisions? It's the right thing to do, Dad!

Don Javier: You have to calm down and be patient, because this is not a problem that can be easily and quickly solved.

Demetrio: If you are not going to let me manage the company by applying the decisions that are required, you are inviting me to leave, is this what you want?

Don Javier: I don't want you to leave, but I don't want you to fire your brother, you can't do that. If you do, you'll lose him forever and he'll never forgive you. Neither will I. If you do, it will be me who will do the same to you for disobeying me. There has to be another solution: your brother deserves another solution.

Demetrio: You're wrong, Dad. You can't treat your 45-year-old son as if he were 17. He is of age, and it is not fair to cover for him or protect him, but to demand that he be responsible, that he assume the consequences of his actions. When are you going to understand that the good of the company comes before the privileges of the family?

Don Javier was visibly upset with his son, because once again he was questioning and offending him with the way he was talking to him. With the intention of putting an end to the conversation and returning to the family gathering, his father said to him:

When are you going to understand, my son, that the CEO is there to execute what the shareholders want? You run the company – and you do it very well, the best by far – but respecting the vision and values of the shareholders. If you don't like the vision and values of the main owners of the company, what you have to do is to imitate your brother and start your own company.

"I thought your company is also your children's company," Demetrio whispered.

Seeing her son very unmotivated, his mother intervened: "We are a family, son, and we must take care of each other. Your brother needs help: let's help him."

Mom, we must help him, but we must differentiate between family issues and company matters. As CEO, I cannot allow or tolerate a person like Xavier stepping on the company's toes, because what he is doing is a serious offense and sets a bad example. Or do you think people don't comment on his growing concern for the game? Xavier gets irritated when you try to help him, he uses gambling as an escape route to alleviate his marital and business failures, he lies to everyone, denying his problem. We must help him as a family, but not as a company, which should not assume his growing and periodic need for financial support. The future of many families is at stake, not only your son's. You cannot be so blind and selfish!

His father replied:

> I ask you to find another way to solve the problem. Family is cared for and protected, not abandoned or betrayed. You must and can find another way, Demetrio. I will not accept the one you want. I will never support you in abandoning your older brother, nor will your mother. We are a family before we are a company.

Demetrio left the meeting, determined to start his own company. He felt that the fairest thing to do was to keep the production business and create his own network of sales outlets. He only had to talk to his friend Sebas to confirm that the land lease, which was signed in his name for 50 years, would not be in jeopardy. He knew exactly how to make the business highly profitable. But there was only one thing holding him back: losing his family. Demetrio had to resolve the dilemma as soon as possible because the situation was untenable. On one hand, it seemed the fairest thing to him to keep the part of the business he had created and developed, practically alone; but, on the other hand, he knew this decision would mean a rupture with his family that would be very difficult to heal, and to explain to third parties without telling them all the intimacies of his family.

DISCUSSION QUESTIONS

1. What should Demetrio do? What are the pros and cons associated with each course of action he could take?
2. Identify elements of Frutas y Verduras San Miguel's history, culture, policies, and evolution that contributed to the difficult position of decision makers of the business and the family.
3. Which are the main origins of the conflict in Frutas y Verduras San Miguel and what role could emotional intelligence play?
4. Which is the leadership style that best fits with the current situation? Why?

EPILOGUE

Demetrio decided to remain in the family business and not trigger a business and family conflict with serious consequences. In addition, he complied with his parents' decision not to fire his brother. This fact has meant that he must periodically seek psychological help to assertively and resiliently manage a situation that generates high levels of stress, triggering other health problems of a minor nature or at least not life-threatening. Faced with the disenchantment generated by the attitude of his parents and a good part of his family, Demetrio has also taken refuge in religion, as he maintains that it helps him to have an attitude of forgiveness, acceptance, and greater empathy with others, especially with his father and brother.

NOTE

1. This case is based on confidential in-depth interviews with the protagonists using data collection techniques from primary sources as well as access to information open to the public, media accounts, and direct observation by the authors. The characters of the business family and the events recounted are real. Some names and minor details have been changed to avoid the case being identified with a specific company or family.

SUGGESTED READING

Caputo, A., Marzi, G., Pellegrini, M.M. and Rialti, R. (2018). Conflict management in family businesses: A bibliometric analysis and systematic literature review. *International Journal of Conflict Management*, 29(4), 519–42.

Kourgiantakis, T., Saint-Jacques, M.C. and Tremblay, J. (2018). Facilitators and barriers to family involvement in problem gambling treatment. *International Journal of Mental Health and Addiction*, 16(2), 291–312.

Richmond, M.K., Stocker, C.M. and Rienks, S.L. (2005). Longitudinal associations between sibling relationship quality, parental differential treatment, and children's adjustment. *Journal of Family Psychology*, 19(4), 550–59.

19

Blinded by trust: a cousin's fraud threatens a family business[1]

Ellison Howard

CASE SUMMARY

The future of a family medical practice is threatened due to theft and insurance fraud committed by the owner's family member. Though the family member had a history of being involved in illegal activities, the owner trusted him and gave him what he hoped would be an opportunity for a fresh beginning. The case counters the popular belief that trust can be assumed among family members within a business in a way that it cannot among nonfamily members. Furthermore, the case shows the potential blind spot that can develop when the history of previous family relationships impacts family firm owners' decision-making, and subsequently the firm and the family itself. This case study takes readers inside the complicated web of family loyalty, family business stewardship, and professional responsibility to explore how deviance can emerge within family firms and how owners can respond accordingly.

LEARNING OUTCOMES

After reading and analyzing this case, students will be able to:

- Explain the boundaries of kinship and the influence of kinship on family firm owner decision-making regarding the discipline and protection of family members within the firm.
- Describe the balance of a family firm owner's responsibility to the family, the firm, and society at large (professional responsibility).
- Explain the preconceived beliefs of the function of trust and loyalty within family firms and describe the level of influence that both should have on compensation and general governance within the firm.

As he heard the words escape from his lawyer's mouth, he was still in disbelief. Jackson couldn't believe that all his years of hard work – not to mention the studying, the bank loans, the family loans for which his mother kept extensive records, the further studying, the testing – had resulted in him having to choose between his hard-earned career and a family member who was also his best friend.

A GROWING FRIENDSHIP BETWEEN FAMILY MEMBERS

Jackson and Terry spent their childhood years during the late 1980s and early 1990s as cousins in Guyana. Jackson lived with his parents, Bernard and Grace, and his sister, Rachel. Terry grew up with his parents, Colin and Pearl, who separated shortly after Terry's birth. Jackson's uncle and father's brother, Benjamin, and Terry's father, Colin, had been partners in one or two failed business ventures of which details were vague, even to the adult versions of both men, or to Jackson at least. Bernard never seemed to interact with Benjamin as much as he did with his other siblings, and often made comments about Benjamin's "get-rich-quick" schemes, but Jackson didn't think much about that rather distant relationship between his father and his uncle. Similarly, Bernard often referred to Colin as a crook. However, given that Bernard would occasionally have drinks with both Benjamin and Colin, and his remarks seemed to be made in jest, Jackson didn't take his father's comments about either of the men seriously.

Although they attended different schools, Jackson and Terry spent as much time together as they could, playing together every couple of months and developing a close friendship. Their interests, from Marvel Comics to Star Wars to their love of geography, connected the boys in a way that kept them engaged for hours on end at every opportunity. This continued until Jackson and Terry were about 8 and 10 years old, respectively, when Terry moved out of Guyana to the US.

DRIFTING APART THEN TOGETHER AGAIN

Terry's parents made the decision to send him to live with his aunt in New York in the hope that he'd have access to more social and educational opportunities. Once in New York, Terry struggled with school, and soon began to spend more time with friends outside of school than with his studies. He soon found himself involved in criminal activities, including theft and drug sales. Though Terry had many close calls, and accumulated a few criminal charges, he managed to avoid jail. Though most of the activities in which Terry engaged felt inconsistent with what he'd been taught, the inclusion from his new friends in his new country, and the attention they received from the money they gained, kept Terry engaged. It was difficult for Terry and Jackson to keep in touch given the expense associated with international calling, and both young men's reluctance to engage in letter writing.

Jackson's path in Guyana since falling out of touch with Terry was one that mainly revolved around academics and sports. He performed well in school, being particularly interested in science and mathematics. He also became a good distance runner, and balanced running competitively with his academic studies. Jackson's later adolescent years also included time spent traveling the world with his family, and a social life that included many friends. Though

Jackson received a few updates about Terry's life in the US via his father, those reports were typically just details about Terry's legal troubles that had made their way through the family-friend "grapevine". As Jackson grew older and developed stronger friendships within Guyana, he thought of Terry less often.

Jackson's academic performance earned him a scholarship to attend a prestigious college in Florida. When Terry heard that Jackson had moved to begin college in Florida, Terry saw it as an opportunity for a fresh start and made the move also. Though Jackson had several friends who'd also traveled to the same college, he was glad to reconnect with Terry in a new country and city. Jackson was often busy with his studies and sports, but he still found time for Terry; Terry provided a sense of "home" and "family" that was quite far away from Jackson's own.

Jackson continued to excel throughout his undergraduate career, both in academics and track and field. Terry found an office job with a large credit card company and took information technology classes at a local community college. Many of Jackson's friends, particularly those he'd known from Guyana, became Terry's friends also. Terry's father frequently visited, and often treated both Terry and Jackson to dinner whenever he did. Both families were pleased with the positive influence Jackson seemingly had on Terry.

LAYING GROUNDWORK FOR THE FUTURE FAMILY BUSINESS

Eventually, Jackson was accepted into medical school in Virginia. He spent the first two years of medical school living in a graduate student dorm and focusing on his studies. Terry, not sure at the time how he fit into Jackson's plans, returned to New York, his old friends, and a few of his old habits. However, when Jackson decided to move to an apartment, Terry moved to Virginia to live with him. The money that Jackson had received to fund the first part of his medical education had run dry and he welcomed the prospect of having someone with whom to share expenses. While Jackson secured loans from family members to fund medical school, as time went on, he couldn't contribute much to rent and general living expenses. During this time, Terry handled most of the household expenses using funds from a series of temporary jobs, as well as from activities about which Jackson had few details, but often suspected were similar to the activities in which Terry had engaged in his younger years.

During his third year of medical school, Jackson met and married his wife, DeAnna, subsequently moving out of the shared apartment with Terry. In doing so, Jackson's social circle revolved around his classmates and his and his wife's mutual friends throughout his last year of medical school and his residency at a different university hospital in Virginia. During this time, Terry remained in Virginia, continuing to take temporary jobs as needed. Jackson kept in contact with Terry, but kept the interactions relatively limited as Terry didn't fit in well with Jackson's wife or his current friends.

PUTTING THE FAMILY IN FAMILY BUSINESS

After completing his residency and briefly practicing within other offices, Jackson decided to partner with his former medical school classmate, Rick, to start their own medical practice. However, during the planning process, Jackson and Rick discovered that their general managerial ideas were not aligned. One sore spot was Jackson's insistence on hiring Terry as office staff. Rick had met Terry years prior through Jackson and wasn't confident in his abilities to help them run their office. Jackson and Rick made the amicable decision to pursue separate practices. Jackson initially looked to DeAnna to help him with the practice, but the birth of their first child meant that she couldn't devote as much time as was needed to the new practice.

Most of the practitioners in Jackson's specialty employed family members in their private practices for managerial roles, as the prevailing thought was that family members can be trusted to have the practitioner's best interest at heart. Motivated by this industry norm, but more so by the prospect of providing Terry with the opportunity to make an honest and lucrative living, Jackson hired Terry as a billing specialist, and eventually office and human resources manager.

For the first few years, Jackson felt that hiring Terry had proved to be a good idea. Both Jackson's and Terry's families were happy with the direction in which Terry seemed to be headed. Furthermore, Jackson's family and the larger community often commended Jackson for providing an opportunity for Terry to excel. Careful that Terry was able to earn enough to provide for his burgeoning family, Jackson had designed a compensation package for Terry that included a generous base salary, as well as bonuses based on the amount of insurance funds collected. The bonus was structured such that as the amount of billings collected increased, so did the bonus percentage. The practice produced more money than young practices typically did, yet to Jackson it didn't seem outside the realm of normal for others in his field, nor the banks with which he had relationships.

SIGNS OF TROUBLE

As time went on, Jackson added two more locations, and at that point was bringing in significantly more than his peers were producing, even though he remained the sole practitioner. Jackson focused on running the clinical aspect of his practice and had all but completely entrusted the financial aspect to Terry. At one point, Jackson attempted to add an additional billing person to the practice who could also help manage the growing staff. The woman, a friend of his wife, was successfully hired, yet quit after about five months, citing that Terry was difficult to work with. Jackson attempted to hire a college friend, Jeffrey, who had a finance background and who he thought would make an excellent addition to the team and lessen Terry's workload. However, shortly before he was due to start, Jeffrey told Jackson that the payroll company had not contacted him to complete his application. Jackson contacted the payroll company and was informed that Terry had told them that Jeffrey's hire had been reversed, and that no further action was needed. While Jackson was mildly concerned, he didn't mention it, and he chalked it up to Terry being territorial about the strong billing system that he'd created.

Terry appeared to thrive in his position and eventually made a point of initiating contact with other local medical practitioners in the hope of creating more business for himself as a biller. However, those practitioners were skeptical. As Terry was seen driving luxury vehicles, and engaging in other luxury purchases and experiences, Jackson's peers and colleagues began to whisper to him that given Terry's past, Jackson should pay more attention to his office finances. Jackson often met these concerns with assertions that his cousin was simply well paid and appreciated, and that their concerns were biased, given Terry's past. The whispers continued to get louder and evolved into full-on chatter within the local medical community. Eventually, even Jackson's parents became concerned with what they observed to be excessive spending by Terry, as well as Terry often referring to Jackson's practice as "our practice", and reporting to his own parents that he was the secret to the business's success. Jackson continued to defiantly ignore the chatter of concerns … until he no longer could.

A DOUBLE BIND AND A DECISION

One February afternoon, Jackson was served notice that he was being investigated for suspicion of defrauding the state's Medicare program. Investigations by Medicare were not unheard of, yet the mention of fraud left Jackson gravely concerned. Given that all billing was filed using Jackson's medical license number, as is the law, he was ultimately responsible for all of the billing done in his office. Initially, Jackson was quick to hire an attorney and was initially eager to cooperate with the investigation by providing any paperwork they needed. Terry was initially apprehensive about providing documents, and his apprehension quickly turned to a defiance toward the investigation process.

Unbeknownst to Jackson or Terry, the state had been investigating the office and its billing practices over the past few years. Their investigation uncovered that Jackson's billing of one type of procedure was over twice that of all other practitioners within his specialty combined. Additionally, the investigation produced specific patient billing incidences that were over-billed, and therefore over-collected. Jackson's reaction was one of shock, then anger, and eventually confusion. He was shocked that this could happen under his nose and angry that Terry would show such "ungratefulness" by engaging in fraud and theft from both the state government and subsequently from Jackson himself. And finally, he was confused, because Terry was still considered family. That confusion led to Jackson deciding to do his own internal investigation. He went through a year's worth of his procedures and associated billing and calculated just how much Terry had inflated the billings, collections, and ultimately Terry's own bonuses. Jackson was devastated, and no less confused than before his own investigation.

Jackson also had to decide whether and how to let his family know what had happened. Not only could these revelations impact how the family viewed Terry, but how the family viewed Jackson as well.

DISCUSSION QUESTIONS

1. How far does the concept of kinship extend across family members? What do you owe family members? Particularly those who may have assisted you during your journey. How does the responsibility to family compare to the responsibility of maintaining your career or business?
2. How might cultural norms – individualist vs. collectivist ideals – have contributed to Jackson's decision to hire Terry? How might those same norms influence Jackson's decision to report Terry?
3. What are the potential negative effects of psychological ownership as exhibited in this case?
4. Was this a matter of mutual exploitation that went too far? Jackson previously, if briefly, benefited from Terry's illegal activities. Terry took advantage of Jackson's trust and of his position in the business. Perhaps Terry felt he was entitled? (Prior to the discovery of the above crime, Terry did tell an attorney in a private conversation that he felt entitled to reap any rewards related to the success of his cousin and the business.)
5. In taking an agency theory approach, how might the contract design have influenced Terry's actions? Was the fraud a result of insufficient oversight or competing incentives with regard to Terry?
6. How are the elements that contribute to fraud, according to the fraud triangle, evident in this case (pressure, opportunity, rationalization)? Could these have been controlled for? And if so, how?

EPILOGUE

The resulting process was a long one, which was carried out mostly behind the scenes with attorneys. Even considering the evidence, Terry insisted on his innocence and stressed to Jackson that they need to stick together and resist cooperating with investigators. Jackson struggled with how to defend himself and his medical license without explicitly blaming Terry, yet he ultimately agreed to continue to cooperate with the authorities. Though the judge was sympathetic regarding Jackson's story and Jackson avoided criminal prosecution, the eventual decision was made to strip Jackson of his state medical license, and he was fined about $2 million, an amount that included the stolen funds and a penalty fee. His attorney delivered the news, assuring him that it was the best possible outcome that Jackson could have hoped to have. Jackson was forced to shutter all of his practices. Everything that he'd built over the course of over 20 years evaporated within a matter of months, leaving him, his family, and the community that had once supported him disappointed.

This initial investigation led to authorities looking further into Terry and his wife's other activities. They found that while conducting billing for Jackson's office, Terry was stealing the social security numbers of Jackson's patients. Terry and his wife (a licensed therapist with no physical practice, but a "Medicare" billing number) had been fraudulently billing nonexistent services using the stolen social security numbers. Both Terry and his wife were eventually found guilty and sentenced to prison. It was determined that Jackson was not involved in that billing scheme.

NOTE

1. This case is based on the author's personal observations, interviews with the key characters in the case, and public records. The case depicts an actual incident, but names and some details have been disguised to protect the identities of the individuals involved.

SUGGESTED READING

O'Brien, K.E., Minjock, R.M., Colarelli, S.M. and Yang, C. (2018). Kinship ties and employee theft perceptions in family-owned businesses. *European Management Journal*, *36*(3), 421–30.

Sundaramurthy, C. (2008). Sustaining trust within family businesses. *Family Business Review*, *21*(1), 89–102.

Yu, X., Stanley, L., Li, Y., Eddleston, K. and Kellermanns, F.W. (2020). The invisible hand of evolutionary psychology: The importance of kinship in first generation family firms. *Entrepreneurship Theory and Practice*, *44*(1), 134–57.

AFTERWORD

The cases in this book provide insights into the workings of business families and family businesses for better or worse. It is important for various stakeholders (family members, owners, employees, instructors, consultants, and students) to have a greater understanding of what does (and doesn't) work in family firms in terms of handling conflicts and dysfunctional behavior. This is so because of the position family businesses have in driving so much of the world's economy, from giants such as Samsung, Walmart, and Royal Jumbo to mid-range companies and small businesses that are largely represented in this book. Families operating small businesses may not have their dysfunctional behaviors revealed to the world by media as some of the larger corporations do, but it is more crucial for these smaller firms to deal with underlying conflict, personality issues, and bad behavior because the consequences of not doing so can more easily result in the death of the small business than the large corporation.

One key takeaway from this case book is that no matter where a family firm is located – Germany, Paraguay, United States, Nigeria, the Netherlands – the family owners face similar sets of challenges including relationship conflict, succession difficulties, professionalization and growth problems, family disharmony, working effectively with nonfamily members and so on. However, another element to consider is the extent to which the culture in which the family firm is located has an impact on how these tests are met. Underlying each case is the external environment in which the firm operates; for instance, problems can arise regarding female succession in a culture where it is not the norm. In other cultures, the lack of community values within the culture can harm family business owners who need to seek outside help in addressing serious issues.

Case studies have proven useful sources of data that generate theory about particular phenomena. It is hoped that the cases in this book will inspire researchers to continue to investigate business families and the conflicts, disputes, and negative behaviors that sometimes occur within them. In this research, the unique nature of each family and its family system will provide an important basis to consider these issues, not only from the business side but the family side as well. Meanwhile cases that provide insights into different types of family firms in different industries and in different cultures continue to provide building blocks to our understanding of why and how conflict and dysfunction are experienced and handled in a variety of ways by family firms and the families who own and manage them.

INDEX